LESBIAN MODERNISM

Edinburgh Critical Studies in Modernist Culture
Series Editors: Tim Armstrong and Rebecca Beasley

Available:

Modernism and Magic: Experiments with Spiritualism, Theosophy and the Occult
Leigh Wilson

Sonic Modernity: Representing Sound in Literature, Culture and the Arts
Sam Halliday

Modernism and the Frankfurt School
Tyrus Miller

Lesbian Modernism: Censorship, Sexuality and Genre Fiction
Elizabeth English

Forthcoming:

Modernism, Space and the City
Andrew Thacker

Late Modernism
Laura Salisbury

Primordial Modernism: Animals, Ideas, transition (1927–1938)
Cathryn Setz

Modernism and the Idea of Everyday Life
Leena Kore-Schroder

LESBIAN MODERNISM
Censorship, Sexuality and Genre Fiction

Elizabeth English

EDINBURGH
University Press

For my parents, Susan and Stephen English, with love

Edinburgh University Press is one of the leading university presses in the UK. We publish academic books and journals in our selected subject areas across the humanities and social sciences, combining cutting-edge scholarship with high editorial and production values to produce academic works of lasting importance. For more information visit our website: www.edinburghuniversitypress.com

© Elizabeth English, 2015, 2017

Edinburgh University Press Ltd
The Tun – Holyrood Road
12(2f) Jackson's Entry
Edinburgh EH8 8PJ
www.euppublishing.com

First published in hardback by Edinburgh University Press 2015

Typeset in Sabon and Gill Sans by
Servis Filmsetting Ltd, Stockport, Cheshire.

A CIP record for this book is available from the British Library

ISBN 978 0 7486 9373 3 (hardback)
ISBN 978 1 4744 2449 3 (paperback)
ISBN 978 1 4744 2450 9 (epub)
ISBN 978 0 7486 9374 0 (webready PDF)

The right of Elizabeth English to be identified as Author of this work has been asserted in accordance with the Copyright, Designs and Patents Act 1988, and the Copyright and Related Rights Regulations 2003 (SI No. 2498).

CONTENTS

Acknowledgements   vii
Series Editors' Preface   ix

Introduction: Foul Minds and Foul Mouths – Censorship and a Turn to
Genre Fiction   1

Part I: Fantasy
Part I Introduction   27
1 'The book is a sort of touch-stone to <u>other</u> people': Sexology, the
   Invert and Desire in Katharine Burdekin's Utopian Fiction   31
2 'Ghost desire': The Lesbian Occult and Natalie Clifford Barney's
   The One Who is Legion or A.D.'s After-life   59

Part II: History
Part II Introduction   83
3 'Spiritual progenitors' and the Historical Biographies of Margaret
   Goldsmith and Mary Gordon   90
4 'I dislike the correct thing in clothes': Virginia Woolf's *Orlando:
   A Biography* and the Cross-Dressing Historical Romance   108

Part III: Crime
Part III Introduction 137
5 'Murder is a queer crime': The Lesbian Criminal and Female
   Communities in Detective Fiction 144
6 'Lizzie Borden took an axe': Repetition and Heterosexual Crime in
   Gertrude Stein's Detective Fiction 169

Coda 189

Bibliography 194
Index 215

ACKNOWLEDGEMENTS

I am indebted to a number of people who have helped to bring this project to fruition. My gratitude goes to Tim Armstrong for his patience, unfailing support and encouragement from the very beginning. Numerous friends and colleagues have provided excellent comments on early drafts of my work as well as advice and support, and for this I thank Georgina Colby, Benjamin Craggs, Robert Eaglestone, Betty Jay, Tom Slevin, and Peter Welchman, as well as my colleagues at Cardiff Metropolitan University. My work has benefited from the editorial guidance of Tim Armstrong and Rebecca Beasley, as well as the support of the editorial team at Edinburgh University Press, in particular Dhara Patel and Jenny Daly, and my copy-editor Christine Barton. My work on Katharine Burdekin would not have been possible without the Arts and Humanities Research Council funding that enabled me to visit Burdekin's archive at the Dobkin Family Collection of Feminism in New York City. I would like to thank the Dobkin Family and Glenn Horowitz Bookseller for allowing me access to these archives. I am grateful to Daphne Patai for her interest in my work on Burdekin and for the generosity with which she has given her time and shared her knowledge. I am also indebted to Harriet Northway who, as literary executor of Burdekin's estate, provided permission to quote from unpublished material that proved pivotal to my study and who also gave me insight into Burdekin's life and work.

Finally, I am deeply thankful to my family and friends for the invaluable and unconditional support they have provided along the way.

The image on the cover of this book is an illustration by Marcelle Kahane reproduced from the cover of Norah C. James's *Sleeveless Errand* (Paris: Henry Babou & Jack Kahane, 1929).

Every attempt has been made to trace the copyright holder.

An earlier version of Chapter 1 was published in *Utopianism, Modernism, and Literature in the Twentieth Century* (Basingstoke: Palgrave Macmillan, 2013), edited by Alice Reeve-Tucker and Nathan Wadell. This is reproduced with permission of Palgrave Macmillan. The full published version of this publication is available from: http://www.palgrave.com/products/title.aspx?pid=541685

The author wishes to thank the following for permission to use copyright material:

Darcie Rives-East, for the extracts from her unpublished doctoral dissertation, 'Fantastic Writing, Real Lives: Gender, Race, and Sexuality in Early Twentieth-Century American Women's Speculative fiction' (University of Nebraska, 2006) <http://digitalcommons.unl.edu/dissertations/AAI3216433>

Harriet Northway, literary executor to the estate of Katharine Burdekin, for the extracts from Katharine Burdekin's unpublished 'Dolly', 'The Stars Shine in Daylight', 'Two in a Sack', 'Walking to Mark'; extracts from Havelock Ellis's letters to Katharine Burdekin; extracts from letters from Isobel Allan-Burns to Daphne Patai.

The Estate of Rebecca West, for the extracts from 'Man and Religion' by Rebecca West from *Man, Proud Man*, ed. Mabel Ulrich (London: Hamish Hamilton) reprinted by permission of Peters Fraser & Dunlop (www.petersfraserdunlop.com) on behalf of the Estate of Rebecca West.

The Estate of Storm Jameson, for the extracts from 'Man the Helpmate' by Storm Jameson from *Man, Proud Man*, ed. Mabel Ulrich (London: Hamish Hamilton) reprinted by permission of Peters Fraser & Dunlop (www.petersfraserdunlop.com) on behalf of the Estate of Storm Jameson.

New Directions Publishing, for permission to reproduce extracts from *Analyzing Freud: Letters of H.D., Bryher, and Their Circle*, ed. Susan Stanford Friedman (New York: New Directions Publishing, 2002).

SERIES EDITORS' PREFACE

This series of monographs on selected topics in modernism is designed to reflect and extend the range of new work in modernist studies. The studies in the series aim for a breadth of scope and for an expanded sense of the canon of modernism, rather than focusing on individual authors. Literary texts will be considered in terms of contexts including recent cultural histories (modernism and magic; sonic modernity; media studies) and topics of theoretical interest (the everyday; postmodernism; the Frankfurt School); but the series will also re-consider more familiar routes into modernism (modernism and gender; sexuality; politics). The works published will be attentive to the various cultural, intellectual and historical contexts of British, American and European modernisms, and to inter-disciplinary possibilities within modernism, including performance and the visual and plastic arts.

INTRODUCTION: FOUL MINDS AND FOUL MOUTHS – CENSORSHIP AND A TURN TO GENRE FICTION

Wolfskins and Togas

When faced with the prospect of censorship in the 1930s, Naomi Mitchison made the decision to go 'back to writing historical fiction'.[1] In her memoir, *You May Well Ask*, the writer describes wrangling with publishers over the decency of her writing and her struggle to bring an uncensored version of *We Have Been Warned* – a novel that discusses abortion, contraception, and rape – to print. Jonathan Cape and Constable were both willing to publish the novel on the condition that it be sanitised; John Lane flatly rejected it; and while Victor Gollancz believed it to be 'the first piece of genuinely social art [. . . and] immensely valuable as such – the sexual parts no less than the political and economic', he feared the damage to his reputation should the book be denounced as '"filthy"'.[2] Somewhat disheartened, but adamant that the novel could not be further bowdlerised, Mitchison made the decision to return to a familiar form of writing – historical fiction – for the protection that it offered.[3] As she observes:

> In some of the stories in *The Delicate Fire* there is, I would have thought, far more overt sex than in *We Have Been Warned*, but apparently it's all right when people wear wolfskins and togas.[4]

Mitchison's choice to revert to the historical narrative, and the freedom she felt this gave her to talk about sex, speaks loudly of the licence and safe haven that a myriad of genre fictions offered writers at this time of artistic and sexual repression. It is this reaction, this turn to generic forms, that I am interested in here, and it is this nexus of forces – the popular and the sexual – with which this study is concerned. More specifically, I propose that at a time of intense censorship, genre fiction served as a strategy for writing the lesbian and provided a language for modernist and mainstream authors alike to navigate and make sense of the social and cultural complexities of the time.

The censorship of obscene literary material began in the mid to late nineteenth century with the 1857 Obscene Publications Act, created to control the import of pornographic publications from Paris. But it was not until the 1868 Hicklin test that the legal definition of obscenity was established as 'the tendency to deprave and corrupt the minds and morals of those who are open to such immoral influences, and into whose hands a publication of this sort might fall'.[5] This definition was applied without regard for literary merit or authorial intention and it acted as what Katherine Mullin calls a 'watershed moment' that marked 'the beginnings of a legal crusade against the literary "obscene"'.[6] In the early decades of the twentieth century, and in particular at the onset of the First World War, the British government increased its scrutiny of, and its action against, what it believed to be offensive literary material.[7] The drive to police literature thus began to attract significant public interest, provoking both comment and protest. By the 1920s, then, book publishing had become a rather hazardous business with literature subject to various modes of official and unofficial control. Those who published and sold 'obscene' books were of course at risk of legal prosecution, but censorship also operated in other, more subtle forms. As Mitchison's experience shows, authors often struggled to find an outlet for their work and if they were successful this was often at the cost of their writing since anxious publishers and printers might only accept the text in an expurgated form. If a book did reach print, it could still be seized and destroyed by the police, postal service, or customs officials if considered indecent. Similarly, libraries and booksellers could refuse to stock a title if they thought it was offensive or a threat to their livelihood. James Joyce's *Ulysses* (1922) and D. H. Lawrence's *Lady Chatterley's Lover* (1928) are two better-known examples of books that were censored for obscenity around this time, although numerous other lesser-known works also fell foul of the censor.[8] Just as infamous as Lawrence's and Joyce's works – and undoubtedly as seismic – was the 1928 prosecution and ban of Radclyffe Hall's lesbian novel *The Well of Loneliness* (1928) for obscene libel. The work traces the sexual development of Stephen Gordon and, ultimately, the sacrifice of her own happiness for what she believes to be the good of the woman she loves. Originally prefaced with a commentary by the sexologist Havelock Ellis, Hall's novel is heavily informed by sexology, the nineteenth-century study of sexual science that offered a theory of homosexuality that it called sexual inversion. Many sexologists intended their work to serve as a defence of inverts, and Hall drew on these ideas to do the same by delivering what she saw as a serious study of homosexuality.⁹ As she wrote to Ellis, 'the book is a cry for better understanding, for a wider and more merciful toleration, for acceptance of these people as God has made them'.¹⁰ Like other writers such as Mitchison, Joyce, and Lawrence, Hall struggled to find a willing publisher, finally settling on Jonathan Cape with the agreement that she would add £150 to the £300 advertising budget and share legal costs if Cape were prosecuted.¹¹ Although not everyone was convinced of its aesthetic value (Leonard Woolf was not alone in his opinion that 'the book fails completely as a work of art'), reviews of the novel were generally positive, praised Hall's 'sincerity', 'frankness', 'courageousness' and 'honesty' on the subject and applauded the campaign she waged on the behalf of all inverts.¹²

How and why the book came to be banned – an event sparked by James Douglas's review 'A Book That Must Be Suppressed' – is a topic compellingly explored by numerous literary and cultural historians.¹³ But I believe that the question of what was at stake in the text's treatment bears further scrutiny and that British Government records on the subject have more to yield. It is clear from these archived papers that sexually dissident material of any kind, whether that was of a homosexual or heterosexual nature, authored by men or women, had the potential to be construed as obscene and to provoke the authorities, purity organisations, and vocal members of the reading public to take action. Texts deemed objectionable were those that referred to sexually unconventional or taboo behaviours – prostitution, adultery, homosexuality, lesbianism, masturbation, birth control, sex outside of marriage, and abortion.¹⁴ As her prospective publishers had originally feared, Mitchison's *We Have Been Warned* was reported by a member of the public to the Metropolitan Police for its 'pornographic concoction' and 'communistic propaganda', and flagged up by the police for the attention of the Director of Public Prosecutions for its discussion of abortion amongst other things.¹⁵ It is clear that, as Celia Marshik points out, although women were not necessarily targeted during this phase, the standards by which the authorities judged texts were certainly gendered.¹⁶ Hall's *The Well of Loneliness* and Norah James's *Sleeveless Errand* (banned shortly before its publication in 1929), for example, fared badly because of the connection they both made between the First World War and radically altered female sexual behaviour.¹⁷ As Marshik states:

> both texts indicate that young, unmarried women were particularly vulnerable to wartime and postwar transformations. The relative freedom that war work offers these protagonists enables them to engage in homosexual or promiscuous activity that would otherwise be prevented by the policing actions of family and local communities. [...] While most officials regarded sexual 'deviance' during wartime as a necessary evil,

they acknowledged that the majority of the public did not hold this view and that the perception of wartime sexual perversion could undermine national morale.[18]

Hall's protagonist, Stephen Gordon, meets and falls in love with Mary when working as part of a war ambulance unit, while James's book about the sexual lifestyles of a group of London women and men establishes a link between their hedonism and the opportunities that the war brought.[19] The brief sent by the Director of Public Prosecutions to its legal counsel in application for *Sleeveless Errand*'s destruction makes evident the anxiety over the shifting social and sexual roles of women. Its author makes the following statement:

> Can it doubted that to either [a boy or girl] the book would have a corrupting influence not in the sense of causing them to imitate the disgusting beasts who are characterized in the book, but by making them acquainted with filthy language, unnatural practices and immoral incidents? Imagine a daughter in a respectable English household [. . . asking] the question 'Father, what is buggery? Don't understand it' [. . .] What a foul mind, what a foul mouth the woman who wrote this book must possess! There are people still existing who look upon women as delicate and refined, and yet into the mouth of the principal character of this book there are odious words and odious sentences. It is no good being mealy-mouthed in such a case, and the Director hopes that Counsel will use some plain honest English in expressing indignation at such a production as 'Sleeveless Errand'.[20]

We cannot fail to see that what is at stake here is essentially female knowledge and experience, both James's and the female reader's – *Sleeveless Errand* dares to suggest that women are not 'delicate', 'refined' or innocent. Moreover, the extract shows that it is James's, and indeed any woman's, ability to speak candidly about such topics that proves threatening. James's excess of inappropriate language, the 'odious words and odious sentences' she puts into the mouths of her characters, must be silenced; the censor, in contrast, must be verbose rather than 'mealy-mouthed', he should embrace 'some plain honest English' in his fight against James's work. Shortly after *Sleeveless Errand*'s initial censorship, Henry Babon & Jack Kahane published an unexpurgated version of the book from Paris. What fronts this second edition is an illustration by Kahane's wife, Marcelle, depicting a seated female figure. Literally without a mouth, the woman in this image is deprived of a voice, unable to utter the foul words and odious sentences that caused such outrage. As such, she seems to inadvertently, or perhaps ironically, embody the sentiment expressed in the above government document, with its aggressive urge to silence James's 'foul mouth' via an articulation of the law's, and arguably male, authority.

Also patent in this extract is the fact that it was a specifically English brand of femininity at risk of being damaged by indecent literature. As Deborah Cohler states, 'twentieth-century lesbian representations were produced not only through the medical discourse of late-nineteenth-century sexology and female homosocial traditions [. . .] but also through discourses of xenophobic nationalism'.[21] With this in mind, it is interesting to note the inclusion of an inflammatory magazine article titled 'Current Literature: The Vulgarity of Lesbianism' amongst the Home Office papers on Compton Mackenzie's *Extraordinary Women* (1928). The article taken from the *New Statesman* claims that:

> Twenty years ago such a theme [of lesbianism] would have seems *outré* and altogether unsuitable for treatment in a novel; but it is impossible to dismiss it quite so confidently in these post-war days of boy-girls and girl-boys. Then it was merely a problem for the psychopath – and the less said about it the better. Now it is a comparatively widespread social phenomenon, having its original roots no doubt in the professional man-hating of the Pankhurst Suffragette movement, but owing very much to wider causes arising out of the war and its *sequelæ*.[22] [emphasis added in pencil on cutting]

The reviewer makes an explicit link between the First World War, changing gender roles, lesbianism and the suffragettes, and in response, an anonymous official hones in on, and literally underscores, the proposition that the feminist movement lies at the root of this causal chain. Literary censorship, then, was partly driven by the fear of female sexual knowledge and experience, as well as the concern that increasing liberty and the rejection of conventional heteronormative roles would threaten national morale and weaken England as an institution.[23] It is, after all, the 'daughter in a respectable English household' that might be corrupted by *Sleeveless Errand*.[24]

The definition of obscenity at this time clearly traded on assumptions about gender identity and mapped the integrity of womanhood onto that of Englishness. This connection is made explicit in a contemporary parody of James's and Hall's novels, P. R. Stephensen's *The Well of Sleevelessness: A Tale for the Least of These Little Ones* (1929), which combines verse and illustrations to mock both censors and authors. When the author features a Dame, 'nicknamed DORA because [. . .] / When she was born it was a Dreadful / Orrible Rotten Act', who incites an idle policeman to act against obscene literature, he refers to the 1918 Defence of the Realm Act, which revived the Victorian Contagious Diseases Act.[25] Intended to protect military personnel from venereal disease, the act gave men in H. M. Forces the power to report women they believed to have passed on a sexually transmitted disease. A woman could be imprisoned if, when made to undergo a medical examination, she was diagnosed with gonorrhoea or syphilis, and, even if healthy, her name could be registered with the police.²⁶ The reference to this legislation hints at the wider forces at work in this cultural scenario, as we also see from Douglas's diatribe against *The Well of Loneliness*:

> I know that the battle has been lost in France and Germany, but it has not yet been lost in England, and I do not believe that it will be lost. The English people are slow to rise in their wrath and strike down the armies of evil, but when they are aroused they show no mercy and they give no quarter to those who exploit their tolerance and their indulgence.²⁷

Framed through the lens of patriotism, he aligns the battle against the obscene lesbian text with that against Germany because both are 'armies of evil' that the 'English people' must destroy. As Adam Parkes points out, a similar connection was made in relation to Lawrence's work during a time when fears arose that modernism was somehow degenerate and Germanic.²⁸ Public response to Lawrence's *The Rainbow* (1915), published and banned in the midst of war, reflects this concern in the way that it formed a link between the sexual themes that Lawrence explored and the influence of German ideas.²⁹ In both literary cases, sexual 'deviance' is aligned with disloyalty to one's country, with the aim of censorship being to curtail both forms of rebellion.

A memo preserved in the Home Office archive on *The Well of Loneliness* reveals as much fascination with Hall's biography as with James's, as well as an interest in Hall's first-hand knowledge of the subject matter. Writing on 21 August 1928 to the Under-Secretary of State, Sir George Stephenson (the Deputy to the Director of Public Prosecutions) notes that '[i]incidentally it would appear to be clear that the authoress is herself what I believe is known as a homo-sexualist, or as she prefers to describe it an "invert"'.³⁰ Hall's identification as a lesbian was evidently not at all 'incidental', as is more than apparent from the starkly different treatment that Mackenzie's satire of a lesbian coterie, *Extraordinary Women*, received. Published in the same year as *The Well of Loneliness*, the novel was also considered for censorship.³¹ Contemplating the damage that Mackenzie's book might do, the Director of Public Prosecutions, Sir Archibald Bodkin, notes that:

> It is disturbing to think that the books were produced independently, as two books on the same subject so produced indicate the extent to which <u>Miss Hall knew, and Compton Mackenzie supposed</u>, abnormal sexual relations had developed, and these two books are not the only ones which have been brought to the attention of the Home Office dealing with or at least referring to this most unsavoury subject.³² [my emphasis]

With other more risqué texts such as *Extraordinary Women* escaping censure, it is feasible that *The Well of Loneliness* fared badly partly because Hall 'knew' while Mackenzie only 'supposed' when it came to lesbian sexuality. The problem that both James and Hall posed for the censors, then, and what made their texts so abhorrent, was their own knowledge, as women and lesbians, of the things of which they wrote. Thus, the fear of the obscene text is informed heavily by a fear of the obscene authorial body – gender-bending, politicised, and sexually conscious and active – and the threat that she, and women like her, might pose to the social and moral order of 'England'.[33]

But it is also apparent that what plays a part in this scenario, and the disparity between the treatment of Hall's novel and Mackenzie's, is certain assumptions about the value of literature and the work that it undertakes. The Chief Magistrate, Sir Chartres Biron's judgement on *The Well of Loneliness* implied that the sticking point with Hall's fictional offering was its sincerity and affirmative representation of the invert because it portrayed her as deserving of equality, acceptance, respect and happiness. Biron concludes that:

> There is not a single word from beginning to end of this book which suggests that anyone with these horrible tendencies is in the least blameworthy or that they should in any way resist them. Everybody, all the characters in this book, who indulge in these horrible vices are presented to us as attractive people and put forward for our admiration; and those who object to these vices are sneered at in the book as prejudiced, foolish and cruel. Not merely that, but there is a much more serious matter, the actual physical acts of these women indulging in unnatural vices are described in the most alluring terms; their result is described as giving these women extraordinary rest, contentment and pleasure; and not merely that, but it is actually put forward that it improves their mental balance and capacity.[34]

The distinction made here, then, is between subject and treatment.[35] It was indeed the book's sincerity and realism that incensed Hall's detractors, as much as it invoked praise from her supporters. As Jonathan Dollimore points out, Douglas penned condemnatory reviews of both Lawrence's *The Rainbow* and Hall's *The Well of Loneliness*. In his 1915 piece on the former, Douglas argued that the artist has a moral responsibility, that is a duty not to expose the unappealing truth about society.[36] But Hall's novel refused to abide by this dictate. Debating whether or not Mackenzie's *Extraordinary Women* should be censored, the Home Office noted that, while preoccupied with the same subject, Mackenzie's book 'lacks the earnestness of the "Well of Loneliness"' and 'may therefore be less dangerous'.[37] This sentiment is echoed in a minute dated 15 October 1928, written by Bodkin and addressed to the Home Office Under-Secretary of State: Bodkin compares the two texts and claims that while Mackenzie's is a 'satire' of a 'lesbian cult' which 'draws a most distasteful and detestable picture of practitioners in vice and the degraded condition into which they ultimately fall', Hall's text 'extols or at least finds excuses for indulgence in vice'.[38] Moreover, as Laura Doan and Jay Prosser point out, the book's materiality – its formal appearance and high price – positioned *The Well of Loneliness* as a novel intended to enlighten a highbrow audience rather than entertain a middlebrow one.[39] Hall's is hardly a novel with an affirmative ending, but the crucial difference between these texts is that while Mackenzie's is flippant and draws caricatures of lesbian women intended to entertain and amuse, Hall's presents a serious and ardent defence of the female invert intended to change society.[40] James recognised this difference when she commented in an interview regarding her banned novel *Sleeveless Errand* that:

> I believe in frankness, and I have books that excite not by what they say but by what they hint at and leave unsaid. It simply means that you cannot write a really sincere book in Britain without having the police down on you.[41]

The events of the 1920s signalled that serious, sincere and frank works concerning sexuality, and in particular lesbian sexuality, had no place in literature as far as the authorities were concerned, but that the frivolous, pleasurable text might be deemed benign and therefore less vulnerable to censure.

It is evident that artistic sexual expression risked social, legal and financial censure during this period. Inevitably this coloured what it meant to write, although such a state of affairs can both stymie and stimulate cultural production at the same time, and can remove a work from the market as well as 'guarantee its place in cultural history', as Dollimore puts it.[42] Thinking about how this crisis shaped literary output, scholars have concentrated on the role of modernist or avant-garde writing to argue that the experimental text navigated censorship by strategically encoding sexual material. Parkes, for instance, claims that the repressive air of the 1920s galvanised the modernist aesthetic by creating a 'theater of censorship':

> while Hall's direct attempt to terminate the lesbian's enforced silence and invisibility resulted only in an unsuccessful court battle, Woolf's *Orlando* shows how the theatrical strategies of an experimental modern narrative can imply the possibility of illicit lesbian desires and quietly undermine censorious legal and sexological discourses. Where public discourses block the route, modernism takes another path, which, though indirect and sometimes barely perceptible, disturbs discursive conventions more radically than a more direct or polemical approach.[43]

Parkes equates the obscene with the experimental and argues that censorship engineers the conditions under which modernism flourishes because, forced into evasive stylistic strategies, the truly radical and rebellious text mocks the censor through its artistry. Leigh Gilmore and Sashi Nair both make similar claims on behalf of Djuna Barnes's *Nightwood*, proposing that this 1936 novella escaped censure because T. S. Eliot's editorial preface positioned the book in the literary realm of artistic experimentation and so, as Gilmore states, '[h]is relatively vague literary/critical judgement, in effect, preempted a legal judgement'.[44] Claims such as these should nevertheless be qualified, in part because they risk privileging stylistic experimentation at the cost of a wider range of responses.[45] *Orlando: A Biography* (1928) is praised by critics for its witty and insolent artistry, for instance, but assumptions that Virginia Woolf's novel avoided persecution because, as Diana Souhami puts it, '[t]he lesbian allusions in *Orlando*, its flights of gender, were too aerial and implicit, too clever and concealed, to interest the Home Secretary or the editor of the *Express*' are mistaken.[46] As Marshik has pointed out, a register of incoming Home Office correspondence for 1928 reveals that a complaint requesting *Orlando*'s suppression was received on 16 October.[47] Since any further documentation is either missing or destroyed, we can only speculate on the forces at work in the novel's escape, but the incident serves to remind us that obscenity prosecutions were often sparked by complaints from members of the reading public, the press and the London Public Morality Council, who notified the Home Office and the police of books they believed required suppression. Even if figures in authority were blind to the lesbian content of texts like *Orlando*, that is philistines unable to comprehend the 'obscenity' of a more sophisticated text, outraged but perceptive members of the public were more than willing to enlighten them.[48] Neither were officials entirely incapable of playing the role of literary critic, as we see from the fact that much of Biron's legal judgement on *The Well of Loneliness* is dedicated to interpreting evasiveness and pointing out evidence of obscene practices between women. Regarding one particular passage he notes that '[i]n order that there may be no mistake what is meant by that passage there are four asterisks placed directly after it'.[49] Biron clearly did not intend to be fooled by blanks and silences.

The assumption that experimental modernist texts evaded censorship by masking transgressive material in obscurity warrants caution for other reasons as well. Archival evidence reveals that after 1929, in light of their experiences with *The Well of Loneliness* (its censorship was not an easy task, and public opinion was generally against such heavy-handed regulation of the arts), officials became increasingly reluctant to pursue a prosecution unless they were convinced of a successful outcome, meaning that experimental texts, and perhaps literature in general, was not at risk in the way that we might imagine.[50] A Home Office file from 1936 records the decision not to suppress Dr Laura Hutton's *The Single Woman and Her Emotional Problems*, an advice book that recommends masturbation or lesbianism for the numerous 'surplus' single women of the postwar period, because:

> It is notorious that the prosecution of the 'Well of Loneliness' resulted in infinitely greater publicity about lesbianism than if there had been no prosecution and if the object of suppression is to prevent women getting to know that these practices exist & adopting them, then I think there is no doubt whatever that the object would be defeated by prosecution and its attendant publicity.[51]

As other government files from the 1930s attest, this sentiment was by no means uncommon. While writers would not necessarily have been aware of this change of tack, this renders suspect the assumption that experimental texts simply went unnoticed.[52]

After the outright suppression of the 1920s, a more insidious form of what Marshik calls 'repressive tolerance' took hold, with unofficial censorship operating in libraries, universities and shops, so making books unavailable in a way that was hard to contest.[53] But this does not mean that the 'censorship dialectic', as she puts it, entirely died away.[54] Indeed, as late as 1939 Woolf wrote in her diary that 'I've been thinking about Censors. How visionary figures admonish us. [. . .] All books now seem to me surrounded by a circle of invisible censors'.[55] The authorities had cultivated an environment of fear, so much so that printers, publishers and authors had begun to police themselves. This is evident from a 1933 *Time and Tide* article in which the editor, Lady Rhondda, complains of the difficulty of finding a willing printer for Sean O'Casey's short story 'I Wanna Woman':

> So much of this kind of unofficial censorship happens in the dark and is never heard of except by the people immediately concerned [. . .] It may be that either to this paper or some other of the organs whose function it is to try to lead opinion will presently come a further opportunity of drawing attention to the most unsatisfactory state of our law – whose inevitable effect is to cause printers and publishers, in self-defence, to impose of themselves a far stricter censorship than the police could openly either impose or justify.[56]

Clippings of this article are included in an early 1930s Home Office file concerned with cases of indecent literature, and this and other archive records from the decade indicate that the government, now reticent to take action itself, looked to publishers to take stricter control of their titles. In one file containing Home Office minutes dated 23 December 1930, the suggestion that the Secretary of State should collaborate with a 'Committee of Publishers & others for consultation (when required) in matters of doubt regarding publications' is quickly dismissed because:

> S. of S. is not a censor, and does not need any consultative body in these matters – other than his legal advisors. [. . .] What he <u>would</u> like would

be some kind of private censorship set up by the publishers themselves, if they would do it.[57]

Similarly, it was hoped that the London Public Morality Council would alleviate the burden by independently taking cases to court, because '[e]xperience of recent prosecutions must lead any Home Secretary to be cautious'.[58] Records show that in 1935 Stanley Unwin (of Allen & Unwin Publishers and also a senior member of the Publishers' Association) met with a Home Office figure (most likely the Home Secretary or his Under Secretary) to discuss the procedure for prosecuting publishing houses.[59] Possibly as a consequence of this meeting a 1936 Obscene Books Bill was drafted to establish an Obscene Books Commission.[60] Literature, if considered obscene, was still under threat throughout the 1930s. Autumn 1934 saw the raid and seizure of 100 titles from the Fortune Press/Sequana book shop, many of which were established 'classics' deemed obscene due to the fact that they dealt with sexual themes such as 'homosexuality', 'masturbation', 'flagellation', 'immorality in a convent' and 'lesbianism'.[61] Representations of lesbian sexuality also continued to be flagged up and considered for censorship: G. Sheila Donisthorpe's *Loveliest of Friends!*, published in 1931, seems to have been considered for suppression, while the Home Office created files on D. L. Loddon's lesbian novel *Do They Remember?* in 1934 and Dr Laura Hutton's *The Single Woman and Her Emotional Problems* in 1936.[62] Suppression of these texts was not pursued because it was believed that any publicity would defeat the object of a prosecution, namely 'to prevent women getting to know that these practices exist & adopting them'.[63] Similarly, the difficulty of obtaining a copy of *Do They Remember?* reassured officials of its lack of impact and reminded them of the need to minimise any publicity surrounding the book.[64] Even as late as 1946, almost twenty years after its initial ban, Una Troubridge's attempt to republish the late Hall's novel as part of a complete edition of her work met with resistance both from the Home Office and her chosen publisher.[65] It deserves repeating that what is clearly at stake in these and other examples, and what continues to be at stake for some years, is female knowledge of sexual practices and the question of how best to curtail its circulation.

But the ban of *The Well of Loneliness* had far-reaching consequences in ways that the authorities could not have anticipated, not least because publishers became savvy to the beginnings of a marketable category of 'lesbian fiction'. Home Office minutes from August 1933 reveal that the *Daily Mail* had reported being approached by the Mitre Press and asked to publish an attack on an upcoming novel demanding its suppression. In exchange for increased book sales, the publisher pointed out, the *Daily Mail* could claim the credit for exposing the latest obscene book before any other paper. A copy of this letter from the Mitre Press is included in the file, and although details of the book and author are not disclosed, it is said to be a novel of the same 'type' as *The Well of Loneliness* and *Loveliest of Friends!*.⁶⁶ In the same vein, an advertisement for *Do They Remember?* (1933) in *The Book-Dealers' Weekly* in 1934 (six years after the publication of *The Well of Loneliness*) promotes the book as 'more revealing' than *The Well of Loneliness* and *Loveliest of Friends!*, and it reminds potential buyers of the book's ban by the Irish government.⁶⁷ Publishers traded on the excitement of procuring and consuming a censored book, but more importantly they used *The Well of Loneliness* as a touchstone against which other 'lesbian' texts were now measured and promoted.⁶⁸ What all of the above evidence seems to indicate is that more complex forces were at work behind the scenes of Whitehall, both feeding and starving censorship, determining which texts were targeted and which survived unscathed. What is also evident is that while the government had privately backed down, the threat of censorship remained as potent, and in some cases as productive, a force as ever for writers, publishers and printers.

Escape or Expression

The government's assumption that only serious work posed a threat to decency, and the critical tendency to romanticise the experimental text's capacity to resist censorship should come as little surprise. These judgements are to some extent symptomatic of an endemic belief in the value of artistic production and indicative of the way in which culture is dichotomised into the high/low, difficult/easy, original/formulaic and good/bad. Traditionally, we privilege the serious, the high, the difficult and the original because they are thought to constitute genuine, lasting and worthwhile art, while the frivolous, the low, the easy and the formulaic are dismissed as mere entertainment or diversion for the masses. When the detective fiction writer Dorothy L. Sayers warns the reader of her introduction to an anthology of detective, mystery and horror stories to 'make no mistake about it, the detective-story is part of the literature of escape, and not of expression', she implies that genre fiction is aside from serious literary concerns, somehow less challenging than its more intellectual, highbrow counterpart.⁶⁹ Woolf and Hall make similarly pejorative comments about their own forays into the popular realm. Woolf privately dismisses *Orlando* as 'all a joke; & yet gay & quick reading I think; a writers holiday', while Hall claims that with her supernatural short story 'Miss Ogilvy Finds Herself', exploring sexual inversion through the theme of reincarnation, she 'permitted [. . . herself] a brief excursion into the realms of the fantastic' before going on to pen 'a serious study of congenital sexual inversion'.⁷⁰ Judging from these statements, the generic text is as much an escape for the author as it is the reader, a holiday from the less appealing, or rigorous, demands of everyday life and potentially onerous task of writing serious fiction. The charge of escapism is commonly levied against 'low' culture, and to some extent is not unfounded since we enjoy genre fiction partly because it is detached from the structures of reality and tends to provide us with what we want and expect. But for commentators like Sayers, there is an evident suspicion and embarrassment of this textual pleasure, or fun.[71] What Sayers' comments bring to the fore, then, are assumptions about what qualifies as 'genuine culture', as the art critic Clement Greenberg puts it in his 1939 essay on the avant-garde.[72] According to Greenberg, it is the difficult, avant-garde artwork that is capable of challenging dominant structures of power and is most valuable to society for this reason. In contrast, kitsch or mass culture 'pretends to demand nothing of its customers except their money – not even their time' and is used by those in power as a tool for propaganda.[73]

The sense that there is a correlation between stylistic originality, cultural worth and political value persists in modernist studies. Critics have spent a great deal of time and energy debating the definition of modernism without a consensus being reached, but the concept of modernism by which we as scholars and students work, in the traditional sense at least, is built on the premise that the modernist aesthetic is one of stylistic innovation. The reason for this might well be that, as Geoff Gilbert has maintained, 'the only history that "modernism" has is an institutional history', meaning that modernism as a period, movement and style has been made cohesive and navigable only through the narrative that we as scholars impose on it.[74] A consistent strand of this critical story has focused on what Andreas Huyssen terms the 'great divide' between modernism and mass culture, between the 'low' and the 'high'. As Huyssen explains:

> Modernism constituted itself through a conscious strategy of exclusion, an anxiety of contamination by its other: an increasingly consuming and engulfing mass culture. Both the strengths and weaknesses of modernism as an adversary culture derive from that fact.[75]

The modernist work intentionally presented itself as an elite cultural product, as unique and aesthetically innovative, rejecting the supposed banality and uniformity of the mainstream and the demands of the market.

Although this monolithic definition of modernism has been adopted by scholars, for some time now critics have tasked themselves with challenging the traditional concept of modernism by mapping out alternative or marginal modernisms, as well as rethinking modernism's relationship with mass culture to investigate the way that it utilised the strategies of the marketplace to promote itself as an elite cultural product.[76] Scholars of lesbian modernism have made a significant contribution to this sea change by highlighting the importance of lesbian sexuality to the modernist aesthetic and by undermining the boundaries of the traditional modernist canon. Since the field first began to take shape in the late 1980s using models that primarily focused on figures of Left Bank Paris, how we define the lesbian modernist text has also been the subject of debate.[77] Much scholarship would describe it as a text in which modernist experimentation (with language and form, for instance) meets the expression of lesbian identity and desire to challenge the conventions of heteronormative society. Moreover, these are often understood as symbiotic conditions in the sense that the text's modernism encodes its lesbianism, while its lesbianism is indicative of its modernity. By bringing certain neglected but significant modernist writers to the fore – Djuna Barnes, Dorothy Richardson, H.D., Gertrude Stein, for example – and insisting upon the importance of female-oriented sexuality for the modernist aesthetic, scholars of lesbian modernism have repositioned the boundaries of modernist studies. But what still dominates the field to some extent is the sense that, as Jonathan Goldman puts it, '[w]hat makes modernism modernism is style'.[78] There remains a focus on high art, radical politics and ideas, as well as a privileging of stylistically experimental texts for their encrypted representation of sexuality. This is not to say that such an interpretative framework lacks foundation – for many writers, 'the fragmented, dissimulating techniques of modernism' posed as what Joanne Winning calls 'a kind of "escape route" for lesbian representation' and presented the opportunity to communicate a meaning which could not be directly articulated.[79] But even in the field's nascent stages, the need for the evolution of its methodology in order to expand the remit of modernism, and to take a more holistic investigative view, was acknowledged. As early as 1989, Shari Benstock posed the following questions:

> What of women writers who did not pursue Modernist experiments? What motivated Natalie Barney and Renée Vivien to adopt archaic poetic forms? Or Radclyffe Hall to employ outdated didactic narrative forms? Or Winifred Bryher to write children's narratives? Or Janet Flanner to adapt architectural forms to her novel *The Cubical City*? Much more work on these, and other, women writers is needed before we can graph the varieties of women's literary contributions to 'Modernism.'[80]

While Benstock is primarily concerned with the gender of modernism here, her central question holds true – how and why are non-modernist forms of writing significant in the narrative of lesbian modernism?

A number of scholars have responded to Benstock's rallying cry: Erin G. Carlston, Robin Hackett and Doan have, for example, all expressed an interest in the conservative strands of lesbian modernism, while others have drawn attention to more marginal figures.[81] Scholars have also broached the topic of genre fiction in a selective way. Gay Wachman self-consciously rejects 'high-modernism' in favour of a 'predominantly satirical, alternative modernist tradition' of fantasy in her study of lesbian crosswriting, and Jane Garrity, Jane Marcus and Terry Castle have all commented upon the appeal of fantasy to lesbian writers, although one might argue that fantasy, as it is framed there, is akin to the slipperiness of modernist writing that we are wont to celebrate.[82] Julie Abraham similarly sees history, although not exclusively historical fiction, as an 'alternative source of narrative structure' with which lesbian writers compensate for the dominance of the heterosexual romance plot.[83] More recent studies have continued with this project. Nair addresses the same dilemma attended to in this study to suggest that the *roman à clef* offered writers such as Virginia Woolf, Gertrude Stein, Djuna Barnes and H.D. a way to encrypt lesbian desire.[84] While these studies deliver compelling and significant readings that have broadened the radius of lesbian modernism, it is the working writer, popular culture, and ideas that sit less comfortably with a recuperative agenda, that remain overlooked. For this reason, it is important to attend to the idiosyncrasies and categorisations of generic forms and the part that they played in early twentieth-century cultural production and the lesbian modernist aesthetic. According to Doan's essay on conservative sapphic modernity, 'our reading strategies of transgression have been extremely limiting, in terms of foreclosing the multiplicity of interpretive possibilities, by ignoring the ways that sexual radicalism may coexist with a certain class-based political conservatism'.[85] My concern here is not primarily the same as Doan's (although lesbian conservatism does feature here), but I am interested in the multiplicity of ways that 'sexual radicalism' finds expression through conventional and popular genre fictions, those that we might initially assume to be conservative, non-political, frivolous, escapist, or even banal. What this book does, then, is loosen the category of lesbian modernism by 'graphing' (as Benstock once advised) the varieties of lesbian literary production.[86]

The censorship of Hall's *The Well of Loneliness* serves as the cultural scenario that allows me to do this, and so I use its publication history – its ban in 1928 and legal republication in 1949 – to loosely demarcate the boundaries of this study and to serve as symbolic bookends of a period in literary history when realist, serious and sincere depictions of lesbianism were under attack and when writers had to second-guess their aesthetic choices. It is clear that what emerges from the events of 1928 is the question of how best to represent the lesbian when literature is policed so strictly. Winning articulates that dilemma in the following terms:

> Effectively, the 'lesbian text' (if we can talk about such a thing), where it seeks to take either a fictional or poetic form (as opposed to scientific case history, or social document), underwent a profound attack in 1928. After such spectacular public condemnation, authors had to pick a course somewhere between a literal formulation which would sink beneath a wave of social outrage and a subversive 'silence' which employed an aesthetics of dissimulation and displacement.[87]

But I propose that a third trajectory, that of genre fiction, offered itself to the lesbian writer as a viable alternative to both realism and modernism, the literal and the dissimulative, and that this allowed women to write about lesbian sexuality and identity when faced with the threat of reprisals. Archive evidence suggests that a distinction was made between the serious and the frivolous text, the threatening and the benign. Thus, if we are to praise Woolf's evasion of censorship in *Orlando*, it might be the novel's multivalent generic status (it is a biography, history, fantasy and romance all at once), and moreover its light-hearted tone, as much as its experimental style that obscures its lesbian content. If, as Pierre Bourdieu states, '[t]aste classifies, and it classifies the classifier' then the consumption of culture is performative in the sense that the type of artwork we consume (and that which we reject) makes a statement about, and constitutes, who we are and our social position.[88] Those of a higher social status are in possession of what Bourdieu calls cultural capital, that is the knowledge, understanding and experience necessary to read the codes of genuine art and so to gain a true appreciation of 'legitimate' culture.[89] But if only 'legitimate' culture is taken seriously, what opportunities might this create for popular culture? Lacking in cultural capital, and in its illegitimate state, genre fiction might be thought to pose little threat or be of little import. It is, after all, when Mitchison goes back to writing about 'wolfskins and togas', or historical fiction, that she manages to write about sex and its associated topics.[90] It is arguably this inclination to underestimate genre fiction that endows it with the manoeuvrability and freedom to explore dangerous topics during the period with which I am here concerned.

This book, then, works to re-politicise a body of work that has in the past been dismissed as conservative, banal and frivolous. Through a selection of texts I show that twentieth-century genre fiction is capable of bursts of agency and that despite, or because of, an escapist façade, it undertakes significant and serious cultural work that needs to be factored into our concept of modernism, both in terms of the influence it has over modernist writers and its significance in its own right. And it is only by charting these varieties that we can achieve a holistic understanding of the cultural landscape at that time. It is with this rationale in mind that I perform a parallel reading practice – examining canonical writers against mainstream or popular – to show that both groups utilised genre in their portrayal of lesbian sexuality and identity and to dissolve barriers between the modernist and mainstream, the experimental and formulaic, and the radical and conservative.[91] Such an approach does not render the category of modernism meaningless – I am not suggesting that we consider all literature of the early twentieth century to be modernist – but neither is modernism a hermetically sealed body of work. The comparison between the experimental and mainstream serves to suggest that while these forms retain distinct characteristics, and while they are certainly not reducible to one another, they do seem to be intimately connected. What we witness, then, is not a clear separation but a mutual reciprocity between the high and the low, the serious and the fun, and an indication that the boundaries between these forms (and across the divide) are permeable. I argue, then, that cultural stratification is neither desirable nor possible and that it is productive and valid to think about modernism as much in terms of content as style.[92]

I begin this book with three aims in mind. Primarily, it focuses upon the hitherto ignored role of genre fiction – literature that is recognisable from its replication of formulaic patterns or conventions – for lesbian modernism.[93] Secondly, I move away from the critical agenda to recuperate texts on the basis of their affirmative, radical content and experimental style, and instead insist upon the significance of literary texts whose ideological positions are nuanced, paradoxical, and at times ostensibly conservative. Finally, such an interpretive strategy aims to expose buried networks of women working outside the cultural and geographical centres of modernism. Moving away from the well-heeled figures of the usual metropolitan social and artistic coteries, I turn to consider groupings of women not afforded such social or financial privilege. Apart from the canonical modernists I take into consideration, each of these women writers either subsidised their writing with income from another profession or wrote to support themselves. Josephine Tey and Gladys Mitchell were teachers; Dorothy L. Sayers worked in advertising, amongst other professions; Mary Gordon was one of the first female doctors and a campaigner for prison reform; Margaret Goldsmith was a journalist, translator and literary agent; and Katharine Burdekin, although primarily a writer, also worked in a shoe factory during the Second World War.[94] While this selection is limited to British and American women residing in Europe, and furthermore white, middle-class, educated and professional women, they nevertheless represent a neglected corpus whose examination is long overdue.

The title of this book is also intended to mark a break from sapphic modernism and to reflect this more democratic selection process, since as Tirza True Latimer points out, 'sapphic', associated with classical education, 'articulates a cultural heritage as well as an explicit sexual practice'.[95] This study defines lesbian modernism first and foremost as those texts that explore relationships and desires of an erotic or romantic nature between women, as well as the subject of modern lesbian identification. With the exception of Sayers and Tey, I have focused on women who experienced erotic and/or emotional attachments to women either at some point or throughout their lives. But my remit allows for both the lesbian text and lesbian author to explore the possibility that the text itself can be thought of as lesbian and/or queer, that is concerned with representing lesbian desire and identity from a 'queer' perspective. As Colleen Lamos argues, 'there is not, on the one hand, a "homosexual" modernism and, on the other hand, a "heterosexual" modernism, but a single literary corpus that is torn in various ways by the scission between these (supposedly) incongruent longings. "Queer" describes this uneasy conjunction'.[96] Thus, some chapters in this study are concerned with an individual author and the strategies she used to write about lesbian sexuality across her corpus, while others are more interested in tropes that recur in certain genre fictions.

Why Genre Fiction?

To address the question posed here, I turn briefly to the work of Mary Renault, a contemporary of the writers examined here. In Renault's first novel, *Purposes of Love* (1939), the nurse Colonna Kimball articulates the appeal of genre fiction for the lesbian reader when she picks up a western magazine to alleviate the boredom of a night shift:

> The Western was called *The Two-Gun Dude*, and promised well. Cowboys of the classic kind were a fairyland which Colonna had never outgrown. In their company she dismissed life with its painful compromises, and became her private picture of herself. Flicking open the thumbed pages, and skipping the preliminaries with the ease of practice, she was the Dude in less than a couple of minutes. Clean-limbed, with sinews of steel and whipcord, she toted his silver-mounted guns, knotted his silk bandana, canted his elegant ten-gallon hat, confounded his hairy rivals, shot up his enemies, and kissed his pale-pink, incidental girl.[97]

This passage is remarkable because Colonna's response to *The Two-Gun Dude* emphasises its fantasy qualities and the escape it provides from ordinary life. Similarly this is a text, or textual experience, that can be embarked upon at any favoured point since Colonna is familiar with the formula. But most importantly, the western offers her the opportunity to become 'the private picture of herself', to inhabit the subject position of the Dude, importantly over-endowed with phallic gun power. The tropes of the cowboy – his rugged masculinity, violence and assertive role in heterosexual romance – are adopted by Colonna in a bid to transform them into something meaningful to her and to express her masculine gendered sexual identity. Intriguingly, in Renault's later lesbian novel *Friendly Young Ladies* (1943), Leo Lane is not a reader but an author of the western. The inclusion of this detail is a notable decision on Renault's part, since, as Abraham points out, Leo is one of a number of 'lesbian-writer protagonists' in the modernist period.[98] But, to my knowledge, Leo is unique in her choice of genre fiction and moreover the cowboy novel. Renault's first attempt at fiction was also a western, and she is best known for historical novels that focus on the lives, and homoerotic relationships, of men.[99] That Renault would consistently choose, for both herself and her characters, forms traditionally associated with male action is interesting.[100] Ruth Hoberman believes the reason for this lies in Renault's attempt to destabilise the categories of gender and sexuality, but I suspect that it also speaks of the specific appeal and malleability of genre fiction for the lesbian writer and reader.[101] Indeed, much has been written on the lesbian author and reader's relationship with popular fictions, although this critical scrutiny has generally focused on cultural production of the later twentieth century. Gabrielle Griffin, for instance, states that:

> Lesbians [...] produce popular culture by utilising formulaic patterns. These can be derived from sub-genres existent in heteropatriarchal culture such as the thriller, science fiction and the romance, for instance. [...] One could argue that the use of these popular forms serves to counteract the absence of lesbians from much of heteropopular culture, undercuts the notion that heteropatriarchy 'owns' these popular forms, inscribes lesbians into popular culture and subverts some of the ideological conservatism inherent in formulaic texts[102]

According to Griffin, generic conventions are emptied out of traditional content and invested with affirmative, radical meanings. My study suggests that early twentieth-century lesbian popular fictions (popular in terms of form if not always circulation) are prescient of this self-conscious transformation of genre fiction's meanings, and it is in their more tentative negotiations with conventions that lesbian modernist writers expose their ideological agendas and loyalties. If, as Fredric Jameson has stated, '[g]enres are essentially contracts between a writer and his readers', it is in the amendments or challenges to these agreements that we must read for meaning.[103] The chapters that comprise this book are divided into studies of individual genre fictions collected under the broad categories of fantasy, history and crime, and they are preceded by brief introductions intended to explore what might be at stake in such contractual negotiations.

Notes

1. Mitchison, *You May Well Ask*, p. 179.
2. Gollancz in Mitchison, *You May Well Ask*, pp. 176–7. Mitchison describes her struggles with publishers in pp. 171–81.
3. *We Have Been Warned* was eventually published in 1935 by Constable.
4. Mitchison, *You May Well Ask*, p. 179.
5. Quoted in Mullin, 'Poison More Deadly than Prussic Acid', p. 18. See Mullin's chapter on the history of this legislation and the definition of obscenity.
6. Ibid. p. 18.
7. Marshik's article on this topic suggests that after the end of the First World War and the retraction of the Defence of the Realm Act, which had previously been relied on to suppress literature that was believed to threaten the war effort, prosecutors turned to earlier legislation concerned with obscenity. Marshik, 'History's "Abrupt Revenges"', p. 148.
8. Marshik, Parkes and Vanderham all provide excellent studies of the censorship history of Joyce's and Lawrence's work. See Marshik, *British Modernism and*

Censorship, Parkes, *Modernism and the Theater of Censorship*, and Vanderham, *James Joyce and Censorship*.
9. Interestingly, George Bedborough was taken to court in 1898 for selling Ellis's own first volume of *Studies in the Psychology of Sex*, entitled *Sexual Inversion* and published in English in 1897 (this subsequently became the second volume in the series). See Gilmore, 'Obscenity, Modernity, Identity', pp. 607–8.
10. Letter from Hall to Ellis (2 December 1928), quoted in Parkes, *Modernism and the Theater of Censorship*, p. 144.
11. Souhami, *The Trials of Radclyffe Hall*, p. 168 and p. 171.
12. Leonard Woolf, in *Nation & Athenaeum*, 4 August 1928, collected in Doan and Prosser (eds), *Palatable Poison*, pp. 52–4 (p. 54). For other reviews see 'A Selection of Early Reviews', in Doan and Prosser (eds), *Palatable Poison*, pp. 50–73.
13. For details of the trial see for example, Doan, *Fashioning Sapphism* and Doan and Prosser (eds), *Palatable Poison*.
14. Some of these topics are listed as the offending subjects of books seized from the Fortune Press in 1934 by police. See London, The National Archives (hereafter abbreviated as TNA), HO 144/22430/9.
15. *We Have Been Warned* was reported by Ethel Boileau in a letter dated 29 May 1935. An internal letter within the Metropolitan Police detailing the book's offensive passages is dated 21 June 1935. Mitchison might have been pleased to know that in considering the possibility of censoring *We Have Been Warned*, a government official compares her to Joyce because of her 'brilliant writing'. TNA, HO 144/22430/5.
16. Marshik, *British Modernism and Censorship*, pp. 124–5.
17. It is worth noting that Norah James worked at Cape, the publisher of *The Well of Loneliness*, at the time of the latter novel's prosecution and that she initially attempted to place *Sleeveless Errand* with her employer. See Pearson, *Obelisk: A History of Jack Kahane and the Obelisk Press*, pp. 63–4.
18. Marshik, 'History's "Abrupt Revenges"', p. 146.
19. But, interestingly, as Marshik points out, James's intention was not to valorise these new sexual opportunities but to critique their ill effects. Marshik, 'History's "Abrupt Revenges"', p. 155.
20. TNA, DPP 1/92.
21. Cohler, 'Sapphism and Sedition', p. 68.
22. The article is dated 25 August 1928. TNA, HO 45/15727.
23. Both Wachman and Marshik explore this connection between war, nationalism and female sexuality. See Wachman, *Lesbian Empire* and Marshik, *British Modernism and Censorship*.
24. TNA, DPP 1/92.
25. Stephensen, *The Well of Sleevelessness*, p. 9.
26. Cate Haste points out that by October of the same year there were 201 prosecutions and 102 convictions of women under this legislation. Details of this and DORA are from Marshik, *British Modernism and Censorship*, p. 105.
27. James Douglas, 'A Book That Must Be Suppressed', *Sunday Express*, 19 August 1928, collected in Doan and Prosser (eds), *Palatable Poison*, pp. 36–8 (p. 37).
28. Parkes, *Modernism and the Theater of Censorship*, p. 27.
29. Ibid. p. 28.
30. TNA, HO 144/22547.
31. Cape in fact brought forward the publication of *The Well of Loneliness* so that it appeared before *Extraordinary Women*, which perhaps indicates an awareness

32. of the publicity that the novel would receive as well as the potential for this to be financially profitable. Ingram, 'Unutterable Putrefaction', p. 344.
32. TNA, HO 45/15727.
33. In a similar vein, *The Rainbow* trial set Lawrence up, as he put it, as a 'lurid sexuality specialist'. Quoted in Parkes, *Modernism and the Theater of Censorship*, p. 31.
34. Sir Chartres Biron, Chief Magistrate, 'Judgement', 16 November 1928, collected in Doan and Prosser (eds), *Palatable Poison*, pp. 39–49 (pp. 42–3).
35. The day after the trial, Woolf asks in her diary 'What is obscenity? What is literature? What is the difference between the subject & the treatment? In what cases is evidence allowable?'. 10 November 1928, *Diary Volume 3*, pp. 206–7 (p. 207).
36. Dollimore, *Sex, Literature and Censorship*, p. 101.
37. TNA, HO 45/15727.
38. TNA, HO 45/15727. The fact that *The Well of Loneliness* was treated differently to *Extraordinary Women* was pointed out in letters from the London Public Morality Council complaining about Mackenzie's book (included in this file).
39. Doan and Prosser, 'Introduction: Critical Perspectives Past and Present', *Palatable Poison*, p. 4.
40. Indeed, Cook and Newton, amongst others, lament the visibility of *The Well of Loneliness* at the cost of other, more affirmative, representations of lesbian sexuality. See Cook, 'Women Alone Stir My Imagination', p. 719, and Newton, 'The Mythic Mannish Lesbian', p. 282.
41. James, quoted in Ingram, 'Unutterable Putrefaction', p. 347.
42. Dollimore, *Sex, Literature and Censorship*, p. 95.
43. Parkes, *Modernism and the Theater of Censorship*, p. 19.
44. Gilmore, 'Obscenity, Modernity, Identity', p. 618, and Nair, *Secrecy and Sapphic Modernism*, pp. 2–3. Potter makes a similar point when she states that 'modernist texts, in their more liberatory guises, become identified with radical and obscene transgression'. Potter, *Obscene Modernism*, p. 12.
45. I draw here on Garrity's point that 'the dominant critical discourse on modernism has tended to fetishize formal experimentation'. Garrity, *Step-daughters of England*, p. 148.
46. Souhami, *The Trials of Radclyffe Hall*, p. 186.
47. Marshik, *British Modernism and Censorship*, p. 118.
48. Marshik also makes the point that critics are too quick to assume that *Orlando* escaped censure because of its stylistic evasiveness. Marshik, *British Modernism and Censorship*, p. 114.
49. Biron, 'Judgement', 16 November 1928, collected in Doan and Prosser (eds), *Palatable Poison*, p. 47.
50. The fact that Sir William Joynson-Hicks, part of the driving force behind many of the convictions in the late 1920s, left his office as Home Secretary in 1929 is perhaps also relevant.
51. TNA, HO 144/22430/6.
52. Marshik also mentions that the government was less likely to move against obscene texts after 1929. *British Modernism and Censorship*, p. 8.
53. Ibid. p. 170.
54. Ibid. p. 3.
55. Woolf, 7 August 1939, *Diary Volume 5*, pp. 229–30 (p. 229).
56. TNA, HO 45/24939. Lady Rhondda's article is dated 10 June 1933. It was not possible to print O'Casey's story.
57. TNA, HO 144/14042.
58. Minutes dated 12 March 1930. TNA, HO 144/14042.

59. TNA, HO 144/22430/4.
60. TNA, HO 144/22430/1.
61. TNA, HO 144/22430/9.
62. Donisthorpe's *Loveliest of Friends!* is briefly mentioned in a file dated August 1933 in TNA, HO 45/24939. On Loddon's *Do They Remember?* and Hutton's *The Single Woman and Her Emotional Problems* see TNA, HO 144/22430/8 and HO 144/22430/6 respectively.
63. TNA, HO 144/22430/6.
64. TNA, HO 144/22430/8.
65. Troubridge contacted the Home Office requesting permission to publish *The Well of Loneliness*, which, of course, she did not receive. The prospective publisher, Peter Davies, also made enquiries and was warned of the risk of legal action if he pursued publication. Correspondence suggests that he was not particularly enthusiastic about the prospect of publishing *The Well of Loneliness* and was relieved to receive this advice from the Home Office. See TNA, HO 144/22547.
66. TNA, HO 45/24939.
67. This advertisement is collected with the file TNA, HO 144/22430/8.
68. Censorship could also be commercially profitable for publishers. Shortly after the ban of James's *Sleeveless Errand*, the Paris-based publisher Jack Kahane placed an advert in the London press claiming that he could publish any book banned in England within a month of its suppression. Ingram, 'Unutterable Putrefaction', p. 346.
69. What exactly Sayers means by 'expression' is rather vague. To some extent, she seems to refer here to emotional expression as well as expression of serious topics that are relevant to the reader's life. Sayers, 'Introduction', *Great Short Stories of Detection*, p. 44.
70. Woolf, 18 March 1928, *Diary Volume 3*, pp. 176–7 (p. 177). Hall, 'Author's Forenote' to 'Miss Ogilvy Finds Herself', p. 7. Hall wrote this short story in 1926 but did not publish it until 1934.
71. As Scholes points out '[w]e do not take pleasure seriously enough [...] and Modernism, with its emphasis on the connection between greatness and difficulty, is to some extent responsible for this'. Scholes, *Parodoxy of Modernism*, p. xiii.
72. Greenberg, 'Avant-Garde and Kitsch', p. 12.
73. Ibid. p. 12 and p. 20. On the value of culture and its relationship to pleasure see also Adorno and Horkheimer, 'The Culture Industry: Enlightenment as Mass Deception'.
74. Gilbert, *Before Modernism Was*, p. xiii.
75. Huyssen, *After the Great Divide*, p. vii. Huyssen develops these ideas further in his article 'High/Low in an Expanded Field'.
76. See Dettmar and Watt (eds), *Marketing Modernisms*; Strychacz, *Modernism, Mass Culture, and Professionalism*; and Turner, *Marketing Modernism*.
77. The phrase 'lesbian modernism' is thought to originate with Makiko Minow and her 1989 article 'Versions of Female Modernism: Review Article' (p. 67). For other work on lesbian modernism see, for instance: Benstock, Carlston, Doan, Elliott and Wallace, Garrity, Gubar, Hackett, Jay, Nair, Wachman, and Winning.
78. Goldman, *Modernism is the Literature of Celebrity*, p. 6.
79. Winning, 'Writing by the Light of *The Well*', p. 375.
80. Benstock, 'Expatriate Modernism', p. 37.
81. See Carlston, *Thinking Fascism*; Hackett, *Sapphic Primitivism*; Doan, 'Conservative Sapphic Modernity' on the conservative strands of lesbian modernism. See Castle, 'Sylvia Townsend Warner'; Garrity, 'Encoding Bi-Location'; and Wachman, *Lesbian Empire* on Sylvia Townsend Warner. See Winning, 'Wilde

Identifications' on the Australian writer Eve Langley; Waters, 'Wolfskins and Togas' on the historical novelist Maude Meagher; and Bacon, 'English Lesbians and Irish Devotion' on the Irish middlebrow writer Molly Keane. Other critics have also made advances into the popular: Carlston's *Thinking Fascism* includes work on Marguerite Yourcenar, and Smith's book on *Lesbian Panic* examines Elizabeth Bowen.
82. Wachman, *Lesbian Empire*, p. 2; Garrity, *Step-daughters of England*, p. 142; Marcus, 'A Wilderness of One's Own'; Castle, 'Sylvia Townsend Warner'.
83. Abraham, *Are Girls Necessary?*, p. xxi.
84. Nair, *Secrecy and Sapphic Modernism*.
85. Doan, 'Conservative Sapphic Modernity', p. 95.
86. Benstock, 'Expatriate Modernism', p. 37.
87. Winning, *The Pilgrimage of Dorothy Richardson*, p. 113.
88. Bourdieu, *Distinction: A Social Critique on the Judgement of Taste*, p. 6.
89. On cultural capital see Bourdieu, *The Field of Cultural Production*.
90. Mitchison, *You May Well Ask*, p. 179.
91. My approach is influenced by Wallace's study of women's historical fiction and her comment that we must 'read both "serious" and "popular" historical novels together and against each other if we want fully to understand the range of meanings that history and the historical novel have held for women readers in the twentieth century'. Wallace, *The Woman's Historical Novel*, p. 5.
92. Elliott and Wallace also comment upon the critical assumption that '[r]adical experimentation with form [. . .] is "modernist" while radical experimentation with content is not'. Elliott and Wallace, *Women Artists and Writers*, p. 15.
93. On the theory of genre see for instance Fowler, *Kinds of Literature*; Frye, *Anatomy of Criticism*; as well as Duff's edited collection of seminal genre theories, *Modern Genre Theory*.
94. Although it is possible that Burdekin did this out of principle rather than necessity since, as Patai notes, she 'never liked living on unearned income'. Patai, 'Afterword' to Burdekin, *The End of This Day's Business*, p. 166.
95. Latimer, *Women Together/Women Apart*, p. 3.
96. Lamos, 'Queer Conjunctions in Modernism', pp. 336–7.
97. Renault, *Purposes of Love*, p. 305.
98. Abraham, *Are Girls Necessary?*, p. 15.
99. Hoberman notes that Renault's first novel was a western and also points out the similarity of genre choices between Renault and her characters. Hoberman, *Gendering Classicism*, p. 79.
100. Hoberman raises a similar point with regard to Renault's work. Hoberman, *Gendering Classicism*, p. 73.
101. Ibid. pp. 79–80.
102. Griffin, 'Introduction', in *Outwrite*, p. 3.
103. Jameson, 'Magical Narratives', p. 135.

PART I
FANTASY

In the essay 'Creative Writers and Day-Dreaming', first delivered as a lecture in 1907, Sigmund Freud draws comparisons between adult 'phantasies', or daydreams, and creative writing. Like phantasy, which Freud argues is the 'fulfilment of a wish, a correction of unsatisfying reality', creative writing provides an avenue for the projection of the writer's own unsatisfied wishes and desires into his textual material and onto his hero of the piece.[1] Freud recognises that the release of such psychical material might be unpalatable to the reader, but he believes that the creative writer is able to counteract such hostility:

> Such phantasies, when we learn them, repel us or at least leave us cold. But when a creative writer presents his plays to us or tells us what we are inclined to take to be his personal day-dreams, we experience a great pleasure, and one which probably arises from the confluence of many sources. [. . . The writer uses] the technique of overcoming the feeling of repulsion in us which is undoubtedly connected with the barriers that rise between each single ego and the others. [. . .] The writer softens the character of his egoistic day-dreams by altering and disguising it, and he bribes us by the purely formal – that is, aesthetic – yield of pleasure which he offers us in the presentation of his phantasies.[2]

Freud defines such aesthetically stimulated enjoyment as 'fore-pleasure' and suggests that this is, in part, sourced from the reader's ability to vicariously experience his or her own fantasies.[3] Under Freud's thinking, the foundations of creative writing are indebted to psychical phantasy; by implication, then, literature could be said to be premised on the fantastic (and not just the phantastic) since it is divorced from or at the very least in negotiation with the psychical real.

Freud's essay does not attribute this psychical work to one particular mode of writing, but his model of fiction as an encoded enterprise, disguising unconscious meaning below layers of aesthetically pleasing techniques, or conventions, could be said to resemble any popular genre. More specifically, Freud's theory evokes thoughts of fantasy literature, since this is also a narrative ostensibly about one thing – other worlds in the future for instance – but essentially about another. If, as Rosemary Jackson states, the 'fantastic traces the unsaid and the unseen of culture: that which has been silenced, made invisible, covered over and made "absent"', such subterranean material is unearthed directly from the unconscious and pertains specifically to desire, or as Freud would have it, unfulfilled wishes.[4] With such material at the core, Jackson argues, '[f]antasies are never ideologically "innocent" texts', in the sense that they express socially and culturally ostracised desires and ideologies, and therefore contain the potential for subversion and a radical challenge to normativity.[5]

For critics such as Brian Attebery, the genre's heterodox tendencies gender it as feminine. In what he sees as their mutual exclusion from the canon, their 'disrupt[ion of] some of the same hierarchies of value and conventions of form', Attebery believes there to be an affinity between fantasy and women's writing.[6] Although one may question this idea – might the bond between the literary categories dissolve as one or both forms is appropriated into the mainstream, as they can be said to have done in recent years – many critics have commented on the affiliation between fantasy and the ideas and aims, often feminist, of the women writers choosing to work with it.[7] Although there is undoubtedly a debate regarding the forms of writing which might be classified under the auspices of fantasy, one might think of science fiction, utopian or dystopian narratives, horror, supernatural fiction and fairytales as all falling under this heading.[8] Herein lies the appeal of the genre for women writers and readers, since in its creation of other worlds, temporally and geographically displaced, these fantasy fictions endow writers with the freedom to not only make an ideological stand against their individual and collective hegemonic realities, critiquing those existences from a safe distance, but also to imagine other ways of living (alternative societies, identities, relationships, or bodies etc.) that are more appealing than the status quo. As Anne Cranny Francis states, feminist fantasy writers reject and critique not simply reality, but more pointedly the 'patriarchal real'.[9]

If one pursues Attebery's or Francis' lines of argument – that fantasy's othered status aligns it to women's writing and that the rejection of reality is a rejection of its patriarchal foundations – then it is not too great an imaginative leap to claim that fantasy may also serve as a rejection of heteronormative actuality for lesbian writers. If, as Jackson posits, fantasy is a narrative of desire, it functions as a potentially utopian space, a place where lesbian erotics can evade societal control to be experienced by both the writer and reader in a disguised form. This connection between fantasy, lesbian subjectivity and sexuality has become significantly more explicit in recent decades, with lesbian writers using fantasy to openly explore sexual themes, particularly in science fiction. But, curiously, critics appear reticent to connect modernism with fantasy and often gloss over this period in their discussions. Attebery suggests that 'most narrative literature, except for an aberrant period from the mid-nineteenth to mid-twentieth centuries [. . .], has made use of the fantastic', and while Jackson does examine fantasy during the period concerned, she cites Franz Kafka as the epitome of the 'modern fantastic'.[10] This is interesting if one considers the parallels that exist between fantasy and canonical modernism: both literary forms push towards a rejection of the established understanding of reality, questioning concepts of truth, unities of time and space, and the idea of subjectivity as contained and cohesive. Wachman's study of lesbian 'crosswriting' counters this neglect, turning away from 'high modernism' and instead towards what she terms an 'alternative modernist tradition' of 'writers who used fantasy as a means of escaping, reshaping, and critiquing a world fragmented by loss and pain'.[11] My chapters on fantasy therefore trace elements of this 'alternative' and fantastic modernist tradition, and they appropriate the term fantasy in the broadest and most inclusive sense, opting to consider what Attebery terms the 'fantastic mode' rather than fantasy as a strictly encoded enterprise.[12]

Chapters 1 and 2 examine writers whose works are fantastic in the sense that they create 'other' speculative worlds or modes of existence – futuristic or supernatural in these instances – and reject the common perception of reality, or rather, what is considered plausible and rational within that reality. In Chapter 1, I draw on a range of materials, including unpublished novels and correspondence examined for the first time here, to argue that Katharine Burdekin dovetails her utopian fiction protagonists with models of lesbian and gay inversion. By melding together sexological discourse and tropes of speculative fiction, Burdekin instigates an investigation into the nature of sexuality and strives towards a definition that might be considered controversial in its exclusion of desire. Burdekin handles the subject of sexuality anxiously and tentatively, but across the body of her published and unpublished speculative fiction we witness an attempt to evolve the concept of sexuality into something 'pure', spiritual and idiosyncratic to Burdekin. In Chapter 2, I focus on Natalie Clifford Barney, the epitome of the social, if not cultural, modernist, and her supernatural novel *The One Who is Legion or A. D.'s After-life*. I locate Barney within a tradition of women using the occult or paranormal, both in their actual lives and the imaginary realm, as a vocabulary with which to express the romantic and erotic ties between women. More specifically, I suggest that Barney turns to the occult, and a belief in spiritual existence after death, in order to conceptualise alternative modes of loving, and in doing so she exhumes and fetishises the spectral lesbian body. The work of each writer might appear unrelated and distinct from one another – indeed, the first looks to imagined futures while the second mourns and fixates upon ghosts of the past – but both are driven by similar motivations that are native to fantasy, since both use a fantastical premise to critique the contemporary real and both are dominated by a belief in alternative ways of conceiving societal and identity constructs.

Notes

1. Freud, 'Creative Writers and Day-Dreaming', p. 134.
2. Ibid. pp. 140–1.
3. Ibid. p. 141.
4. Jackson, *Fantasy: The Literature of Subversion*, p. 4.
5. Ibid. p. 122.
6. Attebery, *Strategies of Fantasy*, p. ix.
7. Jackson acknowledges the broad way in which '[a]s a critical term, "fantasy" has been applied rather indiscriminately to any literature which does not give priority to realistic representation [. . .], all presenting realms "other" than the human'. Jackson, *Fantasy: The Literature of Subversion*, pp. 13–14. Attebery offers a similar definition in *The Fantasy Tradition*, p. 2. For Todorov, in contrast, fantasy hinges upon the reader's 'hesitation' between a rational and supernatural explanation of the events taking place during the course of the narrative. See Todorov, *The Fantastic*, p. 31.
8. Attebery draws a sharp distinction between fantasy and science fiction, while Todorov rejects the supernatural as a component of fantasy. See Attebery, *Strategies of Fantasy*, p. 103 and Todorov, *The Fantastic*, p. 34.
9. Francis, *Feminist Fiction*, p. 77.
10. Attebery, *Strategies of Fantasy*, p. 4. Jackson, *Fantasy: The Literature of Subversion*, p. 178.
11. Wachman, *Lesbian Empire*, p. 2. On the importance of fantasy see also Castle, 'Sylvia Townsend Warner', and Marcus, 'A Wilderness of One's Own'.
12. Attebery, *Strategies of Fantasy*, p. 2.

I

'THE BOOK IS A SORT OF TOUCH-STONE TO <u>OTHER</u> PEOPLE': SEXOLOGY, THE INVERT AND DESIRE IN KATHARINE BURDEKIN'S UTOPIAN FICTION

Speculating on the Future

In 1932 Hamish Hamilton published a collection of essays entitled *Man, Proud Man* which featured commentaries addressing the topic of contemporary gender roles. Of these eight essays, three imagine a sex-role reversal to speculate on what the future might hold for women. Mary Borden's 'Man, The Master. An Illusion', Storm Jameson's 'Man the Helpmate' and Rebecca West's 'Man and Religion' each consider the possibility of a matriarchal society. Jameson traces shifting gender conventions from the late nineteenth century onwards with particular attention to the changes that follow the war. With husbands less willing to support wives who are themselves capable of work, she observes the ever-increasing financial dependence of such men on their partners.[1] She worries that if this continues:

> there is nothing (short of a return to barbarism) to save women from taking over the complete control of affairs. They will earn the wages and salaries, take over the reins of business, remove the bauble from the House of Commons [. . .], bring order out of international chaos – in short, make the word their kitchen and do it very well. Woman is the organizer and manager – the ruler.[2]

Men, in contrast, will have 'nothing to do but to paint, write, dream, explore, experiment, research, fly, climb, dive deep under the sea'.[3] Jameson, then, by suggesting that an inversion of power might take place speculates on an alternate world governed by women and a feminine, domestic order. The point of this fictionalised essay is a negotiation of feminism's aims, and it implies that Jameson is concerned that women, striving for equality and power, may ultimately be cheated of liberty and leisure. Her lamentation that '[i]f our men are allowed to become wholly irresponsible, wholly dependent on our public and private efforts, we shall not be a whit better off [. . .] – only a great deal busier', is indeed a statement that continues to resonate loudly.[4]

West's contribution is also a prospective vision of a matriarchal existence, although this is seen via a mediumistic vision. In West's speculative future the behaviour of men has resulted in a system of female domination. While men have become the less educated and less articulate sex, women have exceeded their counterparts with the aid of science and technology, working more efficiently and living significantly longer lives than men. With the aid of technology, for instance, the gestation of children has been reduced to a mere two weeks, which are 'spent in refreshing repose'.[5] In contrast, men's 'highest destiny is to be the husbands and fathers of good women' and their chastity is as precious to them as financial independence is to women.[6] This is not a wholehearted utopia (female and male dissenters do appeal for equal rights), but then neither of these essays is intended as a serious plan for a new society. Rather, West's and Jameson's reversals of societal standards serve to challenge the rationale for patriarchal norms. This collection of essays is significant because it is indicative of the popularity of speculative fiction – utopian and dystopian modes of writing – in the 1930s and surrounding decades, as well as the ideological purpose it served for women writers.

Andy Croft has pointed out that while much critical and commercial emphasis has been placed on George Orwell's 1949 dystopian novel *Nineteen Eighty-Four*, this 'was only the tail-end of a more original and important literary and political development in this country in the late 1930s and 1940s' that saw a range of writers experimenting with the form.[7] The fashion for speculative modes of writing during the interwar years is hardly surprising given that this was a period of dramatic change and uncertainty. Blighted by the shadow of the First World War, and with indications that a second would follow, speculative writing provided a way to look to the future, whether that was with hope or with anxiety. Thought to originate with Thomas More's 1516 *Utopia*, utopian fiction has experienced fluctuations in popularity and, as Tom Moylan points out, these peaks in interest can often be accounted for by periods of social and political upheaval.[8] Using temporal and geographical displacement to construct fantasy worlds and societies, utopian fiction imagines idealised ways of life and corrects the failings and flaws of reality.[9] This can be motivated by an element of wish-fulfilment and a genuine belief in a better existence, but utopian fiction does not necessarily propose a blueprint for a new society, and as Daphne Patai points out, 'the key point that must be understood about utopian fictions is that they are never primarily about "otherness" but are most of all about ourselves'.[10] The genre, then, provides an opportunity to critique the status quo from a safely displaced position. Jameson and West, for instance, use utopian conventions not to sketch out a new system of gender power, but to lambast the current one.

It should come as no surprise, then, that many women writers chose to work in speculative modes around this time. The list is too extensive to be exhaustively detailed here, but one could cite Jameson, Naomi Mitchison, West and Winifred Holtby as a few better-known authors writing in this way. Many of these women, Nan Bowman Albinski points out, were journalists and internationalists, engaged in political debate during the interwar period and travelling to Communist Russia and Nazi Germany.[11] Evocatively titled texts such as Charlotte Haldane's 1926 *Man's World*, Victoria Cross's 1935 *Martha Brown, M.P. A Girl of Tomorrow*, or Elise Kay Gresswell's 1935 *When Yvonne Was Dictator* indicate that many of these writers were concerned not only with the state of Europe and the immediate dangers it faced but also with the question of what gender and feminist politics could add to the debate.

Frances Bartowski summarises the appeal of utopian fiction for women when she states that '[t]he feminist utopian model is a place where theories of power can be addressed through the construction of narratives that test and stretch the boundaries of power in its operational details'.[12] Indeed this project is very much underway in the work of the Burdekin (1896–1963), a little-known British writer of fantasy and speculative fiction who turns to the landscapes of the past and of the future to imagine utopian and dystopian worlds. Burdekin uses these terrains to explore contemporary political issues and to dissect the structures of Western society, paying pointed attention along the way to the rise of European Fascism (as seen most explicitly in the 1937 *Swastika Night*) and the oppressiveness of gender constructions. After publishing her first novel, *Anna Colquhoun*, in 1922, she followed this with nine others, six of which, beginning with the 1934 *Proud Man*, were written under the pseudonym Murray Constantine. Burdekin, it would then appear, was fiercely protective of her identity and privacy.[13] The writer and poet H.D. in fact described Burdekin as 'secretive, reticent' and noted her reluctance to reveal even minor details such as her nationality.[14] H.D. suspected that Burdekin was Australian, and although this was not the case, she was not far from the truth.[15] Although born in Derbyshire, Burdekin had settled in Australia with her husband and children in 1920, returning to England in 1922 following the end of her marriage and meeting the woman who would become her 'lifelong companion' in 1926.[16] The reticence H.D. picks up on might well account for the relatively minimal critical attention Burdekin has received, but given that the narratives of modernism and lesbian modernism focus heavily on the cultural production of the metropolis, I suspect that it is also her geographical marginality that has made it difficult to situate her within the usual groupings of women writers, artists and intellectuals. As Burdekin's companion commented in a letter to Patai in 1984, '[w]e always talked a great deal, read very widely, belonged to no coterie . . . We knew many writers but as isolated individuals. Indeed we always lived in the country, very rustic and private with sorties to London'.[17] We might think of Burdekin, then, as a somewhat elusive and intriguing figure, in the sense that while she was well connected to individual modernists and literary figures (Leonard and Virginia Woolf, Bertrand and Dora Russell, H.D., Havelock Ellis, and Radclyffe Hall, as well as such writers as Norah James and Margaret Goldsmith) she also stood outside of the better-known coteries and networks that have received scholarly attention.[18]

Yet it is telling that Burdekin's writing features in the first issue of the literary magazine *Life and Letters To-Day* to be published under the auspices of Bryher's ownership and Robert Herring and Petrie Townshend's joint editorship. Alongside contributions from H.D., Havelock Ellis, André Gide and Gertrude Stein, sits Murray Constantine's fantasy story 'The Power of Merlin'.[19] It is useful to situate Burdekin's piece in the light of the editorial introduction, which maps out the magazine's ethos under its new management. This is, as one might expect, largely optimistic, even utopian, in bent, claiming to look 'forward' to the 'future'.[20] Outlining the rationale behind its choice of contributors, the editors reject literary elitism:

> we shall print no authors whose style outruns their sensibility, and as long as the latter looks forward, we do not care to which school the former belongs. [. . .] But we would declare that any bias we have is not towards experiment for its own sake, but to unrecognised achievement.[21]

Burdekin's inclusion alone is not necessarily evidence of her rightful place amongst modernists – although one could argue this to a certain extent – but it does suggest that, ranked alongside now canonised (as least in terms of modernist studies) writers such as Stein and H.D. for her 'unrecognised achievement', Burdekin's (or Constantine's, rather) work was afforded a degree of literary kudos, and this begs the question of why her work has fallen by the wayside during the intervening years.

Her fascinating relationship with H.D., in particular, deserves further investigation. The latter's correspondence with Havelock Ellis and Bryher mentions Burdekin in intimate detail, and dishes what H.D. terms the '"professional" dirt'.[22] What is evident from these letters is H.D.'s admiration for Burdekin's work, her concern for her friend's mental health and her unsuccessful attempts to recommend she enter into psychoanalysis. They also intimate H.D.'s sense of affinity with this writer: she describes Burdekin's partner as a woman 'whom she is not in love with, a sort of Bryher, who helps her', and she draws parallels between their creative methods and experiences:[23]

> I wrote her myself, that her 'complex' about writing and about being known as a writer, by her readers, was so like mine that it annoyed me. That when I screamed at her, I was really be-rating [sic] myself.[24]

By encouraging Burdekin to seek professional help, H.D. stimulates the already evident, and to her disturbing, sense of romantic and creative synergy. It is therefore not surprising that H.D. nurtures Burdekin's fervent interest in her own friend and correspondent, the renowned sexologist Havelock Ellis. In one letter to Ellis, H.D. sidesteps the question that concerned eager reviewers and readers regarding the author's true sex and identity, by referring to her merely as 'it'.[25] The same letter praises Burdekin's most recently published work, *Proud Man*, by stating that 'I find the book is a sort of touch-stone to other people; it brings out some essential "virtu," or essence by the acid like quality of truth.'[26] Although she does not elaborate, it is both tempting and feasible to argue that H.D.'s emphatically underscored term 'other people' signals her recognition of *Proud Man* as a potentially queer text, and that with this phrase she refers to both the non-heteronormative identities littering the novel and those readers to whom it might appeal.

It is this empathetic relationship between Burdekin's works of fiction and homosexual identities that remains a heretofore unexploited topic in scholarship on the author and is therefore the subject of this chapter. Patai's research in the 1980s discovered Burdekin's use of the pseudonym Murray Constantine, and she was responsible for bringing Burdekin's work to light once more through the re-issue of *Proud Man* and *Swastika Night* and the publication of the previously unseen *The End of this Day's Business*. Following Patai's lead, some work has been undertaken on Burdekin's treatment of gender, European politics and Fascist ideology, but this has been to the disregard of her concern with sexuality, which is more tentatively and anxiously tackled in the background of her texts and, to my mind, needs more nuanced and dedicated attention.[27]

By way of reparation for this neglect, this chapter argues that Burdekin's speculative fiction is populated by what H.D. terms 'other people', or sexually dissident identities. Although Burdekin's final novel appeared in 1940, she wrote prolifically until becoming seriously ill in 1955 and this body of material is now housed in her archive in New York City. Drawing on a selection of unpublished writing and correspondence found there but until now critically unexamined, I explore the significance of sexual inversion for this writer. I look to her published novels *The Rebel Passion* (1929), *Proud Man* (1934), and *The End of This Day's Business* (1989), to explore the way that Burdekin casts her characters from the moulds of popular sexological discourses, replicating the widely disseminated paradigm of the sexual invert that would have been decipherable to her readers. Identities that we now recognise as gay and lesbian are intrinsic to Burdekin's deployment of the utopian genre and to her utopian imaginative process in the sense that they are presented as the harbingers of a brighter and evolved future.

Body and Soul

Before looking at the significance of the invert in Burdekin's fiction, I first turn to her source material, the discourse of sexology – the nineteenth-century study of sexual science and theorisation of homosexuality, developed by such figures as Richard von Krafft-Ebing, Havelock Ellis, and Otto Weininger. Karl Heinrich Ulrichs, a lawyer and homosexual rights campaigner, defined inversion in his 1860s publications on homosexuality as an erroneous assignment of soul to body. Ulrich's phrase 'anima muliebris in corpore virili inclusa' – translated as 'a woman's soul trapped in a man's body' – was used to describe what he termed as Uranism, a concept that reappears in much subsequent writing on the subject.[28] Inversion was understood as a congenital identity, innate and ineradicable and so deserving of tolerance and acceptance. This theory relied upon a traditional, and conservative, notion of gender behaviour and, essentially, a heteronormative blueprint of desire to explain and justify homosexuality. As Melanie A. Taylor explains: 'As gender role and behaviour was deemed to be the natural consequence of sex, if an individual's sexual instincts belong to the opposite sex then, it was reasoned, so must her or his gender attributes.'[29] What emerges from this remarkably gender-determined scientific framework is the archetypes of the mannish lesbian and the effeminate homosexual man, those that experience the emotions and behavioural tendencies usually attributed to one sex but that possess the body of another. Ellis's highly influential and popular study of sexual inversion, volume two of *Studies in the Psychology of Sex* states that '[t]he commonest characteristic of the sexually inverted woman is a certain degree of masculinity or boyishness'.[30] As he explains further:

> When they still retain female garments, these usually show some traits of masculine simplicity, and there is nearly always a disdain for the petty feminine artifices of the toilet. Even when this is not obvious, there are all sorts of instinctive gestures and habits which may suggest to female acquaintances the remark that such a person 'ought to have been a man.' The brusque, energetic movements, the attitude of the arms, the direct speech, the inflexions of the voice, the masculine straightforwardness and sense of honor, and especially the attitude toward men, free from any suggestion either of shyness or audacity, will often suggest the underlying

psychic abnormality to a keen observer. [. . .] There is also a dislike and sometimes incapacity for needle-work and other domestic occupations, while there is often some capacity for athletics.[31]

In his 1886 study *Psychopathia Sexualis*, Krafft-Ebing reaches much the same conclusion:

> The female urning may chiefly be found in the haunts of boys. She is the rival in their play, preferring the rocking-horse, playing at soldiers, etc., to dolls and other girlish occupations. The toilet is neglected, and rough boyish manners are affected. Love for arts finds a substitute in the pursuits of the sciences. At times smoking and drinking are cultivated even with passion.
>
> Perfumes and sweetmeats are disdained. The consciousness of being a woman and thus to be deprived of the gay college life, or to be barred out from the military career, produces painful reflections.
>
> The masculine soul, heaving in the female bosom, finds pleasure in the pursuit of manly sports, and in manifestations of courage and bravado. There is a strong desire to imitate the male fashion in dressing the hair and in general attire, under favourable circumstances even to don male attire and impose in it.[32]

These striking excerpts illustrate that for sexologists, sexual difference was both visible and tangible: lesbianism presents itself semaphorically, according to these men, in that it is detectable from sartorial signals – a cropped hairstyle, disdain of feminine *maquillage*, masculine tailoring, or even enjoyment in smoking.[33] Such difference also manifests itself in the rejection of traditional activities of the domestic sphere and in a feminist demand for the right to those realms typically barred to women – the female invert desires access to education (but not simply the concessionary arts degrees) and to the professions. Female inversion, or lesbianism, in this scheme is entangled with political, and distinctly feminist, choices and with a clamouring for the rights and privileges already afforded to men.

Despite the lapse of time since its inception, sexology's currency held firm for an early twentieth-century readership. As Doan notes, sexological works circulated among writers, artists and intellectuals after the First World War, thus reaching an audience who found in these theories a pertinent language for comprehending and articulating gay and lesbian identities.[34] The prosecution and censorship of Hall's *The Well of Loneliness* – what Doan calls '*the* crystallizing moment in the construction of a visible modern English lesbian subculture' – undoubtedly had a significant part to play in promoting knowledge of sexology and the dissemination of the female invert as a recognisable paradigm.[35] Doan's study on the emergence of modern lesbian culture emphasises that although masculine and boyish styles of dress were considered highly modish in the 1920s and were not commonly associated with sexuality, the 1928 trial and the increased visibility of Hall, a lesbian who favoured masculine tailoring, was the moment when signifiers of gender become visibly attached to lesbianism.[36] In the furore surrounding the novel, sexological theories of inversion and Hall's lesbian text enter the public domain hand-in-hand, and the archetype of the mannish lesbian around whom signifiers of dress, body and behaviour had coalesced is marked out as a publicly recognisable and definable figure.[37]

It is with this context of popular sexual theories and cultural events in mind that Burdekin's personal connections to Ellis, H.D. and Hall become relevant once more. In a further letter to Ellis in 1934, H.D. describes Murray Constantine, now named as Burdekin, in detail and in particular expresses concern for her mental state.[38] Encountering difficulties with her friend, H.D. had advised Burdekin to write to Ellis herself, for the reason that 'she worships H.E.'.[39] Of the correspondence that followed between Ellis and Burdekin, four letters from the former, dated between 1934 and 1937, survive and are collected in Burdekin's archive. The content of these is intriguing: Ellis and Burdekin exchange recommendations for psychological, and sexological, reading material (Otto Rank, for instance); they discuss shared experiences of Cornwall and Australia; Ellis sympathises with Burdekin's difficulty working with her editor, Laura Riding; he warns her of the dangers of censorship in the American market; and assuages her fears that she may be experiencing a kind of authorial 'neurosis'.[40] Ellis also relays stories of the mystery surrounding Burdekin's true identity, along with his recommendations of her novels to friends and publishers and their enthusiastic responses. In their wholehearted approval of her work, and in particular of *Proud Man*, Ellis's letters provide Burdekin with creative and emotional support.[41] While Ellis does not detail the specific appeal of Burdekin's writing, he does state that one unnamed and unpublished book 'about women' – most likely 'Snakes and Ladders' – is 'valuable'.[42] The praise heaped upon Burdekin in these missives acts as an endorsement of her fiction and the subjects that she tackles, perhaps in much the same vein, albeit privately, as his preface to Hall's *The Well of Loneliness*.

The uncovering of this correspondence is revelatory since it tells us that Burdekin not only had an interest in sexology but also a relationship with one of its most famous proponents. The discovery that Burdekin wrote but did not publish two realist narratives about sexual inversion, which are now collected in Burdekin's literary archive, gives body to this idea. These narratives can be described as realistic bildungsromane that explicitly imitate Hall's *The Well of Loneliness* and reincarnate her invert protagonist, Stephen Gordon. Burdekin, then, is not only engaging with sexological models of sexual identity but also with Hall's own version of that paradigm.[43] The first of these texts, 'Two in a

Sack', was scheduled for publication in 1928 but withdrawn at the late stage of galley proofs. The publisher, Thornton Butterworth, had gone so far as to include the novel on its advertised list.[44] The rationale behind such a retreat and who instigated the move is unknown, but it seems likely that with its stark similarity to *The Well of Loneliness*, the publisher would have perceived the threat of legal reprisals and withdrawn the potentially offensive text.[45] The protagonist, Blaise Thorwald, loosely follows the same plot trajectory as Hall's Stephen Gordon: in lieu of a son, Blaise adopts the male family name; attracted to athletic pursuits, she longs to be male and feels disaffected by the lot of her biological sex; she adopts a cropped hairstyle to signify her emerging adult identity; on the outbreak of war she longs to fight alongside her comrades; and although attracted to women, her most emotionally intimate relationship is with a figure that resembles Hall's character Martin Hallam. Burdekin also duplicates that pivotal moment of recognition in the original text when Stephen discovers her late father's collection of sexological books and is finally able to decipher her sexual temperament. Blaise's father, intuiting the turmoil that his teenage daughter experiences, explains the gender dissonance that she feels but cannot name:

> Your body more or less conforms to the feminine, though even that is not built quite on the right lines; but your soul, the essential and indestructible part of you, is definitely quite masculine. It is in everlasting revolt against your body. It hates its dwelling place.[46]

The vocabulary and images used here make Blaise recognisable as a female invert, that is a male soul trapped in a despised feminine body.

The later unpublished novel 'The Stars Shine in Daylight', probably composed in the early 1940s, is a sequel to *The Well of Loneliness* and a bolder, more explicit text.[47] Hall's novel concludes with Stephen's decision to sacrifice her own happiness in the belief that only a man, and in this instance her romantic rival Martin, can care for and protect her lover, Mary. 'The Stars Shine in Daylight' details the events immediately subsequent to this tragic ending. Beginning with Stephen's immediate psychological collapse, followed by her immersion into Parisian lesbian society and a series of drunken sexual encounters, the story concludes with her emergence from this hedonistic haze with a renewed understanding of herself. As a nod to the history of the text that inspired it, Burdekin's version of Stephen finds work as a publisher's reader in 1928, the same year of *The Well of Loneliness*'s prosecution. Stephen is duly warned by her new employer to be wary of material that will not withstand the censor's gaze, but is simultaneously informed that the current literary trend is for realism:

> everything ugly must be described in detail, it means that lust is all important and that love can only sneak in at the back door (the way lust used

to) and that bodily functions which used not to be mentioned now take something of a place[48]

This makes reference to the conflicted nature of literary production in the period, the fashion for increasingly candid representations of sexuality and relationships, tempered by a drive against cultural productions of obscenity. More importantly, this extract tells us that Burdekin was particularly conscious of the cultural atmosphere in the late 1920s and discerned the necessity for caution regarding the content of her published work.

However, these texts depart from the example set by *The Well of Loneliness* when they amend the trajectory of Hall's original narrative in utopian ways. Burdekin's Stephen regrets her previously moralistic judgement of other inverts and reconciles with both her mother and her enemy Roger Antrim. Both Blaise and Stephen also ultimately agree to marry their closest male friends, George and Martin, in platonic unions of the soul. But it is Blaise and Stephen's struggle to reconcile their own desire for women with what they believe to be morally good that marks the most intriguing point of negotiation with the archetype, and most certainly signals a deviation from Hall's insistence that the invert is a sexual being.[49] Burdekin's Stephen must unequivocally choose between the love of women on the one hand, and on the other, her sanity, religious faith, and the kinship and comradeship bonds she values so highly. As her friend Brockett explains of her decision to end a passionate affair with Hetty:

> Stephen was getting to the point of chucking Tom and Morton, because she said she was keeping Tom's friendship under false pretences, so you see, it <u>had</u> to be stopped. [...] He's absolutely normal except that he is <u>very</u> masculine, and so Stephen's masculinity never worries him. But Tom's very innocent too, and we want to keep him so. As Stephen rightly says Tom doesn't mind what she <u>is</u>, he likes it.[50]

What is remarkable about this extract is that while Burdekin's work in general suggests a causal relationship between gender identity and desire, Stephen's predicament claims that a rift between what one is and what one does is possible: Tom will accept what Stephen is, a masculine identified woman, but not what she does, that is have sex with women. Stephen chooses homosocial bonds over romantic love when she is reunited with her former friend and rival Martin, the man who once absconded with Mary. Burdekin makes the choice not to reunite the female lovers as one might hope – Mary has since died in childbirth, although Stephen is little grieved by the news – and instead brings Stephen together with Martin, who she describes without any hint of irony as 'my man'.[51] Burdekin concludes this novel with Stephen's renunciation of women and proposal of marriage to Martin, effectively adopting the role of surrogate mother to Mary's child. Blaise of 'Two in a Sack' makes a less starkly framed choice but is also burdened by the conviction that lesbian relationships are somehow exploitative in their lustful nature, steering away from the fulfilment of same-sex encounters. And as with Stephen, Blaise's narrative concludes with her platonic 'spiritual marriage' to her soul mate, George.[52] While marriage is no impediment to the philandering George's heterosexual exploits, we get little sense of whether Blaise has a fulfilling sexual future ahead of her, or whether she, like Stephen, is now destined for a chaste, 'pure' life.

Blaise and Stephen are significant to this discussion on two accounts. Sourced from sexology's archetype of the mannish lesbian, most prominently represented in *The Well of Loneliness*, they demonstrate that Burdekin was creatively engaged by the figure of the sexological invert and interested in extending her narrative in unexpected ways. In the afterword to *The End of this Day's Business*, Patai acknowledges that Burdekin 'toys with the notion that an individual could possess the body of one sex and the soul of the other', but she stresses that:

> it is important to point out, she means a spiritual complementarity, capable of occurring in any two bodies. Her novels repeatedly show same-sex partners whose souls form a perfect whole, as well as male-female couples whose communion and understanding exclude sexual attraction.[53]

Burdekin does indeed believe in a harmony of souls, a meeting of male and female elements, which can occur through any combination of bodies, but it is vital that we do not merely discount this as a vision of an androgynous existence, so disassociating these figures from the context that influenced Burdekin and essentially desexualising her characters. While, as I will later discuss, Burdekin ultimately advocates that these unions should ideally be spiritual rather than corporeal, they do not preclude the inclusion of an erotic component. These texts are also crucial because they serve as a pivotal test case for the premise of this study. After 'Two in a Sack', one of Burdekin's few realist texts, was pulled from publication in 1928, Burdekin turns to speculative fiction in much the same way that Mitchison returned to historical fiction.[54] Blaise is effectively recast in various guises across Burdekin's speculative works, once again suggesting the inadequacy of realist modes for the representation of lesbian sexuality and identity.

All three of Burdekin's published novels examined here map the identity of the modern invert onto the utopian protagonist, signalling that these texts say as much about the contemporary moment as they do about the future. This is particularly explicit in *Proud Man*, a story narrated from the perspective of a traveller sent from the future to observe and report on 1930s England. The visitor hails from an egalitarian and peaceful way of life where war, poverty, hunger and illness have been eradicated. Merely referred to as a Person, this creature represents a single-sexed race that has both physically and mentally evolved. These highly conscious, telepathic beings have achieved the status of true humans in contrast to the primitive subhumans of the present day. Written in the style of a report cataloguing subhuman identities and behaviours, the text mimics the pseudo-scientific tone of sexological writing. A stranger in what is essentially the reader's reality, the traveller experiences everything for the first time and from a seemingly objective perspective, so providing Burdekin with the opportunity to voice her own interpretation of society and to critique social conventions and customs that are often taken for granted. Wars are, for instance, defined as 'large organized killings' and soldiers as 'killing males', while a prostitute is classified quite plainly as 'neither a wife nor a virgin nor a fornicator' but rather a woman who must provide sex 'in order to obtain the necessities of life' (p. 19, p. 22 and p. 45).

Over the course of the novel, the Person befriends three twentieth-century inhabitants, who in turn act as guide and object of study. Each is troubled in their own way and receives emotional and psychological counsel in return for their help: the first guide, a priest called Andrew, experiences a crisis of faith; the second, the grief-stricken writer, Leonora, is stymied by her fear of inferiority; and finally, Gilbert, a murderer, struggles to understand his violent impulses. In separate instances, Andrew and Leonora express concern that the Person's indeterminate, non-gendered, non-sexed identity might impede its investigation by attracting unwanted suspicion. It is then on their advice that the visitor adopts an alias:

> If you were a man your superiority and indifference wouldn't matter so much, because men don't think that there can be anything superior to themselves. They wouldn't for a moment think that you were masquerading, if you were dressed as a man. But your superiority is very wrong for a woman. It's terribly unfeminine. But fortunately your beauty is not specially masculine, you have no beard, and your voice is all right for either sex. You may pass. I think you had better align yourself with the small minority that dislikes men. Look at me with mistrust and defiance. (pp. 146–7)

Andrew suggests that it is only by assuming the guise of the lesbian that the Person's behaviour, and refusal to kowtow to the authority of men, can be made sense of. Having affiliated itself with the 'small minority that dislikes men', the Person continues its research at the British Museum and it is here that it meets its next guide, the writer Leonora. Watching the Person across the desks, Leonora tries to decipher its bodily codes and sartorial markers, and surmises that this individual is indeed a lesbian:

> She wondered why I wore no hat, how old I was, and what climate and blood had given to me my golden-brown colour of skin. She also con-

sidered that my hair would look better cut shorter or else worn much longer, that I was very beautiful, that I took no interest in my clothes, and was probably a homosexual. She looked under the table to see what sort of shoes I had on, and finding them soft, without heels, and far from the fashionable shape either for city females or homosexuals, she thought I might make some kind of a living out of the shape of my feet and would not risk spoiling them with hard shoes. (p. 158)

Having invited this new friend to live with her, Leonora repeats Andrew's warning:

> I was going to suggest that you might find it easier to be homosexual in your behaviour than feminine. If you decide to be that, you can ignore the men and be interested in the women. The steady cold way you stare at people would seem less strange then. It's a very odd way for a feminine woman to look at a man. (p. 198)

Several important points emerge from these extracts and the Person's attempts to 'pass'. Foremost, Andrew and Leonora's recommendations demonstrate an understanding of sexual identity as visual and performative. Moreover, sexuality is defined here by the inversion of conventional gendered behaviour – to be a lesbian is, in Leonora's view, the antithesis of being feminine and, by implication, passive. Burdekin, then, advocates that sexuality and gender intersect and inflect one another: to adopt a lesbian subject-position is to reject conventional femininity and to establish a stance which is essentially feminist and anti-patriarchal.

Such an alliance between politics and sexuality is further evident in the Person's interest in two particular groups – male and female 'homosexual hordes' or 'pack[s]' (p. 34). Burdekin's futuristic anthropologist classifies these 'packs' as:

> two small but ever increasing groups, one of male and the other of females, who from adolescence revolted from their sensual dependence on their opposites, and would seek companionship, solace, and even sexual satisfaction among the members of their own sex. (p. 33)

Yet these men and women who blur the boundary between sociality and sexuality are oddly placed in respectively dystopian and utopian frameworks. While the assembling of such male 'hordes' is motivated by the desire to exclude and denigrate women, so making male homosexuality a natural extension of the abuses of patriarchy, female communities are formed from the evolution of their sex and the drive to advance womanhood. As the Person states, these sororal groupings are based upon the impulse 'to *organize* themselves, to be *loyal* to each other, and to replace their former natural indifference or hostility by feelings of friendship and admiration' (p. 34). The potentially romantic collective is thus motivated by ideological awakening; as they draw together they become 'more conscious and consequently rebellious' and begin to 'organize themselves' as if a burgeoning political movement (p. 34). Such emotionally and sexually independent women, the Person observes, challenge the assurance of the heterosexual male, who believes that they are 'merely *making the best of a bad job*, and would have mated with males if they could' (p. 36). The risk that the lesbian might pose to a male-dominated system is reflected, the Person realises, in the refusal to legislate for female same-sex desire:

> This apparent favouring of females in such a serious matter as *unnatural vice* puzzled me at first, but as I came to a greater knowledge of the subhuman male character and realized men's unwillingness to allow women to be independent of them in any way, I saw that here, perhaps, lay the reason for this unaccountable legal omission. The men, who hitherto have made all the public rules under which they all must live or be punished, preferred that unnatural vice among women should go uncorrected rather than it should have any legal existence. (p. 38)

To make lesbianism illegal would be to acknowledge not only that female desire exists but that it can operate independently from the phallus.[55] The contemporary lesbian, Burdekin would appear to be saying, possesses the power and freedom through her economic, social and sexual independence to abdicate from damaging behavioural patterns imbued within normative male and female psyches.

The importance of this bond between sexual and ideological choices is sharpened in the context of Burdekin's wider corpus. Her dystopian novel *Swastika Night*, which imagines the world as it might be if Hitler's regime were to prevail, pinpoints the heteronormative gender dynamic, and its inherent worship of masculinity, as the foundation for Fascist ideology. As the bearers of children, women in *Swastika Night* and elsewhere in Burdekin's corpus, are complicit with the creation of an environment in which such politics can thrive. If, as is suggested in *Proud Man*, the lesbian woman approaches man as her equal, if she does not comply with the worship of masculinity, then the dynamic on which such political movements are founded, falters and dies. By aligning the contemporary lesbian with this futuristic, evolved and androgynous individual, Burdekin signals that it is her defiance of binary gender categories and patriarchal authority that holds the potential for social and political transformation.

The presence of the invert in *The End of This Day's Business* is similarly patent. In the year 6250 a matriarchal system dominates Western society. Women hold all positions of leadership and skilled employment, along with sole access to knowledge and learning. Although men live healthy, free and seemingly happy lives – they are decidedly better off than the animalistic, caged women in *Swastika Night* – they have degenerated into an inferior and ignorant sex. Praised for their beauty, strength and modesty, men are viewed as sexual objects for gratification and for the continuance of the race. The male sex are unaware of their fallen status, but the novel's protagonist, the artist Grania, hopes for a society based on egalitarian principles, and so imparts to her son the knowledge which is forbidden to all men lest they should attempt to regain power. Educating Neil through a narrative of European history (a common instructional device in Burdekin's fiction), Grania reveals that men were once leaders, inventors, artists, and moreover, the oppressors of the revered female sex. She leads Neil through a survey of history: the Second World War, the persecution of the Jews, the victory of the communists over fascists and the formation of an egalitarian society, a fascist resurgence to reclaim male power and, in retaliation, a surreptitious mission to implement a matriarchal system. Women, Grania informs Neil, secured power by eliminating the father from the family structure, manoeuvring men out of the skilled professions, barring their access to education, and introducing Latin as a cryptic female-owned language. The novel thus reverses patriarchal hegemonic structures: the privileges of masculinity are redistributed, feelings of inadequacy and shame surround the male instead of female body, and the cult of masculinity is replaced by the worship of motherhood. As Grania tells Neil, '[t]he lack is far better than the possession'; the phallus as symbol is replaced with the womb and the once abject female body is now holy and revered (p. 47).

Once again, Burdekin's utopian, revolutionary protagonist is modelled on the female invert, since she is 'far too big for a woman [. . .,] as large as quite a lot of men [. . .,] muscular and heavy-built [. . .,] handsome, but not womanly' (pp. 10–11). Her son notes that she seems ill-suited to the female clothes she must wear, since '[h]er long, ugly, lumpy, masculine thighs would have been better [. . .] in men's loose breeches. And her shoulders too would have fitted a man's coat better than that old orange woman's jacket' (p. 13). Grania herself expresses a belief that she is biologically more masculine than other women, or '*born* muscular', in a way that is reminiscent of the invert's innate bodily dysphoria (p. 97). When Grania attends the men's May Day celebrations, also an arena for courtship, her position as a medial figure is made manifest:

> she stayed there, on the margin, between the noisy physical tumult of the men and the quietness, the cold, spiritual strength and pride of the women, [. . .] a strange and solitary figure, too tall and not tall enough, too strong and not strong enough, too proud, and not proud enough, symbolizing in her position the place, or no-place, or every-place she had in the world. (p. 27)

She watches from the margins and it is evident that Grania occupies an intermediate or third place in society, in terms of gender, desire and politics.

Alienated from her more feminine peers, she has no place within the heterosexual and matriarchal systems she sees at work before her and that she deems inadequate and unequal.

Grania's conspiracy to educate men and instigate social change is soon discovered by the authorities and she is sent to be judged by the European government led by Anna K. who, it is implied, is a past lover. The women have been separated for five years on Grania's instigation because Anna 'may be the only woman in Europe who can, who could, control [...] her] will' (p. 139); such influential attachments, Grania realises, would have stalled her revolutionary plans. Their reunion is a scene of renewed protestations of love, and in the nights leading up to her trial and execution Grania makes the most impassioned and rousing political speeches of the novel. As the women discuss her utopian vision, Anna's body shivers and her 'scalp prickle[s] and tingle[s]', while Grania boils like 'the inside of a volcano' and her heart beats like a 'dynamo' leaving her in 'a wringing sweat' after their exchange (pp. 151–3). Physically expended, in a state of almost post-coital fatigue, Grania bids farewell to her lover and potential ally:

> She lifted Anna off the couch, kissed her, and took her gently to the door. She put her outside, shut it and locked it. Then, finding she was in a wringing sweat, she had a bath and went to bed. (p. 153)

What occurs in this final scene is Anna's simultaneous political and sexual awakening. Grania seduces Anna both intellectually and bodily, exploiting their love to find a guardian for her revolutionary concepts and so planting the seeds of ideological unrest:

> You have the power of this land in you, you have the vitality, the tremendous concentration, the spiritual strength and hardness of a German person. You can use it for the safety and stagnation and injustice and lovelessness of Germany and the world; or you can use it for courage, Anna, for growth, for change, for love, and for a better life. (p. 152)

Grania's rebellion has fatal consequences (so exposing the thin divide between the utopian and dystopian narrative) but Burdekin signals that the utopian impulse – the drive for what Grania terms 'courage', 'growth', 'change', 'love', and finally 'a better life' – will live on and blossom with Anna, compelled by the impetus of same-sex love and desire.

THE INVERT REVOLUTIONARY

The Person and Grania simultaneously occupy utopian and lesbian subject-positions, and they are constructed using a language very much rooted in Burdekin's present moment and in popular sexual discourses. It is evident that Burdekin perceived there to be a link between political consciousness and female-centred sexuality, but even more radical than this, she positions the invert as an agitator, capable of instigating social change and pushing forward the evolution of the species. It is here that Burdekin is arguably indebted to the ideas of another popular theorist of sexuality, Edward Carpenter.[56] Although it is not certain that Burdekin read Carpenter's work, many of her ideas and imagery bear a distinct resemblance to those of this socialist writer.[57] One might point out that both employ the image of the chrysalis and butterfly (or in Carpenter's case the mayfly) as a metaphor for human evolution and spiritual growth; that they imagine the soul as something that will ripen and swell as humanity evolves; that both talk of civilisation not as the epitome of human achievement but as diseased institution bent on self-destruction; and that both advocate a return to nature, a reduced reliance on technology and a dislike of clothes as adornment. However, it is the status of the invert in Carpenter's utopian evolutionary theory that is most fascinating. For him, it is the man or woman who shifts conventional gender paradigms – 'the man [. . .] who did not *want* to fight [. . . and] the woman who did not care about house-work and child-rearing' – who can enable the progress of mankind.[58] With exceptional, often divine, abilities the invert has taken the role of artist, inventor, writer, prophet, priest, diviner, seer, wizard, witch, medicine man and such other supra-natural roles.[59] These men and women have the potential to galvanise human development and to create a fairer, more humane existence:

> The double life and nature certainly, in many cases of inverts observed today, seems to give to them an extraordinary humanity and sympathy, together with a remarkable power of dealing with human beings. It may possibly also point to a further degree of evolution than usually attained, and a higher order of consciousness, very imperfectly realised, of course, but indicated. This interaction in fact, between the masculine and the feminine [. . .] may possibly lead to the development of that third order of perception which has been called the cosmic consciousness, and which may also be termed divination.[60]

Blessed with knowledge of both sexes, the invert is further evolved and possessed of a more sophisticated, even supernatural, level of consciousness. Like Burdekin, Carpenter aligns the invert's determination to buck gender paradigms with his or her politically progressive nature.

Echoes of these ideas can be heard throughout Burdekin's work, most clearly with the Person's observation that '[y]ou may think that these homosexuals, who were physically of one sex and in behaviour of another, might with their dual natures be groping, in a very clumsy and childish way, towards a more human state of existence' (p. 38). Like Carpenter, the Person suggests that it is gendered duality that propagates a higher existence, although this comes with the caveat that such progress is stymied by the persecution they encounter

(p. 63). In *The End of this Day's Business*, Grania also employs an image that references Carpenter when she tries to conceptualise her role in the revolutionary action she has initiated:

> this thing that lies in my mind, *in my mind alone* – as yet – this little embryo of a vast change – it lies there like that little lump of life that was Neil once lay in my womb – will it be born, and grow strong and tall like him, and have a will and power like mine, and *do*? Or will it be stillborn, just a sad little carcass, useless? (p. 29)

Carpenter also makes use of this reproductive metaphor in *The Intermediate Sex*:

> It certainly does not seem impossible to suppose that as the ordinary love has a special function in the propagation of the race, so the other has its special function in social and heroic work, and in the generation – not of bodily children – but of those children of the mind, the philosophical conceptions and ideals which transform our lives and those of society.[61]

Grania and Carpenter conceptualise the invert in much the same vein: far from sterile, the invert's fecundity is found in its ability to propagate intellectual, socially transformative ideas.

Carpenter's concepts similarly filter through another of Burdekin's utopian works, *The Rebel Passion*, in which a twelfth-century monk is visited by a messenger of God and transported to visions of the past, present and future. Unable to conform to the dictates of masculinity, or to silently acquiesce with society's tyranny over women and the subservient classes, Giraldus rebels against social injustice and as a result is exiled to a monastery by his powerful father. This refusal to accept society's hierarchy is accounted for by the dissonance between his body and soul:

> But there was I, a boy in shape, and no boy [. . .] For I would not hunt the deer nor the small game once I had seen the death of a stag, nor fight with the other lads, but only wrestle with them harmlessly. [. . .] So, when I would do none of these things, but passed my days in learning from the old priest, Magnus, and in making friends of the wild creatures, and in harping, and in listening to the women's songs – my father was enraged, and beat me many times, but without avail. And they called me coward and woman, and the boys used me ill and the women despised me, but not all. [. . .] Change the soul within me I could not, and neither could he.[62]

Like Blaise, Stephen, the Person and Grania, Giraldus experiences feelings of bodily dysphoria but he gains an understanding of what this means through his encounter with God's messenger. Once more referring to that revelatory moment in *The Well of Loneliness* when Stephen discovers her sexual identity, the Child explains to Giraldus that he has 'the understanding of a man and the soul of a woman' and presents him with a vision of his birth in which the Spirit of God imbues his newborn body with a female soul and his sister's with a masculine soul (*The Rebel Passion*, p. 17 and p. 56). The heavenly creature reassures Giraldus that his sexual identity is not only inborn and natural but also sanctioned by God, therefore endowing him with a new sense of affinity with others like him, those he calls 'my own people, those wretched ones' (p. 64). Giraldus's status as an invert makes him one of '[t]he chosen servants of Christ' and in this role, the divine child tells him, the inverts 'shall be strong and pure and pitiful, and they shall understand men and women both, by virtue of the nature God has given them. They shall be the priests' (p. 60). Again, the sentiment is indebted to Carpenter, who perceives the invert as an intermediary between God and his people.[63] While the extraordinary resonances between their philosophy and imagery deserve further consideration, what it is crucial to garner from this connection is that for Burdekin, like Carpenter, the invert is a venerated, utopian figure elevated above the throng of (heterosexual) humanity by his or her heterodox nature, acutely perceptive of the structures of society and endowed with the ability to enact social revolution.

A Sexless Society

Although Burdekin dovetails utopian characters with homosexual identities, surprisingly desire is not given free rein as part of this. Instead, it is implicated in a complex process of negotiation over the ideal form sexuality should take. Reading across Burdekin's corpus, it is obvious that she sees sexuality as fractured between the spiritual and the physical, love and lust, but she remains emphatic that the spiritual should be victorious and that, ultimately, sensuality should be expunged from sexual identity. Although Burdekin does not deny that pleasure can be found between women, there are remnants of the belief that satisfaction is reserved for the union of opposing-sexed partners. Grania for instance claims that 'physical sex-love [. . . is] when you want the thing that is opposite, not the thing that's the same' (*The End of This Day's Business*, p. 150), while Leonora believes that 'one can't live with a woman, unless one is homosexual, because she is not a man and therefore inadequate on an important point' (*Proud Man*, p. 174). And although Stephen and Blaise enter into physically satisfying relationships with women, even they face a choice between sensuality and chaste love and ultimately sacrifice their female lovers for heterosexual, but spiritual, unions with men. This is more aggressively, even puritanically, preached in *The Rebel Passion*. While the invert is the servant of God, this privileged position also requires individual sacrifice, as the child informs Giraldus:

> God has made a sweet apple that all men and all women desire, and the apple is the pleasure of the body in its wildest form. And he has granted that the apple may be eaten without sin, and with his blessing and the blessing of his Son, in one way only, and that is in marriage. Will God change his laws for the sake of one or two in every hundred? Surely he will not. So there will always be some who cannot eat the sweet apple without sin, no, not ever in all their lives. It is forbidden to them. (p. 60)

While neither the divine child nor the text itself judges the invert for his desires, it is evident that he should aspire to a chaste existence. As is the case with Stephen in 'The Stars Shine in Daylight', identity and acts are differentiated.

These narratives might initially disappoint us as puritanical, even self-loathing. After all, Burdekin imposes heterosexual romance plots on her lesbian characters and effectively mutes homosexual passion. But it is important to remember that in the context of sexology, this sentiment is not entirely out of character. Many of Ellis's sexological case studies articulate a similar battle between spiritual and physical emanations of love for women, as one woman relates: '[a]t first my feeling for her was almost purely physical, although there were no sexual relations. I hated this feeling and have succeeded in overcoming it pretty largely. [. . .] We both consider sexual feelings degrading and deleterious to real love.'[64] In this respect Burdekin can be said to be participating in what Jo-Ann Wallace has termed, with regard to Edith Ellis (Havelock Ellis's wife), 'sapphic idealism', that is the idealisation and celebration of lesbian love and romance as pure, spiritual, and without shame.[65] Wallace begins her study of Ellis's 'sapphic idealism' by first turning to Suzanne Raitt's essay on the significance of love and emotion, as opposed to sexual acts, in turn-of-the-century sexology. Such theorists as Carpenter, Raitt argues, focused on the role of love and emotion as central to homosexual identities.[66] Burdekin's problematic handling of desire and her focus on lesbian and gay love as a spiritual and emotional bond, is arguably part of this tradition and is testament to her sources. It also serves to remind us that sexology's theory of inversion is, to a certain extent, a theory of gender dysphoria rather than just desire.

Jay Prosser and Melanie A. Taylor have, in separate instances, raised this point in relation to Hall's *The Well of Loneliness*. Taylor and Prosser question the established reading of the novel as a key lesbian text by arguing that this interpretation is founded upon a critical conflation of inversion and homosexuality.[67] For both, *The Well of Loneliness* is not a narrative of emerging lesbian identity but rather one of transgenderism. To some extent this also accounts for the ambiguity present in Burdekin's own work since her texts often express repugnance towards heteronormative feminine identity and the fleshy feminine form. Grania, after all, believes that she, biologically muscular and possessed of an ungainly masculine physiology, should have been a man.[68] Similarly, in the utopian future outlined in *The Rebel Passion*, women have morphed into near-men:

> These women were strange to look at, and it took me some time to get accustomed to them. The whole race was a little taller than it had been, and the women more nearly the size of men [. . .] Their muscle of body had developed so much that their waists had disappeared, and now they were broad-shouldered, broad-hipped and broad in the waist, so that they looked very sturdy and thick-set. (pp. 236–7)

Human progress is here conceived of as the shedding of femininity and the evolution of the female body to a more masculine state.

Burdekin's treatment of male homosexuality supports this split between gender identification and sexuality, since male same-sex desire is often presented as a natural extension of male dominance in its worship of masculinity and denigration of women. In Burdekin's *Swastika Night*, homosexuality is common amongst the male inhabitants of this Fascist dystopia. Similarly Gilbert, the third subhuman who the Person encounters in *Proud Man* and a murderer of young girls, is motivated by a deeply rooted aversion to women and the female body. His method is crudely symbolic: by cutting their throats and letting their blood flow he pre-empts menstruation and prevents his victims from becoming adult women. Remembering his various unsuccessful same-sex relationships at university, Gilbert again raises a connection between his homosexuality and violence against womankind. In contrast, Giraldus, the monk with a female soul, rejects any part in gender and class oppression, and while he loves a fellow monk, he does not act on this. Male inversion is clearly not aligned to gender violence in the same way that male homosexuality is, and while inversion can include same-sex desire, for Burdekin it is by no means synonymous with homosexuality.[69]

These textual instances insist that what is also at work in Burdekin's fiction is a narrative of gender dysphoria and transgenderism. This complicates Burdekin's place as a utopian and feminist writer to a certain extent, given that one might argue that there is something inherently dissonant about the idea that the body at war with itself (at least as it is presented in these texts) acts as the representative of utopia. In *Swastika Night* the female is the most despised creature in the world, caged, derided, and exploited for mere reproductive purposes, but Burdekin's narrative treatment of feminine women – heterosexual and homosexual – arguably possesses some of this same distaste. That is to say, it is solely masculine identified women who are able to step outside and challenge the system, which both serves to reiterate the very patriarchal and misogynist system that Burdekin seeks to critique in the first place and leaves little room for a diversity of gendered identities.

However, this conflation of desire and identification is intrinsic to Burdekin's treatment of sexuality rather than a retrospective critical misinterpretation. Her unpublished inversion narrative 'The Stars Shine in Daylight' employs the terms invert and lesbian as if they were synonymous, and thus for Burdekin desire and transgenderism arguably do overlap.[70] Her suppression of physical pleasure between women and between men is problematic on initial observation, but rather than dismiss her for this, I suggest that this trait is in line with her wider utopian project for sexuality. Although the distinction of sex still exists in the future outlined in *The Rebel Passion*, gender difference has fallen away (largely because women have gradually become more masculine) and in accordance with Christian doctrine, chastity has become revered and practised by all, so much so that the 'touching dances of the old days' are avoided (p. 274). In a similar vein, Grania hopes that they will one day achieve a 'sexless society', which she realises to be 'physically impossible [. . .] but] not morally impossible' (*The End of This Day's Business*, p. 106). The futuristic Person, 'an entity independent of others both physically and emotionally, who is self-fertilizing, and can produce young [. . .] alone and without help', heralds from an impassive society much like the one in *The Rebel Passion*, where the human race has homogenised into a single sex (*Proud Man*, pp. 22–3). If sexual satisfaction is outlawed in the utopian future of *The Rebel Passion*, then it is deemed unnecessary in the Person's more evolved existence.

What stands out in each of these textual instances is the drive to homogenise society, even to create an androgynous ideal. As can be observed from her utopias in which chastity is either institutionalised or biologically enforced, the very distinctions and difference of sex and gender would ideally be rubbed away so rendering the category of sexuality essentially defunct. Her vision for sexual identity is therefore intricately intertwined and reliant upon her hopes for human evolution. It is not that Burdekin believes desire to be pernicious per se, but that we should strive towards an existence of a higher order where such emotions and passions are irrelevant. Burdekin essentially reconceptualises and re-envisions the very nature of sexuality by striving towards what she believes to be the ideal of sexual identity, based not upon carnality but spirituality.

Burdekin's unpublished works, heavily inflected by mysticism, ideas of reincarnation and the afterlife show that she later developed a distinctly spiritual concept of sexual identity. In the late-1940s/early-1950s unpublished novel 'Walking to Mark', reincarnation is transposed onto theories of inversion. Born into a family who long for a daughter, Thomas Wright experiences an unexplainable and 'recurrent queer feeling about women' which he terms his 'woman-misery'.[71] While visiting Glastonbury the origin of such feelings becomes clear as he regresses through visions of his past life as Elizabeth. Her existence is a rather tragic one: she longs for but is denied access to male privileges, although attracted to women she marries a man she neither loves nor desires, and when she is raped and finally abandoned to labour alone, both Elizabeth and her child die. Thomas's guide on this spiritual journey, the Brahmin, Hira Sing, is similarly plagued by a sense of bodily dissonance and tormented by the impossibility of physical union with a man in the female form that he so wishes to inhabit. In this text Burdekin explicitly rejects modern theories of sexuality in favour of a spiritualised framework. As Hira asks Thomas:

> Why, are you so foolish as to suppose that the modern theories of the nature of men – the communist theory, the fascist theory, the Freudian theory, the Jungian theory, the Adlerian theory – to suppose that any of these theories are any nearer the essential truth of the nature of man in his body than the Christian theory of the fourteenth or fifteenth century? ... [A]ny theory about the essential nature of man which denies the soul, denies the justice of God, and cannot face the fact that all our unhappiness is each individual's <u>own fault</u> will always be untrue.[72]

This extract is remarkable on several accounts: while she does not mention sexology specifically, Burdekin signals a rejection of modern scientific and political theories to justify human existence, and instead turns to ideas of the perennial soul and spiritual responsibility. Gender dysphoria under this scheme is, rather troublingly, explained as spiritual debt or punishment for deeds committed in past lives.

The 1936 unpublished novel 'Dolly', set in the afterlife and tracing the journey of the dead to heaven, similarly explores this idea of karmic debt. Margaret, waiting for her female partner Alpha to arrive, considers the implications of our actions while on earth:

> Of course, just the fact that a person thought his action was right, never had made any difference even in that sloppy tattered old thing, the English criminal law, still less could it in this place of clear dispassionate thinking and irrevocable automatic judgement. Whatever happened to you would be right, and you would know it to be right, and her old excuses that she had always half known were invalid, like 'I was born that way' or 'I'd have been different if –'[73]

Margaret's own earthly reasoning for her sexual identity (she notably turns to the rhetoric of sexology and its theory of congenital inversion) is proved defunct in the afterlife and, again, sexual identity is thought to be divinely predestined. Unlike Edith Ellis's rendition of what Wallace terms 'sapphic idealism', Burdekin does not demonstrate a straightforward belief in the purity and innocence of lesbian bonds.[74] However, through her later interest in mysticism that effectively makes a religion of the theory of inversion, her work strives to achieve emotional and spiritual purity between women and between men.

Burdekin's realistic inversion narratives that reincarnate and adjust Hall's archetypal character, Stephen Gordon, mark the beginning of a relationship between sexuality and utopian philosophy. Burdekin amends an established, and of sorts dominant, sexual narrative to be more in line with her own idiosyncratic vision for lesbian and gay identities. She goes on to present a utopian vision of sexuality that rejects lust, and while this is highly subjective, the concept of utopia is always so. Parallel to these unpublished inversion narratives, Burdekin continued to write speculative fiction concerned with sexual utopianism. For each figure – Grania, the Person and Giraldus – homosexuality is dovetailed with gender dissonance and an ideological heterodoxy. Given that Burdekin's first inversion narrative was withdrawn from publication, this implies that when unable to write the lesbian, or to replicate Hall's paradigmatic narrative in realist form, she turned to genre fiction as a vehicle in which to deliver her ideas on sexuality. But utopian fiction is not merely a disguise or form of encryption – her response to genre is more nuanced and less strategic, and her understanding of lesbian sexuality more ambivalent, than this gives credit for. For Burdekin there is something intrinsically utopian, and political, about lesbian identity, or more specifically a sexological version of that identity.

The rationale behind this is not easily defined, but can perhaps be clarified by returning one last time to the connections and resonances between Burdekin, H.D. and popular theorists of sexuality. Carpenter boldly claims that 'I think there *is* an organic connection between the homosexual temperament and unusual psychic or divinatory powers'.[75] It is, then, intriguing that in a letter to Ellis, H.D. mentions asking Burdekin 'if her writing *seems* in any way "mediumistic"' – an unsurprising question given H.D.'s own interest in spiritualism.[76] Burdekin responds, according to H.D., that 'she did at times, seem almost out of herself, or in the hands of a "control"'.[77] A letter to Patai from Burdekin's companion supports this idea of an occult interference: commenting on the nature of Burdekin's writing, her companion describes the writer as an 'automaton' and 'visitant' while in the grip of the authorial process and notes that 'she was a piece of cosmic blotting paper, or sponge, which some power squeezed, and out welled a strange confection'.[78]

Burdekin is thus positioned as a literary spiritualist, privileged with the responsibility of communicating a message from a divine power. Invert protagonist and author alike, then, adopt similar responsibilities: both communicate ideas and observations that possess the potential to galvanise social and political change. For Burdekin the genre of speculative fiction is the means through which to achieve this. In a letter to Ellis, H.D. notes reading some of Burdekin's unpublished 'fables', describes them as 'excellent propaganda', and hints at a plan to distribute these stories by 'just leav[ing] them to be found somewhere'.[79] H.D. treats Burdekin's work as if it were some kind of political tract to be circulated amongst fellow revolutionaries through guerrilla-like tactics. Her interpretation is not at all far-fetched because Burdekin's work candidly dissects the very structures of society and suggests renewing and reworking our political, social and sexual frameworks for living. Yet, perhaps most revolutionary of all, Burdekin suggests that at the very heart of this radical upheaval will be the figure of the sexual invert.

NOTES

1. Jameson, 'Man the Helpmate', p. 111.
2. Ibid. pp. 124–5.
3. Ibid. p. 126.
4. Ibid. p. 128.
5. West, 'Man and Religion', pp. 280–1.
6. Ibid. p. 282 and p. 271.
7. Croft, 'Worlds Without End', p. 186.
8. Moylan, *Demand the Impossible*, p. 3.
9. I draw here on Suvin's definition: 'Utopia is the verbal construction of a particular quasi-human community where sociopolitical institutions, norms, and individual relationships are organized according to a more perfect principle than in the author's community'. Suvin, *Defined by a Hollow*, p. 29.
10. Patai, 'Imagining Reality', p. 229.
11. Albinski, *Women's Utopias*, p. 78.
12. Bartowski, *Feminist Utopias*, p. 5.
13. Burdekin also published under the names Katharine Penelope Cade (her maiden name) and Kay Burdekin.
14. Letter from H.D. to Havelock Ellis (25 November 1934), Friedman (ed.), *Analyzing Freud*, pp. 500–2 (p. 501).
15. Ibid. p. 501.
16. Patai, 'Afterword' to Burdekin, *The End of This Day's Business*, p. 163. Subsequent references are noted in parenthesis.
17. Burdekin's companion quoted in the 'Afterword' to *The End of This Day's Business*, p. 164.
18. Selected biographical information from Friedman, *Analyzing Freud*, p. 551, and from Patai's invaluable forewords and afterwords to Burdekin's reissued novels *The End of This Day's Business*, *Proud Man*, and *Swastika Night*. Subsequent references are noted in parenthesis.
19. Constantine, 'The Power of Merlin'.
20. Herring and Townshend, 'Editorial', pp. 1–2.
21. Ibid. p. 2.
22. Letter from H.D. to Ellis (25 November 1934), Friedman (ed.), *Analyzing Freud*, p. 501. As far as I can ascertain only one letter from Burdekin to H.D. survives and this is housed in the latter's archive in the Beinecke Library. This letter is marked 'destroy', although I am not certain in whose hand, but it suggests that Burdekin may well have instructed correspondents to discard her missives. See letter from Burdekin to H.D., YCAL MSS 24 Box 9 f.298. Beinecke Rare Book and Manuscript Library, Yale University.
23. Letter from H.D. to Ellis (25 November 1934), Friedman (ed.), *Analyzing Freud*, p. 502.
24. Letter from H.D. to Ellis (20 December 1934), Friedman (ed.), *Analyzing Freud*, pp. 523–4 (p. 523).
25. Letter from H.D. to Ellis (24 July 1934), Friedman (ed.), *Analyzing Freud*, pp. 403–4 (p. 404).
26. Ibid. p. 404.

27. See for instance: Patai, 'Imagining Reality'; Stec, 'Dystopian Modernism vs. Utopian Feminism'; Payne, 'Grania, "a mad woman . . . Doomed to attempt the impossible"'.
28. Ulrichs quoted in Ellis, *Studies in the Psychology of Sex*, p. 68. Translation from Sedgwick, *Epistemology of the Closet*, p. 87.
29. Taylor, 'The Masculine Soul Heaving in the Female Bosom', p. 288.
30. Ellis, *Studies in the Psychology of Sex*, p. 244. This was originally published as the first volume of *Studies in the Psychology of Sex* in 1897.
31. Ibid. p. 250.
32. Krafft-Ebing, *Psychopathia Sexualis*, pp. 398–9.
33. For Ellis, the invert's body is tangibly different. While he claims that 'there are no invariable anatomical characteristics associated with this impression [of masculinity]', he contradicts this statement by providing evidence of identifiable physical difference, such as the increased appearance of body hair, the higher proportion of muscle to soft tissue (which give inverts 'an unfeminine impression to the sense of touch'), and atrophied sexual organs and genitals. Ellis, *Studies in the Psychology of Sex*, p. 251 and pp. 253–6.
34. Doan, *Fashioning Sapphism*, p. 130.
35. Doan, *Fashioning Sapphism*, pp. xii–xiii. On this point see also Taylor, 'The Masculine Soul Heaving in the Female Bosom', p. 287, and Newton, 'The Mythic Mannish Lesbian', p. 283.
36. Doan, *Fashioning Sapphism*, p. xiv.
37. For other work on the emergence of the mannish lesbian around this time see Newton, 'The Mythic Mannish Lesbian' and Smith-Rosenberg, 'Discourses of Sexuality and Subjectivity'.
38. H.D. tells Ellis that Burdekin 'has a deep and perturbing "gloom" or "suicide" fixation of sorts – But when I suggest a spot of analysis, she screams. She apparently identifies in part, with a brother, called Murray, who had a bad time in war – had <u>some</u> analysis [. . .] and who is now shut up in an asylum. She evidently has some sort of fear of some like fate for herself.' Letter to Ellis (25 November 1934), Friedman (ed.), *Analyzing Freud*, p. 501.
39. Ibid. p. 501.
40. New York City, The Dobkin Family Collection of Feminism (DFC), Archive of Katharine Burdekin, Letters from Ellis dated 4 December 1934, 20 January 1935, 14 May 1937 and 24 June 1937. Ellis reassures Burdekin about her 'neurosis' in a letter dated 20 January 1935.
41. DFC, Letters from Ellis to Burdekin dated 4 December 1934, 20 January 1935, 14 May 1937 and 24 June 1937.
42. Ellis goes on to note that 'I am not surprised that its arrangement with Laura Riding failed to come off.' Laura Riding, under the auspices of editor, returned Burdekin's 1935 novel 'Snakes and Ladders' strewn with amendments and suggestions for changes. Burdekin did not respond well to such editorial guidance and did not proceed with attempts to publish the novel. DFC, Letter from Ellis to Burdekin dated 14 May 1927. On details of the rift with Riding see Patai, 'Imagining Reality', p. 242.
43. Patai mentions that Hall wrote to Burdekin in praise of her 1927 novel *The Burning Ring*, and that subsequent to this they met around 1930. Patai, 'Afterword' to *The End of This Day's Business*, p. 164. There is no evidence in Burdekin's archive of any correspondence with Hall.
44. 'Two in a Sack' is advertised as a future publication in the back matter of Richard Dehan's *The Lovers of the Market-Place*.
45. The catalogue of the Burdekin archives, whose author is unknown, claims that its

portrayal of androgyny led to its withdrawal from publication. Yet it is unlikely that it was something this innocuous that led to the retreat.
46. DFC, TS 'Two in a Sack', p. 12.
47. The date of composition for 'The Stars Shine in Daylight' is uncertain. The archive catalogue notes that Isobel Allan-Burns (Burdekin's companion) signed and dated the manuscript 'January 1943'.
48. DFC, TS 'The Stars Shine in Daylight', p. 151 and p. 153.
49. Hall was appalled when Norman Birkett, the lawyer defending *The Well of Loneliness*'s publisher, attempted to argue in court that Stephen's relationships were 'purely of an intellectual character'. She forced him to retract his statement. See Souhami, *The Trials of Radclyffe Hall*, p. 207.
50. DFC, TS 'The Stars Shine in Daylight', p. 190.
51. Ibid. p. 265.
52. DFC, TS 'Two in a Sack', p. 77.
53. Patai, 'Afterword' to *The End of This Day's Business*, p. 183.
54. Mitchison, *You May Well Ask*, p. 179.
55. In 1921 a bill was introduced in Parliament to criminalise female homosexuality. It failed because of fears that by making it illegal, they would essentially publicise lesbianism. For details on this see Garrity, *Step-daughters of England*, p. 63.
56. Carpenter does not attempt to account for the female invert and his theories are overwhelmingly geared towards examining the social role of the homosexual man.
57. However, Doan does point out that '[o]f all the treatises on sexuality in the early twentieth century, Carpenter's were by far the easiest to obtain and quite accessible to a nonspecialist reader'. Doan, *Fashioning Sapphism*, p. 143. See also Doan, 'The Outcast of One Age'. Wallace has commented on the recent scholarly work tracing Carpenter's influence on modernist lesbian writers. See Wallace, 'Edith Ellis, Sapphic Idealism', p. 194.
58. Carpenter, *Intermediate Types Among Primitive Folk*, p. 58.
59. Ibid. p. 58.
60. Ibid. p. 63.
61. Carpenter, *The Intermediate Sex*, p. 70.
62. Burdekin, *The Rebel Passion*, pp. 2–3. Subsequent references are noted in parenthesis.
63. Notably as the monk travels through time and sees humanity evolve, he is able to observe the literal growth of the human soul, which takes the form of an aura surrounding each individual. The souls of those in the utopian future have grown ripe and bright and thus appear surrounded by flames. In *Intermediate Types Among Primitive Folk*, Carpenter envisages a similar kind of spiritual growth when he argues that '[i]t may be that with every great onward push of the growing soul, and every great crisis in which as it were a sheath or a husk falls away from the expanding bud, something in the nature of a metamorphosis does really take place; and the new order, the new revelation, the new form of life, is seen for a moment as a Vision in glorious state of a divine being within'. Notably Giraldus's soul, perhaps due to his status as an invert, is already large and bright. See *Intermediate Types Among Primitive Folk*, pp. 64–5.
64. History XXXVIII, in Ellis, *Studies in the Psychology of Sex*, p. 233.
65. Wallace, 'Edith Ellis, Sapphic Idealism'.
66. Raitt, 'Sex, Love and the Homosexual Body', p. 158.
67. See Taylor, 'The Masculine Soul Heaving in the Female Bosom', p. 290, and Prosser, 'Some Primitive Thing', p. 129.
68. Prosser discusses how *The Well of Loneliness*'s narrative 'is driven forward by this "should have been," its direction compelled by this conditional perfect of the

modal auxiliary, by the desire to return to reconstruct a past that failed'. Prosser, 'Some Primitive Thing', p. 134.
69. The difference between 'true' and 'acquired' inversion is a distinction applied throughout sexological works and found even within the case studies that these works employ. Ellis argues that inversion is 'a narrower term than homosexuality, which includes all sexual attractions between persons of the same sex, even when seemingly due to the accidental absence of the natural objects of sexual attraction, a phenomenon of wide occurrence among all human races and among most of the higher animals'. Carpenter, in defence of the invert, attempts to ward off accusations of reprobation by stating that 'it should be said here that too much emphasis cannot be laid on the distinction between these born lovers of their own kind, and that class of persons, with whom they are so often confused, who out of mere carnal curiosity or extravagance of desire, or from the dearth of opportunities for a more normal satisfaction (as in schools, barracks, etc.) adopt some homosexual practices'. Same-sex attraction is therefore justified and reasoned by the argument that it springs from something innate and uncontrollable within the self and is grounded in the complexities of identity. See Ellis, *Studies in the Psychology of Sex*, p.1, and Carpenter, *The Intermediate Sex*, p. 55.
70. DFC, TS, 'The Stars Shine in Daylight', p. 205.
71. DFC, TS 'Walking to Mark', pp. 9–10.
72. Ibid. pp. 229–30.
73. DFC, TS 'Dolly', p. 22.
74. Wallace, 'Edith Ellis, Sapphic Idealism'.
75. Carpenter, *Intermediate Types Among Primitive Folk*, p. 49.
76. Letter to Ellis (25 November 1934), Friedman (ed.), *Analyzing Freud*, p. 501.
77. Ibid. p. 501.
78. Patai, 'Afterword' to *The End of This Day's Business*, pp. 163–4.
79. Letter to Ellis (26 September 1934), Friedman (ed.), *Analyzing Freud*, p. 423. Friedman also notes that H.D. wrote to her friend Silvia Dobson, a teacher and writer, the same day and requested Dobson's help in distributing one of Burdekin's fables through the post. Friedman suggests that these fables sent to H.D. may have been related to *The End of This Day's Business*. See note 42, p. 423.

2

'GHOST DESIRE': THE LESBIAN OCCULT AND NATALIE CLIFFORD BARNEY'S *THE ONE WHO IS LEGION OR A.D.'S AFTER-LIFE*

SPIRITUAL LOVE

Hall's 1926 short story 'Miss Ogilvy Finds Herself' provided an opportunity for what Hall called 'a brief excursion into the realms of the fantastic' before she turned her hand to write 'a serious study of congenital sexual inversion'.[1] As a fanciful precursor to the 1928 novel *The Well of Loneliness*, there are distinct parallels between the two narratives, and although Miss Ogilvy is never openly labelled an invert, her masculine dress and behaviour, as well as her time spent in the First World War ambulance corps, imply that she is much like Stephen Gordon. Disillusioned and displaced when the war concludes, she returns to the family household and a mundane life with her spinster sisters. However, Miss Ogilvy soon falls under the influence of a mystical magnetism that compels her to travel to a cave on an unnamed island, where she experiences visions of her former incarnation as a caveman, including an erotic encounter with the caveman's, or Miss Ogilvy's, female mate (the titular phrase itself teasingly suggests something of an autoerotic experience). Miss Ogilvy dies immediately after these flashbacks, but as she sits with her hands firmly thrust in her pockets in a final gesture of mannish defiance, her corpse presents a picture of satisfaction and spiritual fulfilment. She discovers, albeit through spiritual regression and death, a sense of identity and self-understanding. Hall's short story is evasive and enigmatic in a way that her later, more didactic novel refuses to be, but it is no less concerned with questions of sexual identity and its relation to constructions of gender. Hall's use of reincarnation serves to legitimise a gender-determined concept of sexual identity and enables a thinly veiled scene of lesbian eros. That is to say, it is an occult premise that allows Miss Ogilvy to 'find herself' or to return in some way to a sense of 'authentic' gender identity and to female-oriented pleasure.

It is fair to say that 'Miss Ogilvy Finds Herself' acts as the germ of Hall's later realist novel, and in this sense she claims recourse to the occult as a space in which to experiment with the theme of sexual inversion. The embargo on the story's publication until 1934 and Hall's own decisive role in the history of literary (and moreover sexual) censorship, as well as her acknowledgment of the developmental connection, support this idea. But to reduce Hall's choice of the fantastic to an escapist textual strategy belies the personal and intimate resonance that the occult held for Hall. On the contrary, 'Miss Ogilvy Finds Herself' is indicative of a broader vogue for occult motifs and doctrine, in both the imaginary and actual worlds, amongst lesbian figures at this time. Occult discourses – by which I refer to a variety of supernatural beliefs and practices such as spiritualism, mysticism and ideas of reincarnation, operating on the premise that the nature and boundaries of human existence and reality are not fully accounted for by rationalist or materialist modes of thinking – offered a compelling relevance for lesbian women's lives and proved to be apt motifs for their fictions.[2]

The affinity between supernatural conventions in fiction and film and the encoded representation of homosexual relationships and desires has been noted by a number of critics, as has the modernist engagement with the occult and in particular with spiritualism.[3] The interest shown at this time by lesbian figures in various branches of the occult is also evident. As Raitt, for instance, argues, the bond between mysticism and lesbianism is 'a social and cultural tradition that is easily overlooked'.[4] While this neglected tradition undoubtedly incorporates mysticism, lesbian figures of the period are arguably drawn to a much wider range of occult interests. Hence my title 'ghost desire', adopted from Barney's *The One Who is Legion or A.D.'s After-life* (1930), encapsulates the significance of the other-worldly or paranormal for the formation and nourishment of female bonds in both literature and life at this time.[5] Castle's study of the *Apparitional Lesbian* in modern culture argues that the lesbian has historically been '"ghosted" – or made to seem invisible – by culture itself', and that such social and cultural repression has translated into ghostly or supernatural metaphors in fiction.[6] Unsurprisingly, as Castle points out, such tropes have commonly served a conservative agenda to contain, control and exorcise the threat of female homosexuality.[7] However, this has been tempered by the possibility that the spectral metaphor might provide joyful erotic opportunities:

What of the spectral metaphor and the lesbian writer? For her, one suspects, 'seeing ghosts' may be a matter – not so much of derealisation – but of rhapsodical embodiment: a ritual calling up, or *apophrades*, in the old mystical sense. The dead are indeed brought back to life; the absent loved one returns. For the spectral vernacular, it turns out, contains its own powerful and perverse magic. Used imaginatively – repossessed, so to speak – the very trope that evaporates can also solidify. In the strangest turn of all, perhaps, the lesbian body itself returns[8]

This hints at the paradoxical sensuality of relationships conducted from beyond the grave: to be haunted by a past lover is to resurrect or bring her back to the flesh, defiantly refusing the impediment of death and raising once again the possibility of an emotional or erotic encounter. The phantasmagorical lesbian is both present and absent, paradoxically corporeal and disembodied, and in this state she becomes a contested and sensitised bodily site. This chapter, then, explores the idea that supernatural motifs and conventions provided a vocabulary with which to express emotional and erotic experiences between women and, furthermore, with which to invest those relationships with legitimacy and liberty at a time when realistic representations suffered close scrutiny. Critics have accounted for *The One Who is Legion*'s preoccupation with death by citing Barney's fascination with styles of decadence and symbolism.[9] But I suggest that Barney's interest in motifs of death and the spiritual afterlife indicates more than just the influence of literary forebears. Instead, I locate Barney's rarely discussed *The One Who is Legion* within this tradition of the lesbian occult to argue that supernatural motifs and conventions serve an urge towards homoerotic nostalgia, make sense of gender and sexual difference, and fetishise the spectral lesbian body.

For many women writers and figures of this period the supernatural provided an avenue for rekindling the happiness and pleasure of a past love as well as facilitating artistic collaboration. The posthumous relationship between Hall, Una Troubridge and Mabel Batten (Hall's deceased lover and Troubridge's cousin) is perhaps the most famous instance of this romantic entanglement with the occult. Hall and Troubridge had begun their relationship while Hall was still romantically involved with Batten and so, to assuage their guilt, the two women turned to the medium Mrs Osborne Leonard for help after Batten's death in 1916. Hall and Troubridge meticulously recorded these séances with 'Mabel', going on to present the results at two meetings for the Society of Psychical Research in 1917 and to publish a heavily edited and veiled version of the sittings in the Society's Journal.[10] Troubridge's jealousy of the time and energy that Hall devoted to 'Mabel' is indicative of this paranormal relationship's intimate nature, as is the fact that Hall dedicated *The Well of Loneliness* not to her living lover alone, but 'To our three selves'.[11] The creative collaboration of the Irish cousins Edith Somerville and Violet Martin who published under the pseudonym Martin Ross similarly thrived despite the death of Martin in 1915. Claiming that she spoke with her through the use of a planchette, Somerville published under their collaborative signature for a further 34 years.[12] Edith Ellis also maintained contact with her lover, the artist Lily Kirkpatrick, after her death in 1902 via a medium and visitations from Lily's spirit.[13] In the preface to her 1912 compilation of love poetry, *The Lover's Calendar*, which her husband Havelock Ellis saw as a 'monument to Lily', she defends relationships conducted across the boundary between life and death:[14]

> In this Anthology I have tried to represent the whole course of Love in its birth, its slow growth, its inevitable sorrow and its joyous fruition. [. . .] Death also, and the union of spirits after death, may make a claim on the reader's desire for romance and adventure as powerful as the passionate love of those who are still on earth[15]

By making an appeal to the reader's conventional sensibilities (their almost generic desire for romance and adventure) Edith Ellis attempts to normalise unions that defy death, making them tantamount to those of an earthly nature.

For these women, spiritualism and communication with a lover beyond death prolonged devotion and generated a space for legitimised and authorised grief. Referring to the Hall-Troubridge-Batten love-triangle, Jodie Medd argues that '[t]he occult offered these lesbian relationships a remarkable form of courtship and affiliation that escaped the heterosexual matrix – the prevailing structure of earthly intimacy – to achieve paranormal allegiances that resisted cultural constraints on ways of loving'.[16] By Medd's account, these dalliances with spiritualism questioned the conventional mode of existence and provided unchartered terrain where normative rules of society held limited sway. This specific appeal was not, however, limited to the lesbian woman in that, as critics such as Pamela Thurschwell have noted, the occult allowed writers 'to create phantasmatic spaces in which they redefine[d] intimate, sexual, familial and national ties between people'.[17] With this in mind it is telling that, as Thurschwell observes, the developmental trajectories at the turn of the nineteenth century of psychoanalysis and psychical research were intertwined.[18] The contents of the journal *Proceedings of the Society for Psychical Research*, for instance, featured the discussion of contemporary psychological theories as well as articles on mediumship and telepathy.[19] Freud's 'Dreams and Occultism' is an example of this intellectual coalition in its tentative exploration of the possible relationship between telepathy, thought-transference and the expression of unconscious psychical material.[20] The intersection of these discourses hints at the specific appeal of the occult at that moment because, like psychoanalysis, these theories offered alternative narratives for human existence and new methods of unearthing the true self.

The boundary between science and occultism was similarly blurred, and as Linda Dalrymple Henderson points out, in contemporary scientific discoveries and technological developments, such as the X-ray and telegraphy, occultists found the rationale to support paranormal ideas.[21] Theories of fourth dimensionalism, both spatial and temporal, influenced the mystical theories of such occultists as P. D. Ouspensky and Rudolph Steiner. Several scholars have compellingly traced the cultural impact, in particular in the realm of art, of the fourth dimension as well as Einstein's highly popularised theories.[22] Indeed, supernatural texts that deploy Einstein's theory of the fourth dimension as well as other scientific ideas (albeit imprecisely) in justification for their paranormal narratives are not uncommon around this time. In Vita Sackville-West's 1932 short story 'The Unborn Visitant' an Edwardian woman, Elsa, is confronted by an apparition of her future, as yet 'unborn', daughter and communicates with her across the gulf of twenty-four years. Elsa understands that this encounter with the supernatural is in no way related to the traditional ghost stories to which she is accustomed, since '[t]his apparition reverted in no way to the past, as portrayed either by Holbein or Winterhalter'.[23] Sackville-West's narrative therefore dismisses prior paradigms to embrace modern, in-vogue scientific discourses as the context in which paranormal experiences become feasible. The futuristic Daphne explains to her confused mother that 'I can't stop to tell you about Einstein now. [. . .] For the moment I can only tell you that I'm living in the fourth dimension – so are you, for that matter' (p. 293). Ostensibly, Daphne materialises to encourage her parents' nuptials 'because I'm in a terrible hurry to get born' (p. 292), although this rationale is nonsensical given that her existence is already guaranteed and were she to speed events along her conception would most likely be compromised. If anything, Daphne jeopardises her life by interfering with the past since Elsa is tempted to cheat her daughter, who she realises she dislikes, out of a future. Catherine Gallagher, writing on what she terms the 'undoing' plot of time-travel narratives, discusses what has become known as the 'grandmother paradox' (the theoretical impossibility of the time traveller's return to the past to murder her grandmother and undo her existence). Gallagher comments upon the erotic possibilities of a return to one's genetic history:

> Although, for example, you cannot have killed your grandparent, you might have gone back in time and copulated with her or him to produce your own parent; if you did, then in the present your parent would always have been your child. This sort of sexual genetic puzzle, in which one engenders oneself and is thus simultaneously biological cause and effect, avoids the flat contradictions of the grandmother paradox while preserving the *frisson* of its play with self-identity.[24]

The sexual frisson of which Gallagher speaks is certainly evident in Sackville-West's story. What she engenders through the time-travel trope is a Freudian psychical scenario, the return to the primal scene, or at least the course of events leading up to it. Returning to the night of her father's proposal, she invades both her mother's and father's respective bedrooms, clothed only in enchanting, flimsy silk pyjamas. Her disappointment in her mother's primness impresses the sense that this is also a narrative concerned with the meeting of two generations of women and the clash of their sexual and gender mores. While her mother is entirely conventional and unremarkable, a slave to tortuous feminine ritual, Daphne is wonderfully fashionable in her modern, 'sexless' appearance and daringly feminist in her refutation of marriage (p. 294).

Another text, in this instance non-fictional, which relies on a combination of occult and scientific theories is Anne Moberly and Eleanor Jourdain's *An Adventure*, which describes the authors' encounters with the spectres of Marie Antoinette and her court at the Palace of Versailles. Originally published in 1911 and followed by numerous editions, this non-fiction text gives the impression of being meticulously researched – perhaps no surprise considering that both women were scholars at St Hugh's College, Oxford – in order to defend the authenticity of the experience. In the course of their investigation, Moberly and Jourdain strive to historicise and locate their visions – the ghosts' dress, Versailles' architectural features, or the origin of a musical refrain, for example, are used to support the veracity of the encounter. In the prefatory matter to the 1931 edition of the text (published after the authors' deaths), Edith Olivier and J. W. Dunne make links between the now thirty-one-year-old vision and scientific theories of time and space. Olivier's Preface sets about defending the reliability and scholarly integrity of Moberly and Jourdain's narrative, but she also refutes the suggestion that the account is merely 'a ghost story':

> It is the record of an unexplained extension of the limits of human experience: and it describes an experience of a type with which science is more and more concerning itself. From the first, Miss Moberly hoped that what she had seen might some day be of value to scientists, and that hoped-for day has now arrived. The theories of Relativity and of Serialism are altering our conceptions of Time and Space, and the new view which is emerging seems to point towards a solution of some of the problems which are raised by the experience described[25]

Dunne, an aeronautical engineer and author of influential works on theories of time, provides a potted scientific explanation to support Olivier's revised and contemporary framework. He makes explicit reference to Einstein's theories of Relativity as well as the concept of Serialism to provide a hypothesis for these events, and while he does not come to any solid conclusion, he raises the possibility of a form of time-travelling telepathy: 'all our individual minds are merely aspects of a universal, common-to-all mind, which mind has for its four-dimensional outlook *all* the individual outlooks' (p. 34). While Moberly and Jourdain lacked access to the linguistic and scientific modernity of Olivier and Dunne when they penned the narrative, they too present this less as a tale of ghosts than a slippage of time. Rather than being haunted by apparitions of the past as you might expect, they experience the events first-hand as if by some kind of trans-historical telepathy connecting them to the memories and mind of Marie Antoinette (or possibly a young girl at court called Marion), or at least so they believe.

It is worth noting that in this same prefatory note, Dunne draws parallels between the fourth dimension and dreams, suggesting that in sleep we may become aware of a further, fourth perspective on reality that entails looking to both the past and future. He concludes that '*a dreamer's attention can travel to and fro in the physicist's alleged fourth-dimensional "time"*' (Dunne's emphasis, p. 33). Developing this idea, he appears to also reference psychoanalytic thought by claiming that:

> Investigation shows that there is nothing beyond the established habit to keep us, when awake, from using our larger outlooks; but every psychologist knows that a fully established habit amounts to, practically, an inhibition. Habit is quite sufficient to render us totally blind to what, otherwise, we should see. (p. 33)

The fourth dimension, then, is described in terms consistent with the unconscious, as a realm that is unexplored and invisible but nonetheless present and powerful. In this instance, there is something undoubtedly utopian about the intersection of the fourth dimension and the occult given that the alliance allows for the release of inhibited or repressed material and, as with the appeal of fantasy more generally, provides an opportunity for the creation of other, unorthodox realities.[26] Such may be the case with Moberly and Jourdain's work. Certainly, Castle's interpretation of the text, by way of knowledge of Moberly and Jourdain's life together, argues that the cult lesbian figure of Marie Antoinette and the tale itself act as a 'lesbian legitimation fantasy' in which 'the queen plays the part of both seductive object of desire and visionary emblem of female-female bonding'.[27] The occult experience with 'Marie Antoinette' and the lengthy investigation that follows are thus framed by Castle as acts that cement Moberly and Jourdain's initial bond and nurture their connection over the subsequent years.

Ghostly Intimacy

Amongst this sample of women engaging in the tradition of the lesbian occult, and more specifically a tradition that is inflected by modern scientific developments and theories, is the prominent figure of Left Bank Paris, Barney. Renowned for her salon gatherings, attempts to recreate a Sapphic artistic community on Lesbos, founding the *Académie des femmes* in 1927, and patronage of modernists such as Djuna Barnes, Barney occupies an intriguing place in the narrative of modernism. A central figure in many cultural histories of the period, such as Benstock's seminal *Women of the Left Bank: Paris, 1900–1940*, she is perhaps appreciated more as a social, rather than artistic, modernist.[28] Several scholars have lamented the tendency to neglect Barney's work in favour of her sensational biography, but although critics have more recently begun to redress this imbalance, the nature of Barney's work has perhaps inhibited scholarly appreciation.[29] Bar *The One Who is Legion*, Barney wrote solely in French, which she thought to be a more poetic language, and her work is infused by a fascination with bygone French literary traditions and styles of decadence and symbolism, as well as an intense interest in the life and work of the Lesbian poet Sappho, thus making for an uncomfortable assimilation under the heading of 'Modernism'.[30] To an extent she embodies the privilege and elitism under which many lesbian modernists were able to produce experimental art and, certainly, her work was intended for a select and discerning, rather than mainstream, audience. Having inherited a family fortune she neither had to navigate the publishing world nor concern herself with the quality of her output. As Tama Lea Engelking notes, Barney avoided the practice of redrafting work and although she sought advice from other writers, she rarely put it into practice.[31] The publication history of *The One Who is Legion* – it was privately published and limited to a print run of 560 books – suggests that Barney was able to write as it suited her.[32]

In Barney's 1951 edited collection of posthumous tributes to Dolly Wilde – her lover, friend, and the niece of Oscar – she includes, perhaps rather narcissistically, a selection of love letters she received from Wilde, and she concludes the anthology with a series of her own poems and musings on the subject of Wilde's self-destructive life and premature death.[33] A reader familiar with Barney's oeuvre might recognise the sentiment of the poems published in *In Memory of Dorothy Ierne Wilde: 'Oscaria'*, and might observe the repetition, almost verbatim at times, of certain phrases and thoughts extracted from *The One Who is Legion*. Amongst other instances of this textual echo is Barney's comment that:

> Almost everything escapes us in some way or other, and have we not always felt that to haunt is more than to possess? [. . .] Must we take our love off and be alone with it, to cherish and make it ours entirely? Sometimes I try to believe that death is but a corporeal accident. (*In Memory of Dorothy Ierne Wilde*, pp. 147–8)

In one poem by Barney, the epigrammatic philosophy of 'let the dead bury their dead' is recycled from both *The One Who is Legion* and originally appropriated from the title of a Renée Vivien poem (*In Memory of Dorothy*

Ierne Wilde, p. 149). Barney's philosophy is prescient of Castle's theory of the apparitional lesbian, in the sense that grief and nostalgia for the loss of a lover is appeased by the hope that death does not mark the end of existence, as well as the belief that romantic bonds may be sustained in spite of, as well as enriched by, the transubstantiation of the lover into an ethereal being.[34] Wilde's collected letters betray a similar philosophy, as she notes in a letter to a lover named Emily:

> you have become such a spirit that there is no slipping a hand into your tender palm, no pressing of sister lips. [. . .] I thought today, how logical if Emily were to die, there's no use in this ghost carrying the burden of life any more – this lovely spirit must escape like a bird and preen its silver wings. I felt no remorse, darling; would have laid you in your shroud without a tear falling, feeling you were no nearer and no farther from me. [. . .] And [. . .] if I heard you were dead one morning, I should put on a frivolous spring hat, new gloves and extra rouge and smile and smile and smile all that day! So you see, Snowdrop, how I love you. (*In Memory of Dorothy Ierne Wilde*, p. 98)

Death preoccupied Wilde also, in that she saw the event as merely the doorway to a more divine and essential existence. The wish for a ghostly union – even the homicidal desire for a lover's death – signifies the highest mark of lesbian, or 'sisterly', devotion.

The One Who is Legion is preoccupied with these very same concerns. What unites these two texts, apart from the partial derivation, is a comparable conceptualisation of the relationship between the lesbian and spirituality. In *The One Who is Legion* Barney turns to the occult or a belief in spiritual existence after death to conceptualise alternative modes of loving and lesbian union, and in the process she fetishises the spectral lesbian body. The text opens in a graveyard with the suicide of its title character by gunshot to the temple, followed by a tussle between spirits of light and dark to possess or reincarnate A.D.'s body. Once inhabited by the legion of spirits, the revivification of A.D. is consummated with a kiss from the evocatively named Glow-woman, who has stumbled across the lifeless body while on a romantic graveyard tryst with both her male lover and husband. The sex of A.D. is tantalisingly indeterminate and never at any point confirmed, and this ambiguity is only heightened when A.D. is brought back to life and transformed into a gothic, inhuman and pluralised figure. The ethereal legion that inhabits A.D.'s body must rediscover the life that has been forfeited and in the process embarks on a relationship with the Glow-woman, A.D.'s saviour and one-time lover. The text concludes with A.D.s rejection of the Glow-woman and transcendental union with the spirit of Stella, a deceased past lover implicated in A.D.'s suicide. This work is nebulous in both form and plot, with prose that is poetic and often paratactic in quality. Filtered through the fragmented and multifarious identity of A.D., the narrative is often impressionistic in nature and affects the experience of a fluid and receptive consciousness.

The supernatural premise of the novel evokes a strange mesh of generic influences. As if a visitor from another world, A.D. is estranged from her/his own existence and must experience everything for the first time, so providing fresh insight and observations on the way we live. Like the detective, A.D. must piece together the clues from the detritus of a forfeited life to grasp at a sense of identity and personal history. But A.D. is also a liminal creature possessed of supernatural abilities. If the claim for the text's place within the supernatural genre appears specious one has only to attend to the host of references to occult modes of thinking and paranormal activities littering the novel. The premise of A.D.'s existence is of course occult, proving that death is but a 'corporeal accident' (*In Memory of Dorothy Ierne Wilde*, p. 148) and that spirits not only exist after the body has withered but that they may be reanimated. The posthumous A.D. is a divine creature endowed with powers beyond that of human perception, and these paranormal abilities are represented using the language of science and motifs of what Thurschwell terms 'occult transmission'.[35] Walking through the streets of Paris, A.D. observes a funeral procession and with 'our inner sight X-rayed through the coffin the ceremonious clothes, the bruised decomposition of the flesh, to the architectural sexless skeleton' (p. 36). Similarly, when returning by train to the city, she/he exhibits signs of telepathic ability: amidst the crowd, A.D. is overwhelmed by a flood of impressions, thoughts and emotions, and fears for the integrity of her/his own consciousness, worrying that she might be '[p]articipating too greatly in others, [. . . feeling] their sensations instead of our own' (p. 65). Examining her/his rediscovered library, A.D., in life a poet, considers the nature of text and the act of writing and envisions the blank paper as 'the mind reader', 'the virgin of receptivity, the white priestess', while writers are construed as 'pure secretaries receiving supreme dictates' (p. 93). Similarly, when reading her/his own letters, A.D. feels so alienated from their content that the experience is like entering 'into communication with [. . .] spirit tracings' (p. 107). Later, on returning to the apartment of the dead lover Stella, A.D. refers to her/himself as both 'medium' and 'clairvoyant' and feels as if Stella's love letters read her/his thoughts as if by 'mind transference' (p. 143 and p. 146). With the writer, and reader, as medium or amanuenses, the creative process is here imagined as a channelling of higher meaning, so producing material akin to automatic writing.

In Thurschwell's discussion of the connection between thought-transference, paranoia and male homosexuality in psychoanalysis, she argues that for Freud, who perceived homosexuality to be a narcissistic drive for non-differentiation or the finding of the self in the other:

> Paranoia results from repressed homosexuality [. . .] because of a deep-rooted, definitionally uncanny, fear of the same that is never questioned. This fear is connected to a constitutive fear of losing one's individual boundaries – a simultaneously seductive and frightening lack of barriers between minds and bodies which is [. . .] at the turn of the century often figured through thought transference. In paranoid logic the desired other, whose similarity fascinates but also threatens the borders of the self, can only be seen as persecuting.[36]

A.D.'s concern that the emotions of others will dominate her/his own is essentially a paranoid fear of collapse of the self into the other. Indeed, Barney's reliance on metaphors of telepathy and thought-transference implies an anxiety that the boundaries of A.D.'s mind have already been breached. A.D.'s battle to order the legion of voices in her/his head might also be seen not necessarily as recognition of the multivalence of identity, but as a paranoid fear of invasion from the thoughts of others. This is one possible reading, but I suggest that for A.D., tropes of 'occult transmission' signify less homosexual paranoia than a drive to forge spectral lesbian bonds. Thurschwell also comments on Freud's collaborator and friend Sándor Ferenczi, who incorporated occult ideas into his psychoanalytic theory and practice. Ferenczi also believed paranoia to be the expression of repressed homosexuality, but unlike Freud he perceived this to be a potentially productive state, as Thurschwell explains:

> For Ferenczi, occult powers are aligned with psychosis; paranormal hypersensitivity and psychic illness issue from the same causes. Paranoia may still be at root a disavowal of homosexual desire, but it is also often an indication of a heightened ability to experience a super-substantive reality. If homosexuality breaks down the barriers between desire and identification, creating for Ferenczi a metaphorics of substantive and cognitive exchange, it follows that paranoids also experience this psychic and physical permeability[37]

It is this, then, that applies most aptly to A.D. These tropes of paranormal exchange come most into effect when A.D. returns to the deceased Stella's apartment. As the barriers to A.D.'s mind and thoughts dissolve, she/he is invaded by the spectral Stella, and in doing so communes with both her/his past and Stella's ghost, forging a renewed romantic and erotic link. Thus, A.D. succumbs to undifferentiation in the final pages as she/he and Stella form a utopic transcendental union.

In Barney's listing of 'Dramatis personae' she features the character of TIME followed by the explanatory description of 'Beyond time' (p. 160). This inclusion is elucidated, by degrees, when we examine Barney's claim in her author's note that:

> In our human composite, part ape and part angel, is there not scope for an extreme realism and spirituality? And might not an Epicurean be defined as a 'Fourth-dimensional Materialist'? In the last sense materiality becomes spiritual, whereas spirits may take human shape. (p. 159)

Barney's statement is rife with contradiction, but it is evident that her character of TIME refers to her understanding of the fourth dimension and, we can surmise, to Einstein's theories. The above extract is intentionally enigmatic: one cannot in the conventional sense of these terms adhere to both 'extreme realism' and 'spirituality', or define oneself as a materialist and yet invest ardently in theories of the fourth dimension. Furthermore, Barney's introduction of the character TIME, after the novel has concluded, can only leave the reader bewildered as no relevant reference is made in the body of the text to 'TIME' and, if anything, Barney's concept of the fourth dimension is spatial (a spectral but unperceived plane of existence) rather than temporal, perhaps suggesting a vague or confused appropriation of these scientific ideas. Her belief that an 'Epicurean [can] be defined as a "Fourth-dimensional Materialist"' refers to the Greek philosopher Epicurus, noted for his thoughts on pleasure, and her alliance of the fourth dimension with the materialist connotes that for Barney this theory provides a lacuna – perhaps a hedonist space – in which she imagines pleasure and corporeality to be indulged in. Einstein's theory of the fourth dimension is put to occult use and, moreover, is transformed into a theory loaded with sexual implications and erotic possibilities. Barney splices together ancient Greek and modern philosophies, scientific theory and spirituality, in order to produce a unique interpretation and ultimately to suggest the potential alliance between the spiritual and corporeal. This appended commentary demonstrates that Barney is intrigued and attracted by modes of thought that question the established version of reality and present innovative modes of conceiving of the self: she advocates a stretching of the mind beyond the frameworks of conventional perception – perhaps literally stretching into another dimension – in search of a more essential and authentic version of the self.

This plethora of references reveal that Barney is not only cognisant of, and indeed heavily influenced by, theories of supernatural existence and that she adopts the language of science for occult purposes, but that such beliefs are used to map out the 'dimensions' and variances of sexuality and gender and to stimulate romantic and erotic scenarios. Returned to life by a legion of spirits, and possessed of supernatural powers of perception, A.D. exists between the states of human and paranormal, alive and dead, and man and woman. The text's accompanying illustrations by Barney's long-term lover, the artist Romaine Brooks, evoke this liminality by depicting haunting, emaciated and epicene bodies suspended between two plains of existence. These naked cadaver-like figures, presumably representing A.D., are androgynous, possibly hermaphroditic, although with obscured genital regions this is intentionally hard to determine. One body, the more corpse-like of the two, is pictured slipping through a physical boundary in a gesture of agony into a plane beneath, while the other, suspended in the ether, is portrayed with bands of light emanating from its fingertips as if resurrected to a higher and celestial realm. Barney's own attention to A.D.'s physicality, like Brooks', both exposes and avoids disclosing the body. Soon after A.D. has been revivified, she/he turns to a mirror to examine this newly corporeal status (an act which echoes the scenes in both Woolf's *Orlando* and Hall's *The Well of Loneliness* where Orlando and Stephen observe and respond to their bodies as reflected in a mirror): while Barney focuses on the scars and wounds of A.D.'s naked form, any other detail is omitted (again, as in Woolf's *Orlando*). Similarly, when bathing with the Glow-woman any description of A.D.'s body is noticeably absent whereas the voluptuous fleshiness of the Glow-woman is described in sensuous detail as she undresses. While there are moments in the text that suggest that A.D. is indeed female, or identifies as feminine, and it is evident that her/his passion is directed solely towards women, the resistance on the part of Barney to categorically define or detail the supernatural A.D.'s physiology indicates a refusal to forge a link between her/his sexuality, sex and gender identification. The ambivalence of A.D.'s existence could therefore be read as an effort to evade the established matrix of gender and sexuality via supernatural means, in much the same manner that Hall uses reincarnation to signify the identification of female invert or that Woolf uses fantasy to alter Orlando's sex. Darcie D. Rives takes this approach in her unpublished thesis, arguing that Barney's choice of 'speculative' fiction creates an opportunity to resist the systematisation of sexuality.[38] For Rives, *The One Who is Legion*'s emphasis upon ambiguity can be accounted for by Barney's desire to 'fight the ways in which sexology studies worked to affix lesbian identity – and the identity of all women – to the body. She would instead insist on the impossibility of categorizing anyone, and she resisted attempts to erase individuality and variation through classification'.[39] Indeed, Barney's 'Author's Note' appears to concur with this in its claim that her work is motivated by the 'idea that I should orchestrate those inner voices which sometimes speak to us in unison [. . .] for have we not several selves and cannot a story arise from their conflicts and harmonies?' (p. 159). A.D., like Barney, is compelled to organise the tangle of identities clamouring from within her/his consciousness:

> We must choose a system of classification – make our inventory, determine our composite. Establish an order where each might exist and serve. Put down every wanderer found in our catacombs, fix them by some

familiar trait and so learn to know and govern our ghosts, our lovers, our low-characters, our martyrs and saints, and any that we might encounter in this journey through ourselves. (p. 97)

This attempt to define the schizophrenic cacophony in such minute detail – in the closing pages, for instance, these voices each take on a definite identity such as 'The Passions', 'The Poet' and 'The Philosopher' – is perhaps a parody of the wider scientific and cultural urge to name and define the sexual other.

The One Who is Legion in fact embraces the erotic potential of a gender fluidity that resists categorisation. A.D. frequently muses upon the delights of the medial creature or 'dual being' such as the centaur, the siren, the sphinx, and the Egyptian Janus (p. 100):

> And on another plane, the angel, the double being guardian over the human duality. [...]
> Following on this too happy state, the separate pair creative of a third, their three dimensional perception, their godhead a trinity.
> The three-in-one leading to four: out of the third the fourth. (p. 100–1)

While duality is lauded, Barney reads androgyny not as a static condition limited to that binary but rather a state which is constitutive of a third and fourth dimensional aspect of gendered and sexual identity, reproducing a plethora of pleasurable avenues and combinations for erotic stimulation. As A.D. states more explicitly:

> Angels are hermaphrodites, self-sufficient. No marrying in heaven.
> On earth they often appear with a woman's body and a man's desire, or vice versa.
> Two needed–No one entirely a woman or a man?
> Infinite variety of couples and couplings.
> That sailor and his girl looked inseparable –
> On long cruises, double nature given a chance.
> A need with men. And what for women? (p. 38)

Barney turns to sexology's vocabulary to align the supernatural being with the sublunary homosexual impulse – an angel when transported to earth is merely one that experiences the desires of the opposite sex. By implication Barney suggests that the gender of the homosexual individual is constantly in flux, producing not only numerous gradations of gender identities, but also an infinite variety of erotic couplings and couples. In a novel heavily laden with biographical material, Barney's reference to the amorous sailor is indicative of her own invested pleasure in gender play, since she herself once dressed in that guise when accompanying her lover, the courtesan Liane de Pougy.[40] The courting sailor of this extract is capable of both heterosexual and homosexual impulses depending on the circumstance, but the potential reference to Barney's own participation in masquerade also raises the possibility that this sailor is not necessarily who he appears to be. If neither sex, gender or sexuality are predetermined then multivalent combinations become feasible depending on what proves most erotically and psychically pleasing in that moment. Such gender ambivalence is central to Barney's unpublished 1926 novel, *Feminine Lovers or the Third Woman* (*Amants féminins ou la troisième*), according to Chelsea Ray:

> Barney implies that femininity and masculinity can be detached from biological categories of male and female, evoking the idea of a 'feminine (male) lover.' At the heart of the novel is a deliberate exploration of gender identity within a lesbian relationship and a study of the ways in which both partners can take on masculine and feminine roles in lesbian lovemaking. Barney's work, then, is a self-conscious exploration of how language is used to represent the erotically-charged gender play within a lesbian relationship.[41]

This same ideological work is underway in *The One Who is Legion*, but while for Ray language is the medium through which gender ambiguity is represented as erotically stimulating, in *The One Who is Legion* this is achieved through the means of A.D.'s supernatural existence.

Any semblance of plot or cohesive narrative linearity in this novel is driven by A.D.'s romantic and erotic development and, as with *Feminine Lovers*, her/his exploration of models of lesbian love. Barney presents a scathing critique of bourgeois, heterosexual monogamy and the stifling intimacy of domestic routine. While on an excursion with the Glow-woman to the beach, A.D. observes with disdain the casualties of such orthodox models of living and loving:

> the women, their drooping breasts too small to be falling, their chins not allowed to double below their cropped hair: youth retained, re-engaged in beauty parlours! [. . .] Fathers, with sleek-brushed, sea-sticky hair, buy the daily news before lunching at little tables with their progeniture and female lot gathered about them; through lack of discernment, paralysed in routine – not minding, having chosen, or been chosen, once for all – and once for all, wrong. (p. 62 and pp. 64–5)

Having eloped with the Glow-woman, A.D. fears and reviles the former's attempts to recreate this heteronormative pattern of intimacy:

> Soon we would be sharing the same toilet utensils – [. . .]
> Intimacy more obscuring than any separation,
> Effacing all points of spiritual contact.

> Slow devourer of the inner life,
> Feeding daily on the vitals.
> Two husks that lean upon one another, propped up by the give of each,
> a contribution to nothingness. (p. 132)

A.D. thus condemns monogamy of all types. Familiarity, it is implied, compromises the integrity and self-worth of individual identity.

The belief that a relationship is better served by separation than intimacy is an important one given that A.D.'s desire for the Glow-woman is driven by an unorthodox impulse to enforce such separation through the means of death (as Wilde imagined for the recipient of her letter, Emily). A.D.'s desire to sexually possess the Glow-woman comingles with an urge to destroy her, to set her alight, flay her, or drown her (p. 76 and p. 78). Yet the Glow-woman reciprocates this urge for destruction by pleading with A.D. to '[m]ake me, kill me, take me, kill me', so requesting to undergo a form of vampiric transportation into the realms of what A.D. calls the 'hidden people', those that live beyond the 'surface world' (pp. 133–4). The Glow-woman's wish to unite with A.D. through supernatural means is a response to dissatisfaction with the passions, specifically heterosexual, of the corporeal world: 'No love has fired me as this new hate of yours. It may exterminate me, make me over . . . be creative of my death. I am so tired of desire – of desire without fulfilment' (p. 133). Death is envisioned not as the end of existence, but in fact a sexual liberation providing orgasmic satisfaction. However, A.D.'s body, rent with self-inflicted scars and wounds, is evidence that she/he is driven by masochist as well as sadist tendencies and even suicide is claimed to be a 'love-declaration to life' (p. 37). The rather macabre book detailing her/his romantic endeavours ('The love lives of A.D.') has been bound with skin cut from A.D.'s own breast (p. 29). Even prior to A.D.'s alliance with the afterlife, then, she/he exhibited a predilection for punishment and cruelty. The literal construction of this romantic tome from the body's material affirms the sense that for A.D. love is somehow dependent on the destruction of the self.

In a bid to win the Glow-woman for himself, Duthiers, the Glow-woman's suitor and ex-husband of A.D.'s dead lover, Stella, offers A.D. possession of the past – the union with the memory or ghost of Stella – in exchange for the present, the seduction of the Glow-woman:

> I will install you in her [Stella's] flat and you can finish your days there going over your past, meeting in the spirit, and other enjoyable makeshifts. Aren't you anxious to refresh your love [. . .]? (p. 139)

The nostalgic reunion with the lost paramour is advocated as a viable and even superior alternative to corporeal romance, and one may easily forgo the present to live in the past, so it seems. In contrast, while A.D. experiences a passionate and destructive desire for the fleshy body of the Glow-woman, their sexual exchanges are shallow and unfulfilling:

> The floor on which we fell together smelt of pine.
> To locate desire – a simplification.
> But too excited to choose a gesture, we battled, finding no issue to each other.
> Surprise her into unwilling pre-nuptial ecstasy – break in through her hand barriers?
> Bedded on the wall, our shadow in close mingling with her shadow cut an audacious figure – a pornographic imitation of love-making. [. . .]
> The defenceless easy coupling of shadows seemed to mock our efforts. (p. 81)

It is not apparent why their lovemaking is unsuccessful, but perhaps it is that the Glow-woman is tainted by heterosexuality – 'existing mostly as men appraised her' and so 'fear[ing] new ways of meeting' – or that their union, based on 'the limited vibrations of the flesh', excludes deeper and more spiritual 'supreme communication' between souls (p. 120, p. 75 and p. 82).

In contrast, A.D.'s union with the deceased and spectral Stella, whose very name evokes the astral plane that she now frequents, is portrayed as a more worthy and evolved romance. Delivering the Glow-woman back into the arms of both her husband and her lover, Duthiers, A.D. returns to the apartment of the dead Stella, the familiarity of which produces the sense for A.D. that she/he is a 'medium' interpreting the communications of a ghostly presence, whereby each sound or movement is imagined to reveal Stella's haunting of the room (p. 143). When her letters fall upon the floor exposing a certain passage, A.D. is reminded that 'surely to haunt is more than to possess' (p. 146). Retreating to Stella's bed with these missives and her/his own book of 'love lives', A.D. reacquaints her/himself with this past lover and their affair. In life, this relationship was destructive and abusive, but in death it is transformed into something divine and pure:

> Our heart caught fire and burned as a sacred lamp within us, and the light shone through us that it might guide us to her. And our lover's arms stretched out to her, wider than the crucified arms of Christ: and we were joined together, and two lovers became one angel. (p. 149)

Barney presents an erotic scene of non-bodily communion, or spiritualised sexual exchange, which takes place in the conventional material context and the site of their previous passionate meetings (Stella's bed). This works to sanctify and legitimise lesbian bonds – A.D. is compared to a prostrate Christ, the lovers to the hermaphroditic angel – by spiritualising this mode of desire and rejecting its carnal form.

This fetishisation of the spectral lesbian, to some extent, grates against what we know of the vibrant and pleasure-seeking Barney, who famously categorised her love affairs into liaisons, demi-liaisons and adventures.[42] In many respects this text more closely resembles Barney's lover, Vivien's obsessive eroticisation of death and in particular her 1904 French text *Une Femme M'apparut* (*A Woman Appeared to Me*), a fictionalised account of the disintegration of her relationship with Barney.[43] San Giovanni (in part representing Vivien), an androgynous poet of little literary renown, who believes herself to have been reincarnated several times, resembles A.D. San Giovanni and the unnamed narrator (also representing Vivien) express the same delight in the deathlike and spectral woman:

> I love you because you are ill. I love you because you are going to die. [. . .] I believe I take from you a bit of your fleeting life when I embrace you. I can see within your flesh the delicate design of your skeleton. [. . .] Oh, how beautiful you are, so wasted and pale! Someone must surely be awaiting you in the tomb (San Giovanni, pp. 16–17)
> [. . .]
> I would strangle her. That would be ugly, brutal, savage, but it would be a brief nightmare, and in the joy of the mystic murder, I would stretch her out on the divan covered in the green of a mossy bank. I would spread about her head the halo of her pale hair. I would fill her hands with white lilies and scatter her body with her favourite roses – white with a tinge of green. [. . .] And I would love her in that superhuman hour more than any other being had ever dared to love. (Narrator, p. 25)

The tenor of both Wilde's earlier comments and of Barney's work is strikingly derivative of Vivien's above extracts. The beloved is eroticised by the taint of sickness and her liminal existence on the borders of death, but San Giovanni/ the narrator/Vivien also express homicidal impulses towards the lover (in the case of the latter extract, towards the unfaithful Vally/Barney). The wish to inflict harm or death upon the lover, so transforming her into a saint-like or angelic figure, is construed as the ultimate act of devotion, the route to a purer existence and supreme union.

The One Who is Legion is so heavily beholden to biographical material and mythology – A.D. is for instance informed on the doorstep of Stella's house that 'Madame vient de mourir' in the same nonchalant manner that Barney claimed to have learnt of Vivien's demise – that the boundary between biography and art blurs (p. 108).[44] *The One Who is Legion* could, from this perspective, be viewed as a novel lamenting Vivien's obsession with death, given that biographical studies of Barney repeatedly comment upon her frustration with Vivien's morbid preoccupations. As Gayle Rubin states in the introduction to Vivien's novella:

Renée's endless mourning was in part an effort to expiate the guilt she felt towards Violet's memory. Natalie, on the other hand, hated to think about death and even avoided funerals. Renée's grief seemed to Natalie to exceed the limits of decency. Renée argued for her right to mourn, and wrote a poem called 'Let the Dead Bury Their Dead.' Natalie commented in the margin, 'But not the Living.'[45]

While Vivien fetishised death and dying, and longed for union with lost lovers in the afterlife, Barney famously embraced life. As is evident from the above passages selected from Vivien's work, desire is provoked both by the urge to commit violence against the female lover and by the wasted female corpse. *The One Who is Legion* is not a condemnation of Vivien, nor of her glorification of death and the afterlife because the emphasis is more upon the spectral woman than the woman in the grip of death, and ghostly union is less a release from life than a way of articulating an idealised vision of spiritual lesbian love. If little else, this text is evidence that Barney was haunted by memories of Vivien and plagued by a sense of nostalgia for her lover. As the character Vally, representing Barney, states in Vivien's *A Woman Appeared to Me*, '[o]ne belongs to one's past', implying that we cannot escape the ghosts of those that we leave behind, however we might try (p. 60). Martha Vicinus comments on the frequency with which nostalgia and, in particular, homoerotic nostalgia appear in late nineteenth-century narratives.[46] She argues that:

> the mediated nature of nostalgia made it an enabling approach to conflicted, awkward, or even unmentionable emotions for writers grappling with how to express different forms and experiences of love. Nostalgia enshrines love, but in a space where it can be repeatedly revisited and perhaps reshaped into a more acceptable form. It frees one to relive an incident or person. The memory is treasured, winnowed, elaborated on, and altered. Constant returning and reshaping are essential elements. For homosexual writers of the late nineteenth century, the nostalgic memory became a tangible possession, the best evidence of one's special love.[47]

Vicinus's approach is equally applicable to this 1930 text in the sense that Barney recalls and fictionalises memories of Vivien, so reshaping and rehashing past experiences. Resurrecting the memory of past lovers, both A.D. and Barney commune with those ghosts (Stella, Vivien, Wilde) to reacquaint themselves with their lovers once again. '[G]host desire' and occult conventions thus serve this urge towards homoerotic nostalgia (*The One Who is Legion*, p. 145).

In *The One Who is Legion*, the occult provides a language for framing gender and sexual differences, including desires of a particularly unorthodox nature such as sadomasochism. A.D. is a divine figure whose gender identity fluctuates as does the nature of her/his desires, but these two states – supernatural and queer – are presented as somehow interdependent. Although fiercely hungry for the Glow-woman, ultimately spiritual love is portrayed as far more desirable than earthly corporeal pleasure. Rives reads A.D.'s sacrifice of the Glow-woman and embrace of Stella as a wholesale rejection of lesbian carnality and of the body 'as a limiting and even destructive casing that must be cast aside in order for lesbian women to be liberated from having their identity bound to a particular physical form'.[48] A.D. does struggle between opposing forms of intimacy, but I believe Rives is mistaken in this assumption. Karla Jay has noted that 'Barney disdained sexuality merely for the sake of carnal enjoyment [. . . H]er affairs led to, expressed, or consummated a friendship: They were not the goals but the means.'[49] A.D. rejects the carnality offered by the Glow-woman but her/his union with Stella is hardly platonic, and their meeting may take place in an ethereal form but it is described in highly sexual terms. As Barney states in the 'Author's Note', she hopes that an Epicurean might become a 'Fourth-dimension Materialist', when 'materiality becomes spiritual [. . . and] spirits may take human shape' (p. 159). The union between Stella and A.D. represents this comingling of the material and the spiritual, or of earthly pleasures and spiritual affinity. This text therefore uses occult motifs and conventions to reconceptualise lesbian identity, for it represents a spiritualised, but importantly still carnal, conception of lesbian bonds.

Notes

1. Hall, 'Author's Note' to 'Miss Ogilvy Finds Herself', p. 7.
2. A number of texts in this period turn to the supernatural to represent lesbian identities. See, for example, Sylvia Townsend Warner's *Lolly Willowes* (1926), Mary Gordon's *Chase of the Wild Goose* (1936), Eve Langley's *The Pea Pickers* (1942), *White Topee* (1954), as well as her unpublished 'Wild Australia', and Katharine Burdekin's unpublished 'Walking to Mark', which I discuss in the first chapter of this book. One might also look to the meeting of spirituality and sexuality in Dorothy Richardson's *Pilgrimage* as evidence of the influence of mysticism on lesbian modernists. While very little is known about The Rope group, it is also worth considering this collection of lesbian women based in Paris who studied under the mystic Gurdjieff. Although it is not clear whether their sexualities had anything to do with their attraction to Gurdjieff's brand of mysticism, the collaboration is an intriguing one that warrants further consideration. On H.D.'s engagement with spiritualism and the occult see Sword, *Ghostwriting Modernism*; on Richardson and mysticism see Winning, *The Pilgrimage of Dorothy Richardson*, pp. 146–51; on Gurdjieff, see Rauve, 'An Intersection of Interests'; and on Langley, see Winning, 'Wilde Identifications'.
3. See Castle, *The Apparitional Lesbian* and *Noël Coward & Radclyffe Hall*; Fuss, 'Inside/Out'; Palmer, *Lesbian Gothic*; Vicinus, 'A Legion of Ghosts'; White, 'Female Spectator, Lesbian Specter'. On modernists and the occult, see London, 'Mediumship, Automatism, and Modernist Authorship'; Sword, *Ghostwriting Modernism*; Wilson, *Modernism and Magic*.
4. Raitt, *Virginia and Vita*, p. 134. Critics who have noted a connection between the

occult and the lesbian in this period are: Castle, *Noël Coward & Radclyffe Hall*, note 69, pp. 123–4; Medd, 'Séances and Slander'; Winning, *The Pilgrimage of Dorothy Richardson*, p. 146.
5. Barney, *The One Who is Legion or A.D.'s After-life*, p. 145. Subsequent references are noted in parenthesis.
6. Castle, *The Apparitional Lesbian*, p. 4.
7. Ibid. p. 34.
8. Ibid. pp. 46–7.
9. Elliott and Wallace argue that the interest shown in these modes by Barney, and such other modernist women as the painter Romaine Brooks, 'has led to a critical devaluation of their work as derivative and second-rate'. Elliott and Wallace, *Women Artists and Writers*, p. 34.
10. See Hall and Troubridge, 'On a Series of Sittings with Mrs. Osborne Leonard'. Hall also published a report in which she relates witnessing the apparition of a friend in a Brighton garage. See 'A Veridical Apparition'. Details from Castle, *Noël Coward & Radclyffe Hall*, note 68, p. 123.
11. On the suggestion that Troubridge found these sittings difficult and experienced jealousy of Hall and Batten's otherworldly relationship, see Medd, 'Séances and Slander', p. 205. For Hall's dedication see *The Well of Loneliness*, p. 5, as well as *Miss Ogilvy Finds Herself*, p. 5.
12. For details of Somerville and Martin's relationship, see Castle, *Noël Coward & Radclyffe Hall*, note 69, pp. 123–4, and London, *Writing Double*, pp. 5–6.
13. For details of this, see Wallace, 'Edith Ellis, Sapphic Idealism', p. 193.
14. Edith Ellis quoted in Wallace, 'Edith Ellis, Sapphic Idealism', p. 188.
15. Edith Ellis quoted in Wallace, 'Edith Ellis, Sapphic Idealism', p. 188.
16. Medd, 'Séances and Slander', p. 205.
17. Thurschwell is specifically concerned with writers of the period 1880–1920. Thurschwell, *Literature, Technology and Magical Thinking*, p. 2.
18. Ibid. p. 4.
19. Seed points this out in '"Psychical" Cases: Transformations of the Supernatural', p. 44.
20. Freud, 'Dreams and Occultism'.
21. Henderson, 'The "Fourth Dimension" as a Sign of Utopia', p. 7.
22. On this topic see work by Henderson; Hoshi, 'Modernism's Fourth Dimension'; Miller, *Einstein, Picasso*; and Robbin, *Shadows of Reality*.
23. Sackville-West, 'The Unborn Visitant: An Edwardian Story', p. 290. Subsequent references are noted in parenthesis.
24. Gallagher, 'Undoing', p. 14.
25. Moberly and Jourdain, *An Adventure*, p. 28. Subsequent references are noted in parenthesis.
26. Henderson has written on the utopian application of the fourth dimension in relation to art in 'The "Fourth Dimension" as a Sign of Utopia'.
27. Castle, *The Apparitional Lesbian*, p. 125 and p. 122.
28. Benstock, *Women of the Left Bank*.
29. On Barney, see for instance Elliott and Wallace, *Women Artists and Writers*, and Ray, 'Decadent Heroines or Modernist Lovers'.
30. Jay, *The Amazon and the Page*, p. 119.
31. Engelking, 'Translating the Lesbian Writer', p. 66.
32. Although it should be acknowledged, as Jay points out, that Barney did not always publish under her own name. See Jay, *The Amazon and The Page*, p. 63.
33. Although the recipient of these love letters is not named as Barney, her identity is made patent by certain references. For instance, Wilde calls her lover 'Amazone',

a name given to Natalie by Remy de Gourmont and by which she became known. Barney, *In Memory of Dorothy Ierne Wilde*, p. 135. Subsequent references are noted in parenthesis.
34. Castle, *The Apparitional Lesbian*.
35. Thurschwell, *Literature, Technology and Magical Thinking*, p. 2.
36. Ibid. p. 141.
37. Ibid. p. 146.
38. Rives, 'Fantastic writing, Real lives'.
39. Ibid. pp. 170–1.
40. Jay, *The Amazon and the Page*, p. 91.
41. Ray, 'Decadent Heroines or Modernist Lovers', p. 37.
42. Souhami, *Wild Girls*, p. 1.
43. Vivien, *A Woman Appeared to Me*. Subsequent references are noted in parenthesis.
44. On Barney's discovery of Vivien's death see Souhami, *Wild Girls*, p. 54.
45. Rubin, 'Introduction to Vivien', *A Woman Appeared to Me*, p. xv.
46. Vicinus, 'A Legion of Ghosts', pp. 599–600.
47. Ibid. pp. 600–1.
48. Rives, 'Fantastic writing, Real lives', p. 192.
49. Jay, *The Amazon and the Page*, pp. 25–6.

PART II
HISTORY

In *A Room of One's Own* (1929) Virginia Woolf contemplates the role played by women in history. In her polemical text, based on papers given at Newnham and Girton women's colleges, Woolf advises her reader, and the female students that comprised her original audience, to:

> rewrite history, though I own that it often seems a little queer as it is, unreal, lop-sided; but why should there not be a supplement to history? calling it, of course, by some inconspicuous name so that women might figure there without impropriety?[1]

Woolf's point is that female lives are barely represented in the narratives of history. When Woolf peruses the chapter headings of one book on the Elizabethan period, she is confronted with such topics as 'The Manor Court and the Methods of Open-Field Agriculture', 'The Crusades', 'The House of Commons', and 'The Hundred Years War' (p. 41). When hunting for female figures, she is only intermittently faced with a queen or a lady, and so reasons that 'by no possible means could middle-class women with nothing but brains and character at their command have taken part in any one of the great movements which, brought together, constitute the historian's view of the world' (p. 41). Woolf astutely perceives that the fault lies with the definition of History, and the inevitable exclusion, by virtue of an unequal social system, of the overwhelming majority of women who are unable to become active participants in that record. Those who have occupied privileged seats of power have created a version of events that is narrowed and skewed by the distinctions of race, gender, nationality, class and, of course, sexuality.

The 1906 unpublished short story 'The Journal of Mistress Joan Martyn' hints that from an early stage in her literary career, Woolf was conscious of the need to shift the narrative emphasis of history's story. In 'The Journal of Mistress Joan Martyn', the historian Rosamond Merridew researches land tenure in Medieval England, but her work is distinguished from that of fellow scholars (much to their disdain) by her creative approach, which is full of 'digressions' and the imaginative portrayal of varied ways of life.[2] On a research expedition in search of undiscovered documentation, Rosamond chances upon a mine of material when touring a farmhouse. When she surveys the wealth of documents before her, she shuns the account ledgers and books detailing the family history to investigate the diary of a young woman named Joan, which the farmer had crudely dismissed. The significance of Rosamond's role as a historian is therefore twofold: her work is averse to relying on facts and instead favours imaginary visions of past lives, and her choice of the journal over the ledgers indicates a shift of emphasis to the private, domestic, quotidian and feminine realm.

Woolf's short story seems to imply that historical fiction, with its synthesis of imagination and fact, could satisfy her desire to 'supplement' and 'rewrite history'. But the classic historical novel has traditionally endorsed the standardised view of history that Woolf tries to reject, since it has been concerned with the public sphere and such subjects as politics, war and the monarchy, so depicting largely male concerns and a heavily patriarchal version of events. Furthermore, historical fiction has traditionally been expected to deliver the historical 'truth' in a realist form, or at the very least plausible scenarios featuring recognisable historical figures (reflected in the writer's tendency to provide documentation of research). Critical definitions of historical fiction vary widely, but it is Georg Lukács's study of the form that has become a fundamental, if not uncontested, reference work. For Lukács, the historical novel is born out of the French Revolution and Napoleonic wars, which he argues transform history into a comprehensible experience and concept for the masses.[3] Lukács cites Sir Walter Scott as the originator of the 'real historical novel' (a claim which has also been challenged by later critics): Scott's characters are not individual personalities but types who 'represent social trends and historical forces' and portray the interaction of high and low social strata to reveal how historical events come to fruition.[4] As Lukács claims:

> What matters therefore in the historical novel is not the re-telling of great historical events, but the poetic awakening of the people who figured in those events. What matters is that we should re-experience the social and

human motives which led men to think, feel and act just as they did in historical reality.⁵

The concept of 'prehistory' is pivotal to this framework, and while the 'real historical novel' should avoid evoking the modern, it must:

> [bring] the past to life as the prehistory of the present, in giving poetic life to those historical, social and human forces which, in the course of a long evolution, have made our present-day life what it is and as we experience it.⁶

Under Lukács's scheme, the historical text should enable the reader to comprehend his or her present social and political condition as the result of a process of events, so positioning the reader as a participant in history.⁷

With women's inevitably marginal role in this traditional narrative, we are forced to question how a woman, and moreover a lesbian woman, as either writer or subject, might stake a claim in historical fiction, in particular when cultural value is mapped onto gender value. Avrom Fleishman distinguishes between '*kitsch* historical novels', 'the popular type', and those written by the 'serious artist' which avoid 'escapism [. . . and] withdraw from the horror of the present to contemplate the horror of the past'.⁸ Surveying the state of the genre from the vantage point of the early 1970s, he optimistically concludes that 'the continued popularity of the genre makes possible the attraction of a number of fine novelists who distinguish themselves from the Georgette Heyers and C. S. Foresters'.⁹ Fleishman's discrimination against popular historical fiction, and in particular against a writer such as Heyer whose work epitomises women's historical romance, makes a palpable statement regarding the form's gendered hierarchy and the assumption that history is antithetical to feminine identity, interests, experiences and creativity.¹⁰ This attitude is to some extent echoed by the historical novelists Mary Renault and Marguerite Yourcenar when they discuss their approach to writing fiction, implying that a feminist interpretation and manipulation of the genre can prove problematic, and even unethical. In her 1963 'Reflections on the Composition of *Memoirs of Hadrian*', Yourcenar argues that:

> Another thing virtually impossible, to take a feminine character as a central figure, to make Plotina, for example, rather than Hadrian, the axis of my narrative. Women's lives are much too limited, or else too secret. If a woman does recount her own life she is promptly reproached for being no longer truly feminine. It is already hard enough to give some element of truth to the utterances of a man.¹¹

Renault makes a similar observation in 'Notes on *The King Must Die*':

> I have never, for any reason, in any historical book of mine, falsified anything deliberately which I knew or believed to be true. [. . .] But one can at least desire the truth; and it is inconceivable to me how anyone can decide deliberately to betray it; to alter some fact which was central to the life of a real human being, however long it is since he ceased to live, in order to make a smoother story, or to exploit him as propaganda for some cause.[12]

Both Renault and Yourcenar, whose fictions portray male historical figures and explore homoerotic relationships, are bound by a traditional sense of what 'history' entails: the private, 'secret', domestic lives of women simply do not come under its rubric, and it is clear that, for Yourcenar at least, one would have to endow women with masculine privilege to change that fact. Women are therefore disqualified as central figures of interest, since their inclusion as active participants is perceived as factually impossible and a betrayal of truth.[13] For Yourcenar and Renault, both lesbian writers, history cannot and should not be rewritten to suit ideological ends or modern concerns.

Yet in the early twentieth century, many women and lesbian historical novelists did, like Woolf's historian Rosamond Merridew, begin to take more liberties with historical 'truth', so evolving the genre under a feminist, or at least woman-centric, regime.[14] Diana Wallace pinpoints the First World War and the changes it wrought for the status of British women (in the same vein as Lukács pinpoints the Napoleonic wars) as the catalyst that transformed women's experience of history:[15]

> This appropriation of the form can be seen as the result of several factors: women's sense of their entry into history as citizens, the rise of the woman historian, and the emergence of university-educated women writers, usually with a degree in History or English (both then considered suitable subjects for women students). [. . .] The rise of the woman's historical novel is thus intimately connected to women's new access to university education.[16]

According to Wallace, women's engagement with the genre is enmeshed with the wider subject of their changing relationship to history and an increasing access to education. Armed with knowledge and expertise, women writers could challenge male privilege to barred realms and attend to occluded material, so rewriting history from a female perspective.

If the First World War altered the female experience of history, the highly publicised censorship of Hall's novel *The Well of Loneliness* incurred a similar, if smaller, shift in the lesbian woman's perception of her place in that narrative. This was a pivotal event for both collective and individual lesbian identity and culture: the lesbian woman entered in a recognisable form into history, so altering the way in which she experienced and understood her role in that record. As with the events of 1928, the discovery of Sappho's lost fragments in 1897 and the translations that followed also altered, less immediately but nonetheless significantly, the lesbian's relation to history through her awareness of sexual forebears.[17] As Vivien's poetry or Barney's recreations of Sapphic community imply, Sappho fuelled artistic and personal responses because she provided a sexual lineage in which women could situate themselves, as well as terms with which to comprehend their collective and individual sexual identities.[18] History as a discourse has thus played a formative role in the definition of modern lesbian and gay identities, as Laura Doan and Sarah Waters argue:

> For as long as 'homosexuality' has been available for meaningful deployment, commentators have traced its history, identifying traditions of same-sex love for purposes of diagnosis, censure, celebration, defence or apology. In a sense, retrospection is a condition of homosexual agency.[19]

An active engagement with history – the claiming of well-known figures as predecessors and the recovery of those who have been neglected and obscured from history – has served to authorise and carve out modern homosexualities. This process of recuperating the past is, as Scott Bravmann sees it, primarily performative rather than descriptive, in the sense that these renderings of history forge contemporary individual and collective sexual identities.[20]

Orlando has been called the first lesbian historical novel, but Woolf was not alone in using the genre to explore sexually dissident themes.[21] Hope Mirrlees' lesser-known *Madeleine: One of Love's Jansenists* is a lesbian historical novel that predates *Orlando* by nine years, and incidentally received a favourable review from Woolf in the *TLS*.[22] In the period of concern here, one might also cite the work of Bryher, D. K. Broster, Katharine Burdekin, Margaret Goldsmith, Mary Gordon, Maude Meagher, Mary Renault, Sylvia Townsend Warner, and Marguerite Yourcenar as merely a few examples of lesbian writers who employed historical fiction to explore sexuality.[23] The following chapters therefore examine various experiments during the 1920s and 1930s with what Bravmann terms the 'lesbian historical imagination', focusing on the popular sub-genres of historical biography and historical romance.[24] I approach these experiments in historical writing as evolutions of the wider umbrella genre in its conventional form: severing ties with any duty to historical truth or accuracy, these texts redress the balance of history, and with varying narrative techniques evolve into 'performative' texts (as Bravmann envisions) by constructing and exploring modern lesbian identities through history.[25] Prompted by the popularity of historical biography during these years, Chapter 3 asserts that women such as Margaret Goldsmith and Mary Gordon delve into the annals of history to retrieve figures whose sexuality has been occluded or misrepresented in past narratives. Goldsmith and Gordon respectively employ psychology and the supernatural to present their subjects, Queen Christina and the Ladies of Llangollen, as modern lesbians within a historical context. Such archaeological excavation serves a dual purpose: it primarily provides the modern lesbian with what Gordon calls 'spiritual progenitors', and thus a sense of sexual lineage, but it also allows the reader the pleasure of 'dressing-up' in history. Chapter 4 continues with the theme of 'dressing-up' by suggesting that Woolf's *Orlando* resembles one of the most popular, feminised forms of historical fiction – the cross-dressing historical romance. Wallace argues that the 'serious' and the 'popular' are inherently linked in women's historical fiction and that we must 'read both "serious" and "popular" historical novels together and against each other if we are to fully understand the range of meanings that history and the historical novel have held for women readers in the twentieth century'.[26] It is precisely this sense of interpretive proportion that I apply to Woolf's novel: rejecting the critical tendency to read *Orlando* as a paragon of modernist evasiveness and cunning, I instead make a case for the influence of popular fiction on Woolf both personally and artistically. I posit that Woolf, like other writers of this genre, turns to the cross-dressing trope in a historical setting to induce moments of non-heteronormative desire and to make a comment upon the nature of sexuality, ultimately resisting the dominance of the heterosexual romance narrative.

Notes

1. Woolf, *A Room of One's Own*, p. 41. Subsequent references are noted in parenthesis.
2. Woolf, 'The Journal of Mistress Joan Martyn', p. 34.
3. Lukács, *The Historical Novel*, p. 23.
4. Lukács, *The Historical Novel*, p. 53 and p. 34. For critics that challenge Lukács see, for instance, Maxwell, 'Historical Novel', p. 545, and Wallace, *The Woman's Historical Novel*.
5. Lukács, *The Historical Novel*, p. 42.
6. Ibid. p. 53.
7. Other critics, such as Fleishman, offer an equally staunch definition reliant upon the assumption that the form delivers historical 'truth' and is made up of socially representative 'types'. See Fleishman, *The English Historical Novel*, Chapter 1.
8. Ibid. p. xvii.
9. Ibid. p. xvii.
10. More recently, critics have begun to form a contemporary, elastic, and inclusive definition of historical fiction that liberates it from gender heavy differentiations of literary value. See, for instance, Wallace, *The Woman's Historical Novel*, p. 4.
11. Yourcenar, 'Reflections on the Composition of *Memoirs of Hadrian*', p. 261.
12. Renault, 'Notes on *The King Must Die*', pp. 84–5.
13. There has been some work done on the importance of male relationships in women's historical fiction, and notably the implications of such a focus on questions of gender and sexuality. See Bell, 'Writing a Man's World'.
14. Numerous critics have commented upon the importance of historical fiction for both women writers and readers. See for instance Wallace, *The Woman's Historical Novel* and Hoberman, *Gendering Classicism*.

15. Wallace, *The Woman's Historical Novel*, p. 25.
16. Women who turned to historical fiction in this manner, according to Wallace, include Rose Macaulay, Margaret Kennedy, Lettice Cooper, Hilda Reid, Margaret Irwin, H. F. M. Prescott, D. K. Broster, Mary Renault, Phyllis Bentley, Helen Waddell, Naomi Mitchison and Mary Butts. Wallace, *The Woman's Historical Novel*, p. 27.
17. Hoberman discusses the significance of this discovery and argues that it offers lesbians a 'counterdiscourse'. Hoberman, *Gendering Classicism*, p. 23.
18. On this topic see also DeJean, *Fictions of Sappho*, and Gubar, 'Sapphistries'.
19. Doan and Waters, 'Making up Lost Time', p. 12.
20. Bravmann, *Queer Fictions of the Past,* p. 24.
21. Miller makes this claim regarding *Orlando* in *Historical Dictionary of Lesbian Literature*, p. 89.
22. For Woolf's 1919 review see 'Madeleine', in *The Essays of Virginia Woolf: Volume III*, pp. 108–10.
23. Other writers who also used the genre to explore lesbian themes are Naomi Mitchison, Norah Lofts and Nora Purtscher-Wydenbruck. On the lesbian historical novel, see Abraham, *Are Girls Necessary?*, Waters, 'Wolfskins and Togas', and Doan and Waters, 'Making up Lost Time'.
24. Bravmann, *Queer Fictions of the Past,* p. 24.
25. Ibid. p. 31.
26. Wallace, *The Woman's Historical Novel*, p. 5.

3

'SPIRITUAL PROGENITORS' AND THE HISTORICAL BIOGRAPHIES OF MARGARET GOLDSMITH AND MARY GORDON

REPRESENTATIVE WOMEN

In the late 1920s Gerald Howe published a series entitled Representative Women, offering brief biographical portraits of such historical female figures as *Aphra Behn: The Incomparable Astrea* by Vita Sackville-West (1927), *Anna Comnena* by Naomi Mitchison (1928), and *Christina of Sweden* by Ada Harrison (1929). The appearance of the series at this time speaks of the popularity of biographies – over two hundred were published in 1930 alone – as well as the swelling current of interest in the narration of individual and collective histories of women.[1] The origin of this could arguably be traced back to the Victorian period when, according to Rohan Maitzen, the historical biography proved to be a popular choice among ambitious women writers with an interest in historical writing.[2] The historical biographer was at pains to mark her distinction from the historian, but this can be understood, Maitzen points out, as a strategic disclaimer since it 'allowed them to treat serious historical material in what might at least appear to be an appropriately ladylike manner'.[3] While the genre was deemed fitting for feminine consumption, it also operated as a literary space in which, as Woolf later hoped, history could be 'rewritten' and 'supplemented' (*A Room of One's Own*, p. 41). Maitzen sees these texts, then, as serving a dual purpose:

> In the first place, they accomplish, in their own way, the goal of restoring at least some women to the body of historical knowledge and of arguing

for new ways of understanding historical significance so as to include women's concerns and the details of everyday life and the private sphere. In the second place, however, these volumes have a crucial pedagogical and ideological function: they contribute to the definition and enforcement of middle-class Victorian ideals of womanhood.[4]

Victorian historical biography succeeded in expanding the scope of history to account for the difference of female lives, altering its focus to take in the private, domestic and quotidian, but this inevitably capitulated to ideals of gender. While biographers insisted that women did indeed have a significant role to play in history, it was their influence and power as wives and mothers that earned them this place.

Maitzen also observes that although this period of the genre is littered with virtuous, feminine role models, amongst these exemplars can be found the odd 'misfit':

> The misfits fall into two categories, both of which reinforce rather than disrupt the basic model of ideal female behavior: masculine heroines and bad examples. The masculine heroines manifest unwomanly traits, such as ambition, strength of purpose, independence, military valor, or personal fortitude. The foremost example of such a figure is, not surprisingly, Elizabeth I. Gloriana's legendary political and military successes are generally accounted for by stressing her manly qualities. Rather than proving by example that women can, in fact, succeed in these masculine arenas, she confirms the general unfitness of women for such work by her exceptional status; she is not like other women.[5]

Despite its concern with an earlier cultural moment, Maitzen's study is an important point of reference for this chapter. Historical biography had traditionally been perceived as a feminine and socially acceptable form of writing, but it also operated as a place of respite from exclusionary male meta-narratives, so suggesting a history of being used strategically. But its tendency to discriminate against the 'masculine heroine', an odd figure by virtue of her professional ambition and rejection of marriage and motherhood, in favour of her more feminine, heteronormative counterpart marks it out from the period with which I am concerned. In what could be deemed reparation for these prior weaknesses, an early twentieth-century wave of female biographers embraced the masculine woman, celebrating her as a heroine rather than reviling her as a misfit, and they allocated her a place in history because of, and not despite, her escape from the private domain. Sackville-West's biographies of the soldier and mystic Joan of Arc, the playwright Aphra Behn, and St Teresa, or Goldsmith's study of the pioneer of modern nursing, Florence Nightingale, are examples of such championing.[6] If the Victorian historical biography was used to 'summon up a historical community, a female tradition', as Maitzen puts it, then early twentieth-century experiments seem to evolve this project to more radical ends by invoking predecessors who break the mould and whose histories resonate loudly with a generation of modern women enjoying freshly won social and political advances.[7]

For a select few writers around this time, the 'masculine heroine' – for which I borrow Maitzen's definition of 'unwomanly traits, such as ambition, strength of purpose, independence, military valor, or personal fortitude' and add to this a rejection of heteronormative roles – took on an idiosyncratic import in that she was used to retrieve a notion of historical lesbian community and tradition.[8] The appeal of the genre in this sense can be understood by turning to Wallace's assessment of the heroine in women's historical fiction. Citing Sophia Lee's 1783 text *The Recess* as an example, she observes that:

> It is Mary Stuart, rather than Elizabeth I, who is central to the early development of the historical novel as a genre. [. . .] If Mary is the feminine ideal, a woman victimised by her gender, Elizabeth is constructed by Lee as a 'masculine' woman because (like a man) she puts the public world of politics above the private world of emotions [9]

Wallace further suggests that by 'taking sides with either Elizabeth or Mary, women historians and novelists signal their allegiance to both a version of female identity and a view of women's place within history'.[10] In this chapter, I examine two writers whose choice of heroine is similarly freighted. Goldsmith's 1933 *Christina of Sweden: A Psychological Biography* and Gordon's 1936 *Chase of the Wild Goose: The Story of Lady Eleanor Butler and Miss Sarah Ponsonby, Known as the Ladies of Llangollen* delve into the annals of history to retrieve figures whose sexuality has been occluded or misrepresented, and in doing so they signal a sexual, as well as gender, 'allegiance'.

The significance of these works is several-fold: the subjects chosen for study (independent, autonomous women, and in the case of Christina, pioneers in traditionally masculine fields) suggest a feminist agenda at work, but more importantly writers such as Gordon and Goldsmith are motivated by a desire to rescue what Gordon terms 'spiritual progenitors'.[11] These women retell their subjects' stories through modern lenses to trace a sense of sexual lineage and inheritance for both lesbian writers and readers. The heroine not only signals the biographer's sexual politics but also enables the reader to recognise herself as reflected, even dressed-up, in history, and so provides her with models of lesbian womanhood to which she can refer. Thus, such historical biographers arguably become the early tastemakers of lesbian culture, and by elevating certain historical women (Queen Christina, Sappho, Marie Antoinette and the Ladies of Llangollen, for instance) as archetypes of identity and lifestyle, they participate in the formation and circulation of cult icons. For Goldsmith this is a wider project spanning the 1930s, in the sense that a number of her other biographical studies – for instance, *Frederick the Great* (1929) and *Sappho: A Psychological Reconstruction of Her Life* (1938) – also bring the non-heteronormative sexualities of her subjects to the fore. While not strictly a biography, Goldsmith's collaborative historical romance novel, *Venus in Scorpio: A Romance of Versailles, 1770–1793* (1940), is another work that chronicles the lives of lesbian figures. Co-authored with her friend Katharine Burdekin (under her pseudonym Murray Constantine), the novel primarily concerns itself with the downfall of King Louis XVI and his Queen but it also charts the evolution of the friendship between Marie Antoinette and her companion Marie de Lamballe. While not overtly physical, the relationship is at times eroticised and the book offers insight into Marie de Lamballe's infatuation, and later love, for the Queen. The American Goldsmith (born 1894), who lived in Europe and worked as a literary translator and agent as well as a journalist and author, clearly favoured historical biography. Between 1929 and 1938 she published twelve biographical studies, covering such figures as Florence Nightingale, Christina of Sweden, Madame de Stael, Sappho of Lesbos, Maria Theresa of Austria, Franz Anton Mesmer and Hindenburg. Her publications *Seven Women Against the World: Biographical Studies of Women Revolutionaries* (1935), *Women at War* (1943), and *Women and the Future* (1946), equally illustrate her determination to highlight the formative role of women in history. Although Goldsmith was married for a period to a fellow journalist and historian, Frederick Voigt, she is also known for her brief but intense affair with Sackville-West in 1928, to whom her 1929 novel *Belated Adventure* is dedicated.[12] It is clear from letters to friends and colleagues that Gordon (1861–1941) also experienced what Barbara Brookes, in her study of the lives of women doctors in the 1890s, calls 'intense emotional relationships with women'.[13] But in contrast to Goldsmith, Gordon was not first and foremost a literary figure. She was in fact the 'first woman inspector of prisons, [. . .] a doctor [. . .] and [. . .] a strong supporter of the suffrage cause', and prior to *Chase of the Wild Goose* (which she published at the age of seventy-five) her only publication had been a non-fiction text on prison reform.[14]

But despite their different backgrounds, Goldsmith's and Gordon's works share a common objective – to rescue neglected and abused figures from history and to reveal the 'truth' of their sexual and romantic lives. Strikingly, both pinpoint the same failing of past historical narratives when they claim that, heretofore, the vocabulary with which to define these women had not existed. Gordon explains that the Ladies' relatives maintained their relationship to be 'romantic', 'since no terrible names were in existence to describe phenomena of the kind' (p. 137), while Goldsmith more explicitly states, with regards to Christina, that 'the words [had not] been invented in which she could have described her inferiority complex at being born a woman, who yet did not feel towards other women as a woman should'.[15] This past inadequacy is identified as linguistic – essentially, the historical lesbian figure could not be named – but Goldsmith and Gordon, writing in the 1930s, have the benefit of a recently circulated discursive language with which to know and represent her. They therefore graft modern and unorthodox frameworks onto historical material (somewhat of a misdemeanour in both historical fiction and biography). For Goldsmith, this is what she loosely terms 'modern psychology' (incorporating competing strands of sexology and psychoanalysis) and for Gordon, a supernatural communication with her subjects' ghosts. Their methodologies allow for a fresh, but not necessarily reliable, perspective and they ask us to reassess our knowledge of these figures in order to focus on the neglected subject of sexual identity.

Reconstructing History

Goldsmith's biographies of Christina of Sweden and Sappho are both subtitled 'psychological reconstructions' and this seemingly acts as a disclaimer that enables imagination to take precedence over historical accuracy. The author's preface to *Sappho: A Psychological Reconstruction of Her Life* (1938) explains that this kind of biography must creatively engage with the few fragments of knowledge available, meaning that Goldsmith can present a subjective vision of how she believed Sappho really lived, so denying the common belief that she committed suicide from unrequited, heterosexual love for Phaon.[16] Goldsmith and Burdekin position *Venus in Scorpio* in a similar way by distinguishing it from 'historical treatise[s]' of nineteenth-century historians and stating that they approach Marie 'psychologically and not morally'.[17] *Christina of Sweden* is not introduced in exactly the same manner, but the sleeve blurb of the first edition does claim that the text deals with Christina's 'sexual peculiarities' from the perspective of 'modern psychology', a broad catch-all term for the nexus of psychoanalytic and sexological theories put to use in the book. Queen Christina (1626–89), reigning as monarch of Sweden between 1644 and 1654, famously refused to marry and produce an heir; she abdicated, naming her cousin, Charles Gustavus, as her successor, and controversially converted to Catholicism after her departure from Sweden. During her lifetime, she was rumoured to have had numerous affairs with both men and women, and this scandalous reputation was fuelled by her reported masculine habits and preference for male attire.[18] Goldsmith claims to strike new territory, tackling what other biographers have shrunk from, by accounting for Christina's aversion to marriage and abdication with details of her psychological nuances, or what Goldsmith explicitly labels as her 'sexual abnormality' (p. 67).

In what appears to be the only published research on Goldsmith's work, Waters argues that this text was merely one of a number of readings of Queen

Christina circulating at the time (including the 1933 film *Queen Christina* starring Greta Garbo and directed by Rouben Mamoulian), with each providing a competing version of her sexual identity.[19] Waters' essay explores the ways that these biographies have been 'inflected by the changing conceptualization of sex, gender and lesbianism itself', so suggesting that dominant or popular models of sexuality have determined the tone of her portraits.[20] Victorian biographers, for instance, tended to focus on Christina's gender identity, while at the turn of the twentieth century and after Edward Carpenter named Christina a 'homogenic female' in his 1906 edition of *Love's Coming-of-Age* (importantly with a new chapter on 'The Intermediate Sex'), renderings of her life turned to questions of homosexuality.[21] There are also obvious echoes between Goldsmith's work and Hall's banned novel *The Well of Loneliness*. Christina's life and identity, and the course that it follows, are heavily informed by Hall's character Stephen Gordon.[22] This implies, Waters believes, that Hall's text had become 'something of a lesbian master narrative' and that 'Goldsmith's presentation of Christina as Stephen Gordon [. . . is] an attempt to reopen a space for the articulation of lesbian desire and an implicit protest against its closure'.[23] Goldsmith's use of genre is strategic, and less concerned with the representation of historical truth than with furthering ideological ends. It is feasible that Goldsmith's invert 'type' is more palatable, and less liable to censorship, than Hall's Stephen Gordon precisely because of her basis in fact or history, as well as her distance (both racially and temporally) from the modern English lesbian for whom Stephen Gordon seemed to speak.

With this affiliation in mind, it is unsurprising that Goldsmith serves up a discursive cocktail – Christina resembles the congenital invert of sexology but is also the product of a damaged psyche, ripe for psychoanalytic treatment – and thus constructs the Queen as a deeply pathologised figure. Christina's parents hope for a boy but when the truth of their child's sex is discovered on her birth, they continue, on the order of her father, to raise her as if she were a prince. As Goldsmith notes:

> Nothing that a Prince would have learned was to be omitted from her curriculum. Military tactics and the science of government, fencing, shooting, and riding, all of these subjects were to be taught to her. [. . .] 'The King,' Christina wrote [. . .] 'expressly declared that, apart from virtue and modesty, no feminine traits were to be developed in my character. [. . .] And my own inclinations were extraordinarily in accord with my father's wishes: for I had an unconquerable aversion, an insurmountable antipathy to everything that women do and talk about'. (pp. 17–18)

Her masculinity, then, is both congenital and nurtured, and as with Stephen Gordon, a possible indicator of transgenderism. Christina suffers emotional abuse at the hands of her mother who, having longed for a male heir, resents her daughter's sex as well as her lack of conventional femininity. It is this parental combination of absent but loving father and abusive, hysterical mother that leads to the psychological difficulties constructing Christina as lesbian:

> Her emotional life, arrested in childhood by the death of her father, whom she loved, and by the antagonism of her mother, whom she hated, was immature and negative. She felt a profound contempt for her own sex; she was disturbed by her own growing physical abhorrence of men, whom she enjoyed so much as companions of the mind. (p. 50)

Starved of love and affection as a child, the adult Christina is haunted by mental trauma and suffers from neurosis often triggered by confrontations with her mother. Goldsmith seems to depict lesbianism, then, as a result of stunted emotional and psychological development or the result of an incomplete Oedipal scenario. During one period of illness she is attended by a French doctor whose treatment is described as 'a seventeenth-century psychoanalysis without the Freudian jargon' (p. 133). Goldsmith further confirms the relevance of this discourse when she claims that had Christina and her mother known of 'modern psychology', the latter 'might have used other methods to achieve her ends [forcing Christina to be feminine], and Christina, as she matured, might have realised that, to some extent as least, her exaggerated mannishness was due to her mother's influence' (p. 35).

Taking recourse to these modern concepts as fresh evidence, Goldsmith rethinks Christina's history and offers an alternative explanation for her abdication:

> Most of Christina's biographers have agreed that her refusal to marry was the decisive factor in her life. And they agree that had she married, she would not have abdicated; she would have become a great ruler instead of a great adventuress. None of them, however, even serious modern writers, venture to discuss the delicate reasons prompting her to remain unmarried. They have shrunk from admitting her sexual abnormality, even though many contemporary documents, and Christina's own letters, make it quite clear that she was attracted by her own sex. (p. 67)

Christina surrenders her throne precisely because she desires women, in this instance meaning that the prospect of marriage and reproduction are repugnant to her, leaving her no choice but to ensure the safety of her country by stepping down. Goldsmith acknowledges various rumours of male lovers but discounts each one as false and impossible (p. 91, p. 138, p. 195). Quoting a letter from the young and as yet uncrowned Christina to her cousin and later successor, Charles Gustavus, she rereads its content and 'wonders why so many of her biographers have interpreted them as love letters' since 'they reflect so little youthful impetuosity or passion' (p. 64). Instead, it is Christina's letters to Ebba Sparre that are privileged as historical sources, and Goldsmith even explains the absence of further correspondence as evidence that the Queen was highly discrete and secretive when it came to her 'personal affairs' (p. 69). Goldsmith thus manipulates the evidence, and even its absence, to support her chosen interpretation. Waters comments on the problematic nature of this methodology when she states that:

> She gives details of the Queen's relationship with Ebba Sparre, and quotations from her passionate letters, left out of earlier biographies; she resurrects scandals about Christina's lesbian flings other commentators play down; but her references are selective, and her sources unreliable – she makes unqualified use of allegations from the slanderous French pamphlets, for example.[24]

The salacious and reputed elements of Christina's history – the male hairdresser who she required to dress as a woman (p. 288) or the Jewess she picked up on her travels, with who she fell in love and 'occasionally slept' (p. 170) – shift the biography into a fictional mode, and with its interest in disguise, romance and adventure, it even begins to resemble something of a historical romance.

Goldsmith's agenda appears to be to cast Christina as the epitome of modernity, 'far more modern than even her recent biographers' (p. 67). Her preference for wearing men's shoes was as radical, Goldsmith tells us, as the suffragettes cutting their long hair (p. 53). Indeed, when Christina immediately crops her hair after she has abdicated from power, she signifies her independence and, implicitly, proclaims her sexual identity (p. 162). Her self-imposed exile from Sweden is also compared to that of the modern expatriate:

> Maladjusted people, whether their inner disharmony is based on a sexual conflict or some other form of ambivalence, often become expatriates. They vaguely hope that their maladjustment is due to their home environment rather than to their own conflicting natures. So they run away to some foreign country, where the symptoms of their personal maladjustment are often put down merely to the natural eccentricities of a foreigner. Montparnasse is crowded with human tragedies of this kind. (pp. 125–6)

Goldsmith locates Christina, with what would seem to be a touch of disdain, in relation to the sexually and artistically bohemian community populating the Parisian Left Bank. Elsewhere, it is suggested that the mature Christina, with her shrewd knowledge of politics, 'would indeed have made a brilliant international journalist', therefore making a comparison to women like Goldsmith herself (p. 303). This version of Christina frames her as a modern woman with access to education and the ability to excel, albeit by virtue of her birth, in traditionally male professions. However, these opportunities are not unproblematic and the tribulations that she faces also align her with the 1930s woman:

> However masculine she was in other ways, Christina was not able, during the first few years of her reign, to develop a really male attitude towards the government of her country. She worked with that intensity with which serious-minded professional women so often approach their jobs. She had that over-consciousness which, even to-day, is such a disadvantage to many professional women, who refuse to forget their work after they have left the office. It is almost as though, being new as a sex to responsible work, they are par-venues in their over-zealousness. Christina seemed constantly aware that she must, in her work, live up to the high standards of efficiency set by her male Vasa ancestors. (pp. 76–7)

No doubt like many women enjoying newly won rights at the time of writing she struggles to prove that she is equal to the task and must negotiate between personal happiness and professional ambition.

But by making Christina akin to the modern, educated and professional woman, Goldsmith also taps into anxieties surrounding the affect that education was having upon women's gender and sexual identities, which is a topic I explore more fully in Chapter 5. Christina receives an education usually reserved for men, and her tutors '[stuff] her brain with facts, never letting her imagination roam about; she was not allowed to develop naturally or spontaneously' (p. 38). It is this excessive and masculine education that Christina's doctor and proto-psychoanalyst Bourdelot believes contributes to her psychological distress, since '[a]ny healthy young woman of twenty-six, he concluded, who filled her life with politics and philosophy must become ill unless she had some relaxation, some emotional outlet' (p. 132). As an antidote, he prescribes frivolous and stereotypically feminine amusements such as 'gay parties' (p. 132). This inadvertently confirms, by setting a historical precedent, that women who are given free reign in the male realm of knowledge risk psychological illness and should therefore content themselves with mere trivialities. It also supports the fear that such educated women who reject the assigned roles of marriage and motherhood for a career, ambition and personal development are made mannish and that they usurp not only the place of men in society (Christina is, after all, monarch and not consort) but also their desires. To return once more to Waters' assessment of Goldsmith's work, the former's claim that the text 'reopen[s] a space for the articulation of lesbian desire' suddenly appears in need of qualification.[25] Goldsmith may take up this narrative, but her sympathetic portrayal is countered by comments that give the impression that Christina's sexual orientation is a result of parental abuse and psychological instability, which might have been cured had modern medicine been available (perhaps suggesting, by implication, that modern lesbians can also be somehow healed of their sexual proclivities). Christina's lesbianism is also defined by her desire to emulate men and her disdain for women: her love for Ebba Sparre, her lady-in-waiting, triggers an 'active aversion to marriage', but this connection is based on an attraction for Ebba's beauty alone, since she was 'not in the least intelligent; she was, in fact, rather dull and extremely conventional minded' (p. 63). Her depiction of Christina thus appears to suffer under its own discursive weight. Goldsmith comments that Christina is unable to articulate her feelings for women since 'the words [had not] been invented' but in some respects this writer is overwhelmed by modern 'words' that describe sexuality (p. 133).

Occult Collaborations

Gordon's *Chase of the Wild Goose* is, in contrast, a celebratory representation of the famous aristocratic Irish women, Eleanor Butler and Sarah Ponsonby, more commonly known as the Ladies of Llangollen. Eleanor and Sarah had, by the time of their elopement together in 1778, known one another for ten years (having met when Sarah was thirteen and Eleanor twenty-nine) and, as Alison Oram states, 'despite the age gap [...] they formed a deep and affectionate friendship, cemented by their love of books' and 'developed a mutual desire to spend their lives together'.[26] The women's first attempt to run away, with the help of servants and in male disguise, was unsuccessful, and as a result Eleanor's family threatened to consign her to a convent. It was only when Eleanor escaped for a second time and met Sarah at her aunt's home that the families allowed the women to leave, whereupon they settled in Wales for the remainder of their lives.[27]

Gordon's biography of the women is divided into three parts. The first two, 'The Ladies Meet One Another' and 'I Meet The Ladies', provide a reasonably standard narrative describing the time from Eleanor and Sarah's meeting to their elopement and lives together in Llangollen. The study concludes with 'The Ladies Meet Me' and an explanation of the supernatural circumstances under which Gordon came to write this tale. The author tells us that in response to a dream of Vale Crucis Abbey, she travelled to Llangollen and met the silent ghosts of Sarah and Eleanor.[28] After researching their history and recently published journal, she returns to the mystical site with the intention of communing with the spectral figures.[29] Gordon makes many of the same gestures as Goldsmith to position her work as an appendage to previous, ill-conceived histories of women, and in particular as a correction to the slander that had beleaguered the Ladies' memory. She tells her subjects' ghosts that:

> I doubt whether much truth is to be obtained by accounts claimed to be authentic of other women's lives. Not much has been obtained through

others' accounts of yours. And after all, when we have read everything we can get about them, what does anyone of us know, for instance, about Madame de Genlis, Madame d'Orleans, Ninon de l'Enclos, Madame de Maintenon, or all the rest. (p. 249)

In her foreword to the text, Gordon explains that this book is necessary because '[t]here still exists no biographical account of them which is not in one particular or another based on hearsay, phantasy, or empty conjecture' (p. 11). In contrast, Gordon proclaims her version to be grounded in the 'things nearest to reality, preserving historical setting where it may be had, as well as genuine incidents when these are available' (p. 11). She aims to provide a faithful rendering, free from 'phantasy', but she soon admits that limited research sources make this difficult to accomplish, meaning that she must resort to paranormal methods. She states that 'I can only do justice to the main feature of the Ladies' lives, their great and abiding love for one another, by calling in the poets and letting them speak as no other writers of their story could do' (p. 13). Gordon does not consider this to be at odds with 'reality', nor does she try to justify or banish it to the fictional realm. Instead, her fantastical framework, which comfortably sits alongside scholarly references, stands as a legitimate research methodology like any other, and she leaves it to her reader to judge its validity 'according to his own opinion of ghosts' (p. 13). This unorthodox method rejects commonplace definitions of historical and biographical accuracy in favour of a truth that is subjective, emotional and whimsical.

The main body of the tale itself, beginning with Sarah and Eleanor's meeting and broadly covering their lives until their deaths, is not of extraordinary interest. Both women are idealised, even idolised, by Gordon who depicts them as blessed with intelligence, beauty and social graces, admired by all in Llangollen, flooded with visitors, and treated with reverence. Both women are abused by their respective parents: Eleanor is exploited as a tool with which to advance the family's position through marriage and harassed by a mother who is 'not quite sane' (p. 128), while the orphan Sarah is subject to the unwelcome advances of her guardian and uncle, and expected to marry whomever her relations deem fit. Yet living by their joint (arguably masculine) code of *'noblesse oblige'*, their actions are always reasonable, just and dignified, and their decision not to marry is made rationally and entirely from choice. The significance lies, then, not in the narration of the minutiae of their lives, nor in the clarification of the details surrounding their elopement, but (as is the case with Goldsmith) in the lens through which Gordon represents these women.

The Ladies wish to know what has occurred since their deaths and so Gordon informs them of a number of social and political advances – the extension of the vote, the availability of birth control, the altered dynamic of marriage, and women's access to education and professions. Gordon reveres the women as the originators of this feminist evolution:

> Had you any idea how many women have been on a pilgrimage to this little old house of yours? Silently, saying nothing to anybody – but they came. [. . .] You made the way straight for the time that we inherited. You meditated among your books and dreamed us into existence. You handed on to us your passionate love of freedom plus honour. We may very well ask our spiritual progenitors how we, discouraged and belittled as we were, came to be born as we were. People like yourselves are the answer to that. (pp. 269–70)

From this perspective, the Ladies' philosophy of *'noblesse oblige'* (the traditional obligation of the nobility to provide an example for others live by) takes on a different hue (p. 222). The Ladies have set a paradigm or point of reference that has enabled modern women to live as they choose and to form their own individual and collective identities. As Gordon assures the Ladies, '[n]o one thinks it remarkable now if two friends prefer to live together' (p. 266). Her representation of the women as pioneers of a feminist lifestyle, then, also implicitly incorporates a lesbian lifestyle, the choice of another woman as a companionate and potentially loving partner. Gordon elides the difference between feminist and lesbian, seeming to suggest that one incorporates the other and that 'we', Gordon's reading audience, are implicated in both.

Gordon's biography expresses an inner conflict in the way that it both promotes and discounts various models of identity that could be applied to the Ladies, one minute representing the women as romantic friends, feminists aligned, while the next minute undercutting the assumption that their relationship is merely platonic. As Oram points out, Gordon turns to models of female friendship and love from turn-of-the-century suffrage feminism partly because she 'wanted to protect the Ladies' reputation against later sexological definitions of them as lesbians', but 'she was also aware that they did not really fit very well into the model of romantic friendship' which provided little space for the erotic potential of female bonds.[30] In the wake of their failed first elopement and consequent separation, Sarah's family see her as the 'unconscious victim of Miss Butler's seductions and odious example' (p. 104) and warn Sarah that, if reunited, the predatory Eleanor will 'entirely dominate you and suck your blood' (p. 121). When their families are finally convinced to let the women live together, they publicly maintain that this is an innocent romantic friendship, but Gordon suggests that this fails to account for their intimacy:

> Whatever, in the eighteenth century, a romantic friendship was supposed to imply, that [. . .] their relations [. . . upheld] And since no terrible scientific names were in existence to describe phenomena of the kind, the

escapade remained romantic, to the entire peace of the subjects themselves. (p. 137)

The unavailable 'terrible scientific names', which we could assume belong to the modern discourse of sexology, would have sexualised, and demonised, their relationship, but at the same time the Ladies know that theirs is not merely a romantic friendship. Asked by the Ladies' ghosts her opinion of the modern women who choose to make lives together, Gordon emphatically answers '[a]s a doctor, nothing. It is not a question for me at all' (p. 267) and so pointedly declines, as a member of the medical establishment, to provide a scientific explanation for same-sex desire or to pathologise the lesbian in the way that Goldsmith does.

Yet Gordon is always hesitant to let her reader assume that the Ladies' relationship was not both loving and erotic. Conversing with their ghosts, she observes the friends look at each other and 'wonder[s] if I had not been present, whether –' (p. 254). This scene of frisson implies through the use of ellipsis that their connection is an intimate one that necessitates privacy. And when the Ladies ask her to tell them of her own life she similarly responds through omission:

> If we are to speak of personal griefs we will do it to one another only. As I said yesterday, look what you left out of your journal; you showed an exquisite taste; and even in our present lives . . . well . . . an imputed superiority obliges one . . . (p. 268)

These few sentences are replete with lacunae: she praises the Ladies for leaving unspecified details out of their journal, which we can assume to be sexual, and she takes a similar stance regarding her own experiences, since if she is to narrate her own lesbian life, it will be outside of the text and to the exclusion of the reader. By placing the Ladies within modern concepts of sexuality, without committing to a particular framework, Gordon signals to her reader that these historical figures should be read not as platonic romantic friends but as lovers. Similarly, she suggests through omission and ellipses that there is erotic material, both in the Ladies' and her own pasts, which cannot and should not be freely articulated in this context.

For Gordon, exhuming this history establishes a lineage, a historical lesbian self, through which to understand the modern lesbian self. From the beginning of the text Gordon believes that 'we', presumably herself and the reader, are the 'spiritual descendants' of the Ladies, who 'never foresaw that the hum they occasioned would join itself to the rumblings of the later volcano which cast up ourselves' (p. 17). This becomes a literal, rather than imagined, lineage in the way that she writes herself into their history.[31] Drawn to the women by a dream, she believes that she has been 'called' to them and that they have 'searched' for her (p. 245 and p. 252). In the text, Gordon implies that she resembles Sarah and, according to Oram, when she used the profits from her book to commission a plaque commemorating the Ladies, she requested that Eleanor be made in her own image (p. 244).[32] If there is truth in this rumour, it affirms the impression that Gordon not only identifies with and models herself on the Ladies (and vice versa) but that all three women, in Gordon's mind at least, are involved in a kind of occult triadic relationship from which the reader is excluded. Gordon, after all, is privy to a moment of intimacy and suggestively promises to later confide her own sexual history to the Ladies. Gordon's interest in the paranormal situates her in a wider tradition of women who found in the occult an apt language for the formation and depiction of lesbian bonds, which is a topic I discuss in more detail in Chapter 2. Indeed, like the women discussed in that chapter, ideas of occult existence allow Gordon to initiate a paranormal romance with the Ladies. Believing the women to have 'called' her, she experiences a kind of spectral seduction and romantic reunion (p. 245); imagining that she closely resembles Sarah, she also assumes the role of Eleanor's lover (and, if she did model Eleanor's statue on herself, as Oram mentions, she doubles as Sarah's partner as well). One could even argue that the act of artistic collaboration (as Gordon tells us, the Ladies are instrumental in the faithful rendering of their own history) itself holds erotic power, as Wayne Koestenbaum's study of the erotics of late nineteenth-century and early twentieth-century male literary collaborations suggests.[33] Focusing on women's literary partnerships, Bette London similarly argues that occult forms of transmission (mediumship and automatic writing) can be thought of as methods of literary collaboration.[34] Gordon's communication with the Ladies is creatively productive but this collaboration is also an act of, or excuse for, occult erotic exchange. Indeed, the very idea of communing with paranormal spirits, with its implied transgression of bodily and psychic borders, is evocative of the intimacy of sex.[35]

Her choice of chapter titles ('I Meet The Ladies' and 'The Ladies Meet Me') further evokes this sentiment in that Gordon extends the narrative of the Ladies' story, albeit into posthumous other-worldly realms, and inscribes herself as an active participant in their romantic history. Oram argues that '[i]n so strongly identifying with the Ladies of Llangollen towards the end of her life, Mary Gordon was publicly asserting her feminist past and also establishing her own identity as a woman who loved women'.[36] Indeed Gordon, who visited the Ladies' house when seventeen and seventy-five years old, so book-ending her adult life, finds personal meaning and definition through allying with the Ladies. But I would suggest that this 'public assertion' is in fact implicit and conflicted, given that something remains obscured and unnamed in Gordon's text. She speaks frequently of the connection between the ideals of modern women and the Ladies, and conjures the symbol of the wild goose as the metaphor for this affinity.[37] Yet the specifics of how these temporally separated women are aligned, and just what this metaphor stands for is glossed over, just as the details of the Ladies' and Gordon's erotic lives are replaced by silence and elision. Gordon flags up various names we could define and know the Ladies by – romantic friend, invert, predatory seductress – and rejects the authority of each, but she also neglects to locate an alternative. In this sense, it is through negation and omission – the impression that there are apt words to describe these women, but Gordon cannot voice them – that the Ladies' sexual identities are conveyed.

Gordon and Goldsmith both note their dissatisfaction with previous ways of articulating lesbian identity, but whether either succeeds in their linguistic reclamation is debatable. In replicating the tropes of sexology and psychoanalysis and echoing Hall's *The Well of Loneliness*, Goldsmith fails to exceed the limits of the invert paradigm and is hemmed in by her own reliance on sexual discourses. Her version of Christina, and by implication a version of the modern lesbian, is deeply pathologised and doomed to a life of unhappiness without love and companionship. Goldsmith's recognition of the limitations of this model of sexuality is evident in *Sappho of Lesbos*, published two years after *Christina of Sweden*. Here she makes a pointed statement that this biography will not present Sappho as a 'type': '[t]he preference that Sappho later showed for women was not in any way due to her relationship with her father. Cleïs, whom she adored, was the centre of her infant world, but she was extremely fond of Scamandronymus' (p. 16). While portrayed as physically unattractive, Sappho is not overtly masculine and takes pleasure, unlike Christina, in her appearance and 'ultra-feminine' fashions and, furthermore, she revels in motherhood (p. 40). While she does suffer from bouts of depression and ultimately commits suicide, this melancholia is not portrayed as a direct result of her sexuality. Gordon, in contrast, finds existing models that account for female same-sex love to be inadequate, but she can only replace these with implicit suggestion and omission, and thus continues to be constrained by linguistic inadequacy and a sense of what cannot be said. With their respective focus on the excess and absence of discourse, both texts reveal that, to some extent, early twentieth-century language remained a limited resource with which to describe and define women's relationships with one another.

Both Goldsmith and Gordon make gestures towards historical accuracy and scholarly style, but although they provide extensive bibliographies and evidence of research (this is less the case for Goldsmith who fails to source the material that she quotes), their works are untenable as historical documents in the traditional sense. In contrast to such historical fiction writers as Renault and Yourcenar who placed great stock in truth and accuracy, Gordon and Goldsmith test the boundaries of how we define and construct history by letting their imaginations roam and more personal motivations take precedent.

In their hands, then, history as a discourse is altered, becoming personal and highly subjective. In this sense, we might think of Goldsmith and Gordon as indebted to, or even part of, what William C. Lubenow calls the 'revolution in biographical writing' inaugurated by Lytton Strachey and in particular his 1918 collection of biographical studies, *Eminent Victorians*. Strachey's work responded to the staid Victorian model of what he termed 'Standard Biographies', and his idiosyncratic style favoured brevity, a focus on the psychology of his subjects, and a selective approach to facts that chose 'certain fragments of the truth which took my fancy and lay to my hand'.[38] His statement that '[h]uman beings are too important to be treated as mere symptoms of the past. They have a value which is independent of any temporal processes – which is eternal, and must be felt for its own sake', chimes with Goldsmith and Gordon's own ambitions.[39] While placing their texts under the heading of historical biography, a retrieval of an individual's past, they effectively dehistoricise their subjects by revealing their 'eternal value', as Strachey called it – they retrieve the lesbian past in order to make comprehensible the lesbian present. In their efforts to make connections between historical and contemporary lesbian identities, their non-heteronormative subjects become cultish emblems of lesbian modernity. In this respect these portraits are less concerned with attaining some essential truth about Christina of Sweden or the Ladies of Llangollen, than with using historical biography to find a way to explore the modern sexual identities of their readers and, it could be added, the writers themselves.

Notes

1. Graves and Hodge note that over 200 biographies were published in 1930 and that these sold well. Graves and Hodge, *The Long Weekend*, p. 233.
2. Maitzen, 'This Feminine Preserve', p. 371.
3. Ibid. p. 374.
4. Ibid. p. 385.
5. Ibid. p. 384.
6. See Sackville-West's *Aphra Behn: The Incomparable Astrea* (1927), *Joan of Arc* (1936), *The Eagle and the Dove: A Study in Contrasts: St. Teresa of Avila, St. Thérèse of Lisieux* (1943), and Goldsmith's *Florence Nightingale: The Woman and the Legend* (1937).
7. Maitzen, 'This Feminine Preserve', p. 382.
8. Ibid. p. 384.
9. Wallace, *The Woman's Historical Novel*, p. 19.
10. Ibid. p. 19. Wallace claims that the tide turns in favour of Elizabeth in the 1940s and early 1950s, although I would suggest that, in historical biography at least, the masculine women becomes popular much earlier than this (pp. 95–6).
11. Gordon, *Chase of the Wild Goose*, p. 269. Subsequent references are noted in parenthesis.
12. Goldsmith met Sackville-West, who had recently accompanied her husband, Harold Nicolson, on a diplomatic posting to Berlin, in early 1928. Goldsmith and Sackville-West embarked on an affair, which continued when Goldsmith later

travelled to England. The affair soon ended when Sackville-West lost interest, but their friendship continued: Goldsmith helped Sackville-West with translations of Rilke; Sackville-West persuaded her husband to write a preface for Goldsmith's 1929 book *Frederick the Great*; and Goldsmith's 1929 novel *Belated Adventure* is both dedicated to and features a character based upon Sackville-West. It is known that Goldsmith divorced her husband in 1935, but little other biographical information is available, including whether she went on to have, or had previously had, romantic or erotic relationships with women. For details of Goldsmith and Sackville-West's relationship, see Glendinning, *Vita*.

13. Brookes refers to a letter from Gordon to Dr Agnes Bennett on 8 December 1925 as evidence of this claim. Oram and Turnbull similarly claim that Gordon lived with a female partner. See Brookes, 'A Corresponding Community', p. 250, and Oram and Turnbull, *The Lesbian History Sourcebook*, p. 37. Oram provides further details in her essay on the Ladies of Llangollen when she notes that Gordon had been 'involved in a close relationship with another woman whom she referred to as "Frank"'. But her letters to friend Dr Agnes Bennett suggest that this relationship ended in 1922, soon after Gordon retired. See Oram, 'Telling Stories', p. 52 and note 40, p. 61.
14. Oram, 'Telling Stories', p. 50.
15. Goldsmith, *Christina of Sweden*, p. 133. Subsequent references are noted in parenthesis.
16. Goldsmith, *Sappho of Lesbos*, p. v. Subsequent references are noted in parenthesis.
17. Constantine and Goldsmith, *Venus in Scorpio,* p. 10.
18. Biographical details from Buckley, *Christina Queen of Sweden*.
19. Waters, 'A Girton Girl', p. 47. Oram's 'Telling Stories' similarly charts the different representations of the Ladies of Llangollen.
20. Waters, 'A Girton Girl', p. 44.
21. Ibid. p. 44.
22. It is interesting to note that Goldsmith's friend and collaborator, Burdekin, also imposed the invert's narrative, lifted from Hall's text, as a structure for several of her unpublished works (see Chapter 1 of this book). Goldsmith explores many issues familiar to Burdekin's work such as identities of sexual inversion, female inferiority complex and questions of social and class inequality.
23. Waters, 'A Girton Girl', p. 57.
24. Ibid. p. 55.
25. Ibid. p. 57.
26. Oram, 'Telling Stories', p. 44.
27 All details of the Ladies' elopement are from Oram, 'Telling Stories', p. 44.
28. Oram makes a connection between the dream that Gordon has and the fact that she was studying under the psychoanalyst Carl Jung at the time. 'Telling Stories', p. 50. The book itself is dedicated to Emma Jung, the psychoanalyst and wife of Carl Jung.
29. *The Hamwood Papers of the Ladies of Llangollen* was published in 1930.
30. Oram, 'Telling Stories', pp. 50–1.
31. Oram makes a similar point when she states that 'Gordon herself enters the Ladies' story'. 'Telling Stories', p. 51.
32. Ibid. note 41, p. 61.
33. Koestenbaum argues that 'men who collaborate engage in a metaphorical sexual intercourse'. *Double Talk*, p. 3.
34. London questions the applicability of Koestenbaum's model for female collaborations because 'the female body subscribes to a different economy of desire and pleasure' and because the act of writing and authorship holds alternative

social, economic and historical meanings for women. See *Writing Double*, p. 66.
35. As I discuss in further detail in Chapter 2, Thurschwell examines the relationship between modes of intimacy and the occult in *Literature, Technology and Magical Thinking*.
36. Oram, 'Telling Stories', p. 52.
37. Woolf also employs the 'wild goose' as an enigmatic symbol in the concluding lines of *Orlando*. The Ladies of Llangollen also appear in Woolf's early germination of the idea for *Orlando*: 'Suddenly between twelve & one I conceived a whole fantasy to be called "The Jessamy Brides" – why, I wonder? I have rayed round it several scenes. Two women, poor, solitary at the top of a house. [. . .] It is to be written as I write letters at the top of my speed: on the ladies of Llangollen; on Mrs Fladgate; on people passing. No attempt is to be made to realise the character. Sapphism is to be suggested.' It is curious that both texts, inspired to different extents by the Ladies' story and their supposed sexualities, use this symbol of the wild goose. Although Gordon's text was published by Woolf's Hogarth Press, Woolf's letters and diaries do not produce evidence of any creative engagement between the women other than the relationship between publisher and author. Jones's essay explores the connection between the two texts, but concludes that '[i]t may just be a fascinating coincidence'. The wild goose is of course of particular import in the history of Ireland and as a symbol evoking exile and loss. The 'Flight of the Wild Geese' refers to the departure of an Irish Jacobite army from Ireland to France in 1691. See Woolf, 14 March 1927, *Diary Volume 3*, pp. 130–2 (p. 131); Jones, 'The Chase of the Wild Goose', p. 187; Callow, 'Jacobite Rebellions', pp. 1034–5; and Finnan, *John Redmond*, p. 8.
38. Strachey, *Eminent Victorians*, p. 6 and p. 5.
39. Ibid. p. 5.

4

'I DISLIKE THE CORRECT THING IN CLOTHES': VIRGINIA WOOLF'S *ORLANDO: A BIOGRAPHY* AND THE CROSS-DRESSING HISTORICAL ROMANCE

The High and the Low Ground

Woolf's famously caustic essay on the cultural 'Middlebrow' struggles to convey in any certain terms how the middlebrow should be defined, but it is evident that her piece is directed at 'brows' as people rather than as texts:[1]

> [Middlebrows] do not live in Bloomsbury which is on high ground; nor in Chelsea which is on low ground. Since they must live somewhere presumably, they live perhaps in South Kensington, which is betwixt and between. The middlebrow is the man, or woman, of middlebred intelligence who ambles and saunters now on this side of the hedge, now on that, in pursuit of no single object, neither art itself nor life itself, but both mixed indistinguishably, and rather nastily, with money, fame, power, or prestige.[2]

Jonathan Rose's survey of British working-class reading habits suggests that the gradual democratisation of the class system, increased literacy, and greater access to affordable literature was in part responsible for derision of this sort:

> By the early twentieth century the Board schools had introduced great literature to the masses, who were buying the shilling classics of Everyman's Library by the million. Workers and clerks had by no means caught up with the educated classes, but some of them were coming uncomfortably close. Many intellectuals felt threatened by the prospect

of a more equal distribution of culture: it is telling that the epithet they loved to spit at the masses was not 'uneducated,' but 'half-educated.' One could feel a patronizing fondness for the unlettered peasant, but in a society where every man supplies his own philosophy, the philosopher becomes redundant.[3]

To a certain extent, Rose's argument is born out in Woolf's comment. For this modernist, the 'battle of the brows' is conducted on territorial terms in that the middlebrows are imagined as ambitious social upstarts who breach the borders of class ghettoes and trespass on the privileged space of society's higher echelons. It is also clear that Woolf's distaste for the middlebrow is rooted in a set of assumptions about how and why culture should be produced and consumed:

> We highbrows, I agree, have to earn our livings; but when we have earned enough to live on, then we live. When the middlebrows, on the contrary, have earned enough to live on, they go on earning enough to buy – what are the things that middlebrows always buy? ('Middlebrow', p. 201)

It is the middlebrow individual's commercialism, as both seller and buyer of goods that, when compared to the detached autonomy of the highbrow, strikes Woolf as crass. She condemns the ambition, even the need, to write for money and in the process produces a definition of what classifies as valuable culture. As Bourdieu's analysis of cultural production suggests, culture earns its producer and its consumer different forms of profit, or capital. As he states:

> 'Symbolic capital' is to be understood as economic or political capital that is disavowed, misrecognised and thereby recognised, hence legitimate, a 'credit' which, under certain conditions, and always in the long run, guarantees 'economic' profits. Producers and vendors of cultural goods who 'go commercial' condemn themselves, and not only from an ethical or aesthetic point of view, because they deprive themselves of the opportunities open to those who can *recognize* the specific demands of this universe and who, by concealing from themselves and others the interests at stake in their practice, obtain the means of deriving profits from disinterestedness.[4]

Bourdieu's point is that highbrow or avant-garde art distinguishes itself through its disdain of economic profit and its affectation of disinterest in the market and so endows itself with legitimacy or symbolic capital, that is in Bourdieu's terms '"prestige" or "authority"'.[5] In contrast, to write for commercial purposes brings short-term financial profit but little if any artistic kudos. But the ability to create art for art's sake, rather than for the market's or the consumer's, is a liberty indicative of one's position within the social, as well as cultural, hierarchy.[6] For Woolf, who lived comfortably on an inheritance left to her by her aunt, as for others engaging in the 'battle of the brows' at this time, elitist ideas of cultural value were fundamentally entwined with distinctions of social class and economic status.[7]

As Woolf's comments show, then, the middlebrow was not a coveted moniker, but as Nicola Humble points out, to be labelled in this way was, to a certain extent, beyond an author's control and instead determined by a book's reception and circulation.[8] Several studies have admirably examined early twentieth-century middlebrow fiction in an attempt to account for its neglect and to repair its reputation.[9] Scholars have acknowledged the difficulty of defining this term and of establishing clear-cut distinctions between high, middle and lowbrow cultural products, but what is evident is that the middlebrow is most of all distinguished by its reception, both in terms of its audience (mostly middle-class and female) and its circulation (through cultural agencies such as lending libraries, book clubs and newspapers' book-of-the-month recommendations).[10] As Humble explains in her study of the feminine middlebrow novel, texts were characterised by an interest in common themes and 'a particular concentration on feminine aspects of life, a fascination with domestic space, a concern with courtship and marriage, a preoccupation with aspects of class and manners'.[11] While the middlebrow is not the equivalent of genre fiction – it is not dependent on recognisable and codified, formulaic conventions in the same way – certain genres, such as detective or romance fiction, become middlebrow in their handling of these themes or in their appropriation by the reading public.

Woolf's condemnation of the middlebrow might, then, also be thought of as an attack on forms of genre fiction. With this in mind, I suggest that despite Woolf's derision of all things middlebrow, she was somewhat implicated in the category herself, both personally and artistically. As I will explore, Woolf was certainly exposed to popular fiction, and more specifically historical fiction, during her time as a book reviewer and through her father's literary tastes. Resisting the temptation to read *Orlando*, published in the same year as Hall's *The Well of Loneliness* (1928), as an isolated novel that evades censorship and encodes lesbian desire in its experimental style, this chapter argues that Woolf's novel references the historical romance, a sub-genre of historical fiction particularly popular during the 1920s. I will highlight some of the generic commonalities between the historical romance and *Orlando* – specifically its use of disguise and the cross-dressed figure, its attention to the feminised detail of costume, and the dominant structure of the romance narrative – in order to question why Woolf shares in such familiar and formulaic tropes and how they are put to work under her care.

On publication, *Orlando* proved to be highly popular, overtaking sales of her previous works. Within three months the novel had entered into its third edition, sold more than 6,000 copies with 50–60 more ordered each day, and had earned Woolf £2,000 in royalties.[12] Of the novel's reception, Sean Latham states that:

> Woolf's novel had itself become a valuable bit of capital eagerly circulated throughout the city. Rather than the aloof high modernist experimenting with narrative form, Woolf suddenly emerged as a fanciful writer of romances accessible to a wide and varied audience.[13]

Woolf was one of the bestselling authors between 1919 and the early 1930s, alongside such writers as Agatha Christie, Rafael Sabatini and P. G. Wodehouse.[14] By virtue of popularity and sales, *Orlando* catapulted Woolf into the mainstream and endowed her 'rather nastily, with [the] money, fame, power, or prestige' that so appalled her ('Middlebrow', p. 199). Woolf condemned the middlebrow writer's ambition to write for profit, but *Orlando*'s success effectively metamorphosised a highbrow artwork into a middlebrow commodity, so troubling the unforgiving boundaries which she had set to determine cultural value. And so, as Laura Marcus states, for Woolf '[t]he popularity of *Orlando* [. . .] led to concern that she would be required to repeat herself rather than engage in new and different experiments', or essentially that she would be forced to become generic or formulaic.[15] Indeed, *Orlando* is to some extent a generic novel extraordinaire, classed since its publication as a biography (and promoted in this vein by booksellers at the time), historical novel, parody, comedy, satire, fantasy, 'elaborate love-letter', and more recently an act of lesbian communication between Woolf and her lover Sackville-West.[16] What is evident is that the novel's mass circulation and its assimilation into popular culture are due, in part, to its stylistic flexibility and broad appeal.[17]

The novel itself mocks the commercialism of the popular when the literary critic Nick Greene complains that 'all our young writers are in the pay of booksellers. They turn out any trash that serves to pay their tailor's bills', so echoing Woolf's dislike of authors who publish to meet market, rather than aesthetic, demands so that they may in turn become consumers (notably, here, of fashion).[18] However, reflecting on *Orlando*'s sales, Woolf's diary entry for 18 December 1928 reveals that she was very much reaping the benefits of her own commercial success and more than simply managing to 'pay [. . . the] tailor's bills':

> For the first time since I married 1912 – 1928 – 16 years – I have been spending money. The spending muscle does not work naturally yet. I feel guilty; put off buying, when I know that I should buy; & yet have an agreeable luxurious sense of coins in my pocket beyond my weekly 13/-

> which was always running out, or being encroached upon. Yesterday I spent 15/- on a steel brooch. I spent £3 on a mother of pearl necklace – & I haven't bought a jewel for 20 years perhaps! I have carpeted the dining room – & so on. I think one's soul is the better for this lubrication; & I am going to spend freely, & then write, & so keep my brain on the boil. [. . .] The important thing is to spend freely, without fuss or anxiety; & to trust to one's power of making more – Indeed, I cannot at this moment very seriously doubt that I shall earn more, this next 5 years, than ever before.[19]

Delightfully, what emerges from this private missive is Woolf's lavish enjoyment of financial independence. Although she mentions few details of her purchases – and these are a mixture of the frivolous and practical – the emphasis is strikingly upon the experience of buying rather than the product bought: '[I] put off buying, when I know that I should buy [. . .] I am going to spend freely [. . .] The important thing is to spend freely'.[20] There is no mention of what exactly Woolf wishes to buy, but this appears to be less significant than the liberty to become an independent consumer. It is evident from *A Room of One's Own* that the financial autonomy of women is more than the freedom to make purchases, but Woolf does acknowledge the interdependence between her role as a consumer of commodities and her cultural output. The claim that 'I am going to spend freely, & then write [. . . and] trust to one's power of making more [money]' is not dissimilar from her invective that '[w]hen the middlebrows [. . .] have earned enough to live on, they go on earning enough to buy – what are the things that middlebrows always buy?' ('Middlebrow', p. 201). Woolf is evidently more heavily invested in middlebrow culture, as both producer and consumer, than she would no doubt have cared to publicly admit.[21]

Woolf's time as a book reviewer, in particular during the early period of her career, also brought about an acquaintance with popular fiction.[22] Jeanne Dubino's catalogue of Woolf's essays reveals that between 1904 and 1909 Woolf wrote 101 essays, twenty-eight of which were concerned with what Dubino calls '[c]ontemporary popular writers' (such as Marjorie Bowen), compared to a mere seven on '[c]ontemporary important popular writers' (such as Henry James).[23] Dubino surmises from this that:

> it is apparent that at this point in her career she had not quite reached the tastemaker stage. The reputations of the 'important' writers – James, Conrad, Galsworthy, Wells – were already established; as a reviewer she was in a position to maintain the status quo and function as a cheerleader. Her own reviews of the popular writers reveal that almost all were, to put it mildly, far from groundbreaking. Indeed, it is amusing to think of the young Virginia Stephen reading a conventional romance, the plot of which sounds little different from today's Harlequins.[24]

It is also worth noting that a number of these reviews were of historical fiction: Woolf, for instance, wrote about Hope Mirrlees' 1919 lesbian historical novel *Madeleine: One of Love's Jansenists*, the work of Vernon Lee, Marjorie Bowen, A. C. Inchbold, and Sir Walter Scott. In one such appraisal of Scott's work, Woolf acknowledges the satisfaction and pleasure that might be gained from the Waverley novels, but confesses that it is a 'vicious [. . .] pleasure; it cannot be defended; it must be enjoyed in secret'.[25] Woolf articulates the guilty pleasure of genre fiction, but at the same time she also appreciates the creative freedom that the distance of time can allow the writer. As she writes in 'Phases of Fiction', '[w]here Scott will go back a hundred years to get the effect of distance, Mrs. Radcliffe will go back three hundred. With one stroke, she frees herself from a host of disagreeables and enjoys her freedom lavishly'.[26] And while Woolf's reading notebooks do not betray a secret penchant for the classic historical novel (beyond Scott and Charlotte Yonge, at least) or historical romance, what can be drawn from this is that, whether willingly or not, her time as a book reviewer and her reading of popular fiction for money, meant that she was far from unfamiliar with the genre.[27]

Woolf was also exposed to her father's own combination of affection and derision for historical fiction. In an essay on Leslie Stephen she recalls childhood evenings spent listening to her father read from Scott's novels:

> I cannot remember any book before *Tom Brown's School Days* and *Treasure Island*; but it must have been very soon that we attacked the first of that long line of red backs – the thirty-two volumes of the Waverley Novels, which provided reading for many years of evenings, because when we had finished the last he was ready to begin the first over again. At the end of a volume my father always gravely asked our opinion as to its merits, and we were required to say which of the characters we liked best and why. I can remember his indignation when one of us preferred the hero to the far more lifelike villain. My father always loved reading aloud, and of all books, I think, he loved Scott's the best. In the last years of his life, when he was tired of reading anything else, he would send one of us to the bookshelf to take down the first of the Waverley Novels that happened to present itself, and this he would open at random and read with quiet satisfaction till bedtime.[28]

Several telling points emerge from this passage: Woolf reveals a familial affinity with historical fiction (as well as the sense that her analysis of it was faulty) and she positions Stephen as a consumer of genre fiction, whose pleasure not only survives, but is also stimulated by, the return to the familiar and formulaic text. It is this fondness for Scott which colours Stephen's otherwise staunch critique of the historical novelist's work and historical fiction in general. In an essay on the subject, Stephen takes issue with the superficiality of Scott's writing and, like Woolf, the idea that literature might be a trade rather than an art.[29] His analysis of historical fiction in the wider sense is equally critical (historical novels are the 'mortal enemies to fiction'), but it is Stephen's focus on costume and clothing that is particularly important in the context of this discussion.[30] As he complains:

> Scott bestows an apparently disproportionate amount of imagination upon the mere scene-painting, the external trappings, the clothes, or dwelling-places of his performers. A traveller into a strange country naturally gives us the external peculiarities which strike him. Scott has to tell us what 'completed the costume' of his Highland chiefs or mediæval barons. He took, in short, to that 'buff-jerkin' business of which Carlyle speaks so contemptuously, and fairly carried away the hearts of his contemporaries by a lavish display of mediæval upholstery.[31]

For Stephen, Scott 'too often manufactures his characters from the materials used by the frequenters of masked balls', implying that his narrative techniques are evidently as meaningless as the costumes worn by the masqueraders themselves.[32] In this reliance on metaphors of clothing as a way to reiterate the frivolity of Scott's work, he derides both the literature under question and the very idea that dress might play a significant role in a narrative. Given that fashion is, stereotypically, deemed a feminine interest, Stephen's implicit critique is of historical fiction as a feminised form. As Wallace argues in her study of the women's historical novel:

> The term 'costume novel' is generally used in a derogatory fashion to distinguish the popular novel [. . .] from the 'serious' historical novel. But the term indicates a key element in the attraction of historical novels for women, which is quite simply the clothes: Elizabethan ruffs and farthingales, Regency pelisses and muffs, even Victorian crinolines and bonnets. Many of these were probably uncomfortable and constraining to wear (and, possibly, of doubtful cleanliness) but can be glamorous and sensual in the imagination.[33]

Stephen's distaste is, then, arguably also for women's reading interests and it quietly voices an underlying anxiety that mass culture was somehow a degraded, feminised form of culture lacking in literary worth.[34] In a 1926 article on the 'The Views of the Great Critics on the Historical Novel' Ernest Bernbaum somewhat dramatically cites Stephen's criticism as the 'most damaging to the genre throughout the English-speaking world'.[35] Bernbaum no doubt overstates the case, but his comment does speak of the influence of Stephen's views, both in his capacity as a critic and as Woolf's father.

Substantial scholarly work has been undertaken on *Orlando* as a revision of patriarchal versions of history and biography, of which Stephen as the first editor of *The Dictionary of National Biography* was merely one representative. Such work focuses on Woolf's shift of narratological emphasis to record the marginalised voices of the domestic, female and lesbian, and while there is also much engaging work on Woolf's complex relationship to dress, it is curious that the two subjects have not been explicitly interwoven. More specifically, the connection between Stephen's vehement dismissal of costume as a convention of historical fiction and Woolf's almost obsessive attention to the intricacies of clothing in *Orlando* has not been commented on, as far as I am aware.[36] From the very first sentence of *Orlando* when the narrator assures the reader that 'there could be no doubt of his sex, though the fashion of the time did something to disguise it', Woolf links period dress to the ambiguity and playfulness of the categories of sex and gender (p. 15). Given that Stephen felt that the attention to the minutiae of costume marred the historical novel and was detrimental to literary value, it is surely significant that Woolf not only embraces the sartorial within her historical fiction but also uses such detail to create cross-gendered identities and to inspire non-heteronormative desires.

Dressing-up in the Past

In her essay on the middlebrow, Woolf claims that 'I dislike the correct thing in clothes' and both Woolf's life and fiction are testament to this ('Middlebrow', p. 199). 'Dressing-up' was a favourite pastime of Woolf's circle of family and friends, as Maggie Humm's catalogue of the Monk House's photo albums reveals.[37] And other instances of such rebellion – her masquerade as an Abyssinian Prince in the Dreadnought Hoax, her commission for a green dress made of upholstery fabric, and her appearance in the fashion magazine *Vogue* wearing her mother's antiquated Victorian dress – all suggest a certain delight in wearing inappropriate clothes and an interest in the playful dissonance between the body, its appearance, and its context.[38] In Woolf's short story 'A Society', the members of a secret sorority venture out from their homes in class, race and gender disguise (as charwoman, Aethiopian Prince, and male book reviewer) to investigate the truth of the world in which they live, before they commit to adding to its population as mothers. The incorrect clothes in this instance allow for a feminist liberation and search for truth and knowledge.[39]

Like Woolf, women writers of historical fiction were also increasingly finding that they disliked the 'correct thing in clothes' and were exploiting its traditional reliance on the detail of costume to provocative ends. By the time of *Orlando*'s publication, historical fiction's shifting focus from adventure and grand events to romance meant that it was generally perceived as a woman's genre.[40] However, as Lisa Fletcher argues, this did not result in an unquestioning acceptance of heteronormativity, but rather 'the beginning of popular historical romance fiction's detailed and ongoing exploration of the patterns and privileges of heterosexuality'.[41] It is of no surprise that disguise and cross-dressing are important motifs that enable writers at this time to achieve that.[42] The popularity of the cross-dressing historical romance that emerged in the 1920s, featuring heroines, and sometimes heroes, in masquerade, no doubt reflected the wider cultural and social interest in cross-dressing and cross-gendering concurrently developing throughout the 1920s and 1930s.[43] *A Narrative of the Life of Mrs. Charlotte Charke Daughter of Colley Cibber*, originally written in 1755 by the actress of the same name whose cross-dressing exploits transgressed from the stage into real life, was republished in 1929, over a century since its last edition in 1827. E. F. Benson's short story 'The Male Impersonator' appeared in 1929, the same year that Valerie Arkell-Smith, living as Colonel Victor Barker, was imprisoned for providing false information on a marriage certificate. Several early 1930s films – *Morocco* (1930), *Queen Christina* (1933), *Sylvia Scarlett* (1935) and *First a Girl* (1935) – also featured cross-dressed women. For the characters in many of these narratives, gender disguise is both pragmatic and liberatory, since it provides protection from danger and access to adventure and freedom; for their authors, the trope serves as a prop with which they can explore questions of class, gender, sexuality and, most importantly, same-sex desire.[44] This is certainly the case with another historical novel that Woolf reviewed – Mackenzie's *The Early Life and Adventures of Sylvia Scarlett* (1918). Woolf's review, entitled 'The "Movie" Novel', discusses the eponymous cross-dressed heroine's failings and criticises the novel's string of superficial adventures and its failure to provide character depth.[45] According to Harold Orel, Mackenzie's earlier work, *Sinister Street* (1913–14), characterises Sylvia as a lesbian and Orel points out that this suggestion is picked up again in the later work.[46] This is perhaps no surprise considering that Mackenzie also penned *Extraordinary Women* in 1928, a satire of a lesbian community. Woolf's dismissal of Mackenzie's work as a 'movie novel' is somewhat prescient of its later adaptation into the 1936 film *Sylvia Scarlett* staring Katharine Hepburn as Sylvia/Sylvester. The film itself makes patent the homoerotic potential of the trope on two particular occasions, when Sylvia, disguised as Sylvester, is kissed by her young stepmother and when she falls in love with her father's criminal accomplice.[47]

The connection made here between Woolf's and Mackenzie's cross-dressing novels is intended to make a case for her familiarity with the motif, but I could have also looked to a range of other texts that Woolf may have been aware of or influenced by. Having reviewed Bowen's *The Glen o' Weeping* (1907), Woolf may have known her other novels *The Viper of Milan* (1906) and *Black Magic* (1909), which feature class and gender disguise. In the first of these, Valentine disguises herself as a page to escape from her despotic brother with his imprisoned wife. She assumes the masculine role with relish and impulsively kisses her sister-in-law during their ultimately failed escape.[48] Being an admirer of Scott's work, it is also possible that Woolf would have read his

1808 historical poem *Marmion* about the Battle of Flodden Field, in which a Marmion's lover travels with him disguised as a page. Similarly, Woolf's lifelong interest and study of Renaissance literature, in which gender masquerade is a common plot device often associated with transgressive desires, would certainly have meant that she was conversant with this trope and its potentially homoerotic renderings.[49]

One other popular writer who made use of the cross-dressing trope was the historical romance novelist Georgette Heyer. Wallace has, in fact, noted a connection between Heyer's 1928 *The Masqueraders* and Woolf's *Orlando* in that 'both writers, in different ways, use history as a fantasy space to suggest that gender is socially constructed'.[50] Heyer's *The Masqueraders* features the cross-dressed siblings Prue and Robin who disguise themselves to evade the law after their involvement in a failed Jacobite rebellion. For this popular historical romance novelist cross-dressing overtly signals that gender is not only performative but that it can easily be learned by rote. Heyer shows, so Wallace believes, that 'only a man can really be convincingly "feminine" because "femininity" itself is a male fantasy projected onto women, which women must then learn to assume in order to satisfy their own desires through men'.[51] This is also born out in Prue's behaviour because although she must adapt her identity if she is to be believed male, she does not have to venture so far from her 'real' self to perform that role. While Robin's disguise exposes and even makes a farce of the artificiality of femininity, Prue's disguise provides her with access to the life she cannot have as a woman, full of daring adventures and political intrigue. This imbalance – that a man pretending to be a woman is a source of amusement and ridicule, while a woman pretending to be a man is simply good sense – is common to many cultural representations of cross-dressing.

For Heyer's characters this disguise also inspires transgressive, homoerotic desires. As part of Robin's feminine role, he takes a particular interest in the clothes he wears and the fashions now available to him. His feminine apparel, which makes him an exemplar of beauty, is not merely a necessary evil but something that he capitalises on in his flirtations with other men. But this use of cross-dressing to create the space where homoerotic desire can emerge is most evident in Prue/Peter's relationship with Sir Anthony. The latter gives his protection to his young 'male' friend but cannot fathom why he is so drawn to this boy, stating that 'I have an odd liking for you, little man. One of these strange twists in one's affections for which there is no accounting.'[52] The suggestive discourse exchanged between Prue/Peter and Sir Anthony could be mistaken for a clichéd romance, complete with longing looks and modest blushes, but this is ostensibly a relationship between two masculine identities. As soon as Prue's true sex is revealed, the heterosexual romance plot takes precedent as her now legitimate suitor seeks to impose his will, forcing her to exchange a life of masquerade for one of marriage. The text, of course, ends with the appropriately attired Prue installed on the arm of her new husband, accompanied by her also newly married brother. Heyer's other cross-dressing novel *These Old Shades* (1926) is perhaps more subversive on this account, since the hero of the text, Justin Alastair, is less content for his cross-dressed heroine to revert to her feminine identity, preferring Léonie in the guise of a boy.[53] But, ultimately, in both novels heterosexuality triumphs over gender and sexual confusion, and 'twists' in affection are neatly ironed out.

The parallel drawn between Heyer and Woolf is useful because although several critics have examined *Orlando*'s ties with the historical novel, this has not been allowed to detract from its definition as a modernist text.[54] In Woolf's first novel, *The Voyage Out*, Terence Hewet contemplates writing a Stuart tragedy, but is determined to leave behind what he terms the 'absurd conventions' of the historical novelist in order to represent the 'beauty in the past' and to 'treat people as though they were exactly the same as we are'.[55] In contrast, *Orlando* embraces many of these 'absurd conventions'. The novel spans a significant period of history from 1586 to the year of publication and features identifiable figures and events, albeit often exaggerated; it includes a preface that credits research sources and an index, both lending it the air of authority and accuracy that historical novelists strive for. As with the heroines of historical romance, Orlando's life is characterised by adventure, travel and love: she attempts to elope, escapes from Turkish rebels, abdicates her social and political status to live as a Gipsy, duels with enemies, must prove her identity and regain her inheritance, is embroiled in a series of love affairs, and ultimately abandons this freedom for marriage, motherhood and modernity. Most important though, is Woolf's fascination with the details of costume (the colours and textures of fabrics, and the choices of jewellery and other accessories) and her characters' frequent escapades in class, race, and gender disguise, which are all motifs common to the historical romance and to Heyer's work.

Like Heyer's main characters, Orlando cross-dresses in the literal sense by using gender and class disguise to achieve specific aims, but Woolf also 'cross-dresses' her creation by transforming her hero into a heroine through an unexplained and fantastical overnight change of sex. It is because of this sudden alteration that Orlando must, like Robin, experience her gender as an alien and artificial role, learning how to be a 'woman'. But at various other points in the novel Orlando also chooses to don gender and class disguise in search of adventure. Wrapping himself in a 'grey cloak to hide the star at his neck and the garter at his knee' he frequents the common pubs of London, and as an Ambassador in Turkey he disguises himself so that he may 'mingle with the crowd on the Galata Bridge; or stroll through the bazaars; or throw aside his shoes and join the worshippers in the Mosques' (p. 29 and p. 114). As a man, it is class, race and nationality that Orlando seeks to escape, but as a woman the import of clothes and their relation to gender identity is heightened, as is evidenced by her more frequent changes of costume:

> So then one may sketch her spending her morning in a China robe of ambiguous gender among her books; then receiving a client or two (for she had many scores of suppliants) in the same garment; then she would take a turn in the garden and clip the nut trees – for which knee-breeches were convenient; then she would change into a flowered taffeta which best suited a drive to Richmond and a proposal of marriage from some great nobleman; and so back again to town, where she would don a snuff-coloured gown like a lawyer's and visit the courts to hear how her cases were doing [. . .] and so, finally, when night came, she would more often than not become a nobleman complete from head to toe and walk the streets in search of adventure.
> [. . .T]here were many stories told at the time, as, that she fought a duel, served on one of the King's ships as a captain, was seen to dance naked on a balcony, and fled with a certain lady to the Low Countries where the lady's husband followed them (pp. 200–1)

As is the case with mainstream historical romance, the female Orlando uses disguise to assume various identities appropriate to her context but otherwise historically impossible for her sex. Woolf, therefore, turns to this generic convention to exceed the realistic boundaries of gender as well as to trouble the very idea that these roles and behaviour are natural.

Perhaps more intriguing is the fact that Orlando resorts to sartorial strategies in response to emotional crises, and usually to either affirm or renounce her current gender identity. Having dismissed the attentions of the Archduke, she suddenly feels the absence of a lover and so takes up her pen in an attempt to turn her emotional impulse into writing. However, she soon discovers a much more effective strategy:

> Then laying her pen aside she went into her bedroom, stood in front of her mirror, and arranged her pearls about her neck. Then since pearls do not show to advantage against a morning gown of sprigged cotton, she changed to a dove grey taffeta; then to one of peach bloom; thence to a wine-coloured brocade. Perhaps a dash of powder was needed, and if her hair were disposed – so – about her brow, it might become her. Then she slipped her feet into pointed slippers, and drew an emerald ring upon her finger. [. . .I]t was a thousand pities that there was no one there to put it in plain English, and say outright, 'Damn it, Madam, you are loveliness incarnate,' which was the truth. (pp. 168–9)

Orlando responds to her loneliness by embracing femininity and adds various appendages until she feels herself to be beautiful. In the psychoanalyst Joan Riviere's 1929 essay 'Womanliness as a Masquerade' she claims that an excessive display, or masquerade, of womanliness is provoked by a psychical denial of female masculinity, and in some cases homosexuality, and is intended to ward off possible condemnation from men.[56] Such psychical work is potentially underway in this extract, since Orlando rejects her suitor – indeed she wishes that she could run him through with a rapier – and her immediate response to this phallic act of (masculine) gender and (homo)sexual independence is to masquerade as feminine and wish that a gentleman would reassure her of her desirability. She responds similarly after receiving an insult from the poet Alexander Pope. She turns to her wardrobe:

> which hung still many of the clothes she had worn as a young man of fashion, and from among them she chose a black velvet suit richly trimmed with Venetian lace. [. . .] She took a turn or two before the mirror to make sure that her petticoats had not lost her the freedom of her legs, and then let herself secretly out of doors. (p. 195)

Orlando ventures out in male clothing in search of female company, which she finds in the figure of a prostitute called Nell. Faced with Pope's misogyny, Orlando renounces her feminine gender and her ostensible heterosexuality and goes in search of some alternative. Writing of Renaissance romance prose that features cross-dressing, Winfried Schleiner argues that the 'prime moments of heightened consciousness of these matters [homosexuality, sex and gender] are the ones when such garments are put on and when they are removed'.[57] These instances of clothing and disrobing the body in *Orlando* create liminal moments between identities that emphasise that those gendered states are tenuous and stitched together. Thus, Woolf suggests that clothes can act as a way of restructuring and refortifying the self, whether this is in confirmation of or rebellion against expectations.

In a letter written shortly after the novel's publication, Woolf posed the question '[w]hy is Orlando difficult?'[58] The answer to this, for critics at least, might well be the text's refusal to commit itself ideologically, and the tangled web it weaves in its approach to identity. Orlando, we are told, remains constant despite his change of sex, suggesting that something essential and sexless is embedded within the self. However, the idea that identity is a wholly performative construction is posited with equal vigour:

> She remembered how, as a young man, she had insisted that women must be obedient, chaste, scented, and exquisitely apparelled. 'Now I shall have to pay in my own person for those desires,' she reflected; 'for women are not (judging by my own short experience of the sex) obedi-

ent, chaste, scented, and exquisitely apparelled by nature. [. . .] There's the hairdressing, [. . .] that alone will take an hour of my morning; there's looking in the looking-glass, another hour; there's staying and lacing; there's washing and powdering; there's changing from silk to lace and from lace to paduasoy; there's being chaste year in year out . . .' (p. 143)

Like Heyer, Woolf here suggests that femininity is inorganic, a systematic layering of acts constructed for the benefit of the viewer rather than the possessor of the identity. The biographer, whose sex is also unknown, sways wildly between paradoxical sartorial philosophies. In one instance, she or he is recorded stating that clothes 'change our view of the world and the world's view of us', for clothes 'mould our hearts, our brains, our tongues to their liking' (pp. 170–1). In another moment, this belief in the formative power of clothes is dismissed as merely 'the view of some philosophers and wise ones' because, in fact, '[c]lothes are but a symbol of something hid deep beneath' and the gendered identities we adopt align to an innately ordained sex (p. 171). Woolf's views on identity and its relation to clothes continue to multiply when the biographer suggests a further possibility to consider:

> Different though the sexes are, they intermix. In every human being a vacillation from one sex to the other takes place, and often it is only the clothes that keep the male or female likeness, while underneath the sex is the very opposite of what it is above. (pp. 171–2)

The biographer now claims either that we each have the metamorphic power to change our biological sex (like Orlando), or more likely that our innate selves have the freedom to oscillate between these two gendered positions at will. We may be wearing the 'right' or the 'wrong' clothes for the innate self at the time but they have no constitutive effect, although Orlando's experience as a Victorian woman arguably proves otherwise. Sandra Gilbert, in an examination of the transvestism metaphor in modernist fiction, reads *Orlando* as a work that 'emphasize[s] that costume, not anatomy, is destiny'.[59] Yet, to some extent this underestimates the discursive maze which Woolf maps across *Orlando*, leading us through intellectual twists and turns and ultimately back to where we began. Orlando's biographer deems that she or he will 'let other pens treat of sex and sexuality', such as those of biologists and psychologists; nonetheless the text is infuriatingly replete with an array of paradoxical ideological positions (p. 128).[60]

Marjorie Garber quite rightly takes issue with *Orlando* in this respect and with any assumption that the novel's politics are particularly radical, when she states that '[w]hatever Orlando *is*, her clothing reflects it: the crossing between male and female may be a mixture (a synthesis), but it is not a confusion, a transgression. The inside always corresponds to the outside.'[61] Woolf claimed that she disliked the 'right' clothes, but Orlando rarely wears the wrong clothes, in that she matches her costume to the 'part' that she wishes to play. Orlando is always male or female beneath, or a man or woman above, leaving limited opportunity for radical play in between. Like Heyer, Woolf uses costume and cross-dressing to reveal that gender is not an inevitable state and should not determine the limits of the lives we lead, but to a certain extent she maintains the binaries that such assumptions are rooted in. But as Garber also suggests, one of the key points in the debate regarding transvestism is the '"confusion," of gender versus sex or sexuality', or essentially whether transvestism is motivated by pleasure or by an expression of gender difference.[62] Garber argues that it is this borderline between gender and sexuality that the transvestite troubles:

> The cultural effect of transvestism is to destabilize all such binaries: not only 'male' and 'female,' but also 'gay' and 'straight,' and 'sex' and 'gender.' This is the sense – the radical sense – in which transvestism is a 'third.'[63]

Orlando admittedly struggles to escape gender binaries, but its most cohesive and radical statement can be said to come on the subject of desire and in its success in blurring the distinction between 'gay' and 'straight', something that it arguably achieves through its play with costume.

Disclosing the Cross-dressed Body

Clare L. Taylor's study of literary female cross-gendering between 1890 and 1950 notably excludes a study of Woolf's novel. Taylor justifies this omission by arguing that the text 'does not speak of the specificities of female fetishistic cross-gendering, but rather addresses male-to-female con-version as opposed to female per-version'.[64] Although cross-dressing in *Orlando* is not fetishistic per se, this does not mean that the novel does not explore the way that pleasure can be found in cross-dressing. As is often the case in historical romance, it is the ambiguity of the cross-dressed body, and the tendency to misread that body, that provide a locus for desire and the opportunity for homoerotic connections. When the young male Orlando first sees Sasha skating upon the ice he cannot decipher her body and while Sasha is not cross-dressed as such, the androgynous nature of her costume inspires the same kind of erotic ambiguity:

> Orlando was ready to tear his hair with vexation that the person was of his own sex, and thus all embraces were out of the question. But the skater came closer. Legs, hands, carriage, were a boy's, but no boy ever had a mouth like that; no boy had those breasts; no boy had eyes which looked as if they had been fished from the bottom of the sea. (p. 37)

With allusions to Shakespeare's androgynous sprite Ariel (and more specifically to *The Tempest*'s line 'Those are pearls that were his eyes') historically played by both male and female actors, this extract confirms that it is the anticipation of the almost supernaturally unstable body, and Orlando's dissection of Sasha's physique into sexed constituents, that inspires frisson.[65] Despite Orlando's insistence that a same-sex relationship is out of the question, this episode serves to show that desire is directed towards what Orlando terms the 'whole person', the essence of an individual rather than an assigned gender or biological sex (p. 36). When Orlando is thirty-six and female, she again meets Sasha (evidently also immortal) in a twentieth-century department store, and it is ambiguity that arouses her still when she receives 'a whiff of scent, waxen, tinted as if from pink candles' because she cannot tell whether it emanates from a boy or a girl (p. 272). The Archduke Harry, posing as Harriet, also inspires lust because of that selfsame ambivalence. With a strange mix of female and male characteristics, the Archduke performs a grotesque, almost animalistic, rendition of femininity, much the same as Heyer's character Robin. Yet Orlando is overcome with such unfathomable passion for this disguised person that he is driven to leave the country.

During a period in which Orlando 'change[d] frequently from one set of clothes to another', the biographer loses tracks of his/her subject (p. 199). The motivation for this masquerade is clearly pleasure since '[f]or the probity of breeches she exchanged the seductiveness of petticoats and enjoyed the love of both sexes equally' (p. 200). With this, Woolf not only infiltrates lesbian desire into the text, but also troubles any understanding of how we desire, since it is unclear whether Orlando enjoys the company of women as a woman or under the guise of a man and so whether these experiences be categorised as homosexual or heterosexual, if they can be categorised at all. Certainly, when Orlando, dressed as a man, meets the prostitute Nell, it is from playing the part of a male lover that she derives enjoyment:

> To feel her hanging lightly yet like a suppliant on her arm, roused in Orlando all the feelings which become a man. She looked, she felt, she talked like one. Yet, having been so lately a woman herself, she suspected that the girl's timidity and her hesitating answers and the very fumbling with the key in the latch and the fold of her cloak and the droop of her wrist were all put on to gratify her masculinity. (p. 196)

In a similar instance, we are told a tale of Orlando's elopement with a woman, yet not the gender guise she adopts for this clichéd romantic scenario (p. 201). Clothes themselves do not necessarily provide erotic stimulation and so do not function as fetishistic in the strict sense, but the ambiguity between the representation of a body and the real body that lies beneath creates moments of uncategorised, and uncategorisable, desire and it is this that destabilises the ease with which sexuality can be defined.

The plot of mainstream cross-dressing historical romance relies upon what Fletcher calls the 'redoubled scene of confession: the revelation of the heroine's true sex and the declaration of love'.[66] Fletcher sees this formulaic scene as one that ultimately drives a plot change, transforming a homosexual romance narrative into a heterosexual one and speeding the way towards closure and most often marriage.[67] This chimes with Francette Pacteau's psychoanalytic interpretation of the androgyne:

> The androgyne dwells in a distance. The androgynous figure has to do with *seduction*, that which comes before undressing, seeing and touching. It can only exist in the shadow area of the image; once unveiled, once we throw a light on it, it becomes a woman or man, and I (myself) resume my position on the side of the female.[68]

While Pacteau is concerned with the androgyne and not the transvestite, her comments apply here in that both figures depend on ambiguity and reject binary gender positions for what could be seen as a third option.[69] The cross-dresser or transvestite does not produce an absolute replica of its opposite sex, but 'performs' that sex's gender, so troubling those very identities. For Pacteau, the sight of the androgyne is a teasingly erotic act characterised by the anticipation of seduction, which can only survive while there is distance between the androgyne and the viewer. The disclosure of the cross-dressed body therefore works to enable the heterosexual narrative by making the body knowable and stable and by cementing that body's place within the heterosexual psychical schematic. The novel's index, detailing the events and people of Orlando's life, enacts this theory and the idea that bodily revelation ignites the heterosexual romance plot. In the last four entries under the listing 'Orlando', Woolf summarises her character's life succinctly: 'declared a woman, 229; engagement, 225; marriage, 235; birth of her first son, 266' (p. 298). No mention is made of Orlando's publication of the *The Oak Tree*, a text she has been working on since her boyhood, which occurs after her marriage and before the birth of her son. This detail serves to demonstrate Woolf's understanding of the way women's lives are documented and the assumption that love, motherhood and domesticity will dominate their narratives. Once Orlando has been legally defined as a woman she will, of course, become engaged, marry and conceive the first of many sons. Even Orlando has a sense that she is fated to submit to the romance plot, as is obvious from her decision to 'buy twenty yards or more of black bombazine [...] to make a skirt. And then (here she blushed), she would have to buy a crinoline, and then (here she blushed) a bassinette, and then another crinoline, and so on' (pp. 212–13).

Orlando is profligate with scenes of bodily disclosure and of clothing and undressing the body. While this should in a conventional historical romance give way to the precedence of the heterosexual romance plot and re-categorise the text's bodies in their supposedly rightful places, Woolf intentionally derails these moments in order to frustrate that plot and exploit the homoerotic potential of the cross-dressed figure, meaning that the scene of seduction essentially exceeds and survives the unveiling of the body. Despite the pressure exerted in the index, the novel itself resists the temptation to be definitive and pays only a cursory attention to the events of marriage and childbirth, avoiding details where possible. Orlando's body similarly refuses to yield itself to the reader, although much time is spent appraising and detailing its flaws and many attractions. The biographer lustily blazons Orlando's 'shapely legs, the handsome body, and the well-set shoulders' and his beautiful androgynous face (p. 16), but as Lisa Rado points out, the biographer limits him or herself to targeted areas of the body, refusing genital confirmation.[70] This is the case immediately after Orlando's metamorphosis into a woman:

> He stretched himself. He rose. He stood upright in complete nakedness before us, and while the trumpets pealed Truth! Truth! Truth! we have no choice left but confess – he was a woman.
>
> The sound of the trumpets died away and Orlando stood stark naked. No human being, since the world began, has ever looked more ravishing. His form combined in one the strength of a man and a woman's grace. [. . .] Chastity, Purity, and Modesty, inspired, no doubt, by Curiosity, peeped in at the door and threw a garment like a towel at the naked form which, unfortunately, fell short by several inches. Orlando looked himself up and down in a long looking-glass, without showing any signs of discomposure, and went, presumably, to his bath. (pp. 126–7)

The biographer seems to have been privy to this pivotal moment of corporeal exposure but the reader is frustratingly excluded from such voyeuristic pleasure or any sense of definitive truth. We are in fact blinded from the supposedly female anatomy and confounded by the array of genital puns (Orlando 'stood upright in complete nakedness' but also 'fell short by several inches'). It can be presumed that an anatomical transformation has taken place, but the biographer emphasises that little about Orlando is actually different because '[t]he change of sex, though it altered their future, did nothing whatever to alter their identity' (p. 127). The public's response to Orlando's metamorphosis is also used to discredit the event because it is claimed that '(1) that Orlando had always been a woman, (2) that Orlando is at this moment a man' (p. 127). It is then assumed that an act of transvestism has been, or is still, taking place.

This confusion works to refuse confirmation of Orlando's sex and as a pointed assertion that desire is not legitimised, or heterosexualised, by its disclosure. On the contrary, each time an attempt at disclosure is made this desire is renewed as homoerotic. As the biographer reminds us after Orlando's sex change, 'though she herself was a woman, it was still a woman she loved; and if the consciousness of being of the same sex had any effect at all, it was to quicken and deepen those feelings which she had had as a man' (p. 147). Bodily revelation also succumbs to the lesbian when Orlando discloses her true sex to Nell. Relieved that she can abandon disingenuity, Nell breaks into intimate conversation with Orlando, who is admitted thereafter into her society of prostitutes who share their tales. Nell may have little wit to boast of but she possesses the 'charm of ease and the seduction of beauty' that appeals to Orlando (p. 198). In a scene similar to that in *A Room of One's Own* when Woolf advises her reader to 'admit in the privacy of our own society that these things sometimes happen. Sometimes women do like women', the biographer wonders what it is that women desire when they are alone (*A Room of One's Own*, p. 74). Interrupted first by the fear that there may be a man eavesdropping on the stairs, and then by a gentleman client who interjects with the claim that women have no desires at all, the biographer concludes that 'Orlando professed great enjoyment in the society of her own sex, and leave it to the gentlemen to prove, as they are very fond of doing, that this is impossible' (p. 199). The biographer states here, as Woolf suggests in *A Room of One's Own*, that sometimes women do enjoy the company of other women, and sometimes this enjoyment is loving and sexual. The disclosure of Orlando's body therefore allows for a scene of domestic female intimacy, the shared narration of female lives, and the forging of a space where desire between women can flourish.

This moment of bodily discovery is repeated when Orlando meets her fiancé Shelmerdine. The two are in such sympathy with one another that they each begin to question the true sex of their partner:

> 'You're a woman, Shel!' she cried.
> 'You're a man, Orlando!' he cried.
> Never was there such a scene of protestation and demonstration as then took place since the world began. [. . .]
> 'Are you positive you aren't a man?' he would ask anxiously, and she would echo.
> 'Can it be possible you're not a woman?' and then they must put it to the proof without more ado. (p. 227 and p. 232)

Both Orlando and Shelmerdine accuse the other of gender masquerade but they also realise the erotic potential that such moments of bodily confession hold. In attempting to disclose the other's true sex, Orlando and Shelmerdine take pleasure in putting that body to the test, and this begs the question of what exactly it is that each finds under the other's costume that necessitates reconfirmation. All manner of combinations become feasible, then, and all fundamentally and wilfully refuse the heteronormative. If the appeal of the androgynous body and the homoerotic potential of the cross-dressed body are conventionally repealed when those bodies are uncovered, Woolf refuses any such categorical definition. Shelmerdine and Orlando prolong the state of anticipation and desire for the ambiguous, possibly same-sexed, partner and find erotic stimulation in inconclusive attempts to define that body.

Orlando is not the only figure to reveal the 'true' self beneath a cross-dressed exterior. The Archduke Harry initially masquerades as Harriet in an unsuccessful attempt to seduce Orlando, and reappears once more in this disguise, despite his knowledge that Orlando is now a woman. In this latter moment, Harry/Harriet chooses to confess the truth, revealing his true sex and his love for Orlando.[71] While Orlando is distracted, he eschews his feminine garb and reveals himself to be 'a tall gentleman in black' (p. 162). Again, the guise under which Harry/Harriet courts Orlando is unclear, as is the classification of his desire. Harry/Harriet initially remarks that the male Orlando is reminiscent of his sister, so suggesting that it is his androgynous looks which appeal, as well as hinting at a more complicated incestuous attraction. The Archduke falls in love with Orlando as both a man and woman, while masquerading as both female and male, and he tells the female Orlando that 'she was and would ever be the Pink, the Pearl, the Perfection of her sex' (p. 163), but which sex she is the exemplar of is not entirely clear. The admission of Harry/Harriet's sex refuses to stabilise or make comprehensible either their sexual and gender identities or the configuration of desire.

The shift in plot and tone we might expect from such revelations of identity is brought about self-consciously and awkwardly, since the biographer is aware that 'when we are writing the life of a woman, we may, it is agreed, waive our demand for action, and substitute love instead' (p. 241). Orlando is rescued by Shelmerdine when she breaks her ankle on the moor – replaying the memorable scene from Charlotte Brontë's *Jane Eyre* (1847) when Jane first encounters Mr Rochester – and falls prey to the clichés of the romance narrative. Perhaps it is her pregnancy and the birth of her son that acts as the ultimate confession in the sense that parturition is an incontestable anatomical act. However, there is no confirmation that Shelmerdine is the father or, given that Orlando begins dressing in crinoline prior to having met her husband (so wearing the 'correct' clothes at inappropriate times), that this child is fathered at all. This is not to suggest that Orlando necessarily bears a child parthogenetically but to note that there is something suspect about his conception and Orlando's seeming compliance with the romance narrative. However, while the biographer deals with Orlando's marriage and childbirth perfunctorily, it is still disappointing that Orlando, much like Prue in Heyer's *The Masqueraders*, must sacrifice her gender play to become a wife and a mother.[72] She must also submit to convention in order to become a successful writer, since Orlando's work (concerned with '[s]ullen and foreign-looking [. . .] Egyptian girls') is rendered less suspect and threatening by virtue of the fact that she is married (p. 239).

Woolf employs disguise and cross-dressing to much the same effect as a historical romance novelist such as Heyer might do. Both use costume as a source of feminine textual pleasure, as a way of deconstructing gender, and to induce moments of non-heteronormative desire. As Kathryn S. Laing and others have explored, Woolf felt ambivalent about what she called her 'clothes complex' in the sense that her enjoyment of fashion was tainted by its association with consumer culture and complicated relationship with feminist values.[73] Indeed, as I pointed out at the beginning of this chapter, Woolf's feelings on middlebrow culture and historical fiction were also conflicted and possibly influenced by her father's own derision. *Orlando* with its focus on costume and arguable debt to historical romance might be seen as a knowing, but guilty, indulgence in two feminised, ephemeral industries – fashion and popular fiction. Rachel Bowlby, in fact, suggests of *Orlando* that:

> the biography could well seem to trace a paradigmatic move from men's to women's values [. . .] And indeed, in the opening scene, Orlando is to be seen 'slicing at the head of a Moor which . . . was the colour of an old football' [. . .]; by the end, she is spending her time in department stores.[74]

But in *Orlando,* Woolf adopts the structures of genre without compromising her writing, and in fact the novel shows that these structures can be constitutive of literary value. Woolf reworks generic conventions to interrogate the nature of sexuality and ultimately to resist the heterosexual romance narrative embedded within much of women's middlebrow and genre fiction at the time. As Doan and Waters argue in their essay on contemporary lesbian historical fiction:

> It is only, perhaps, in such testings of the genre – even, in the jettisoning of generic structures altogether – that we find a sophisticated treatment of lesbian historiographical issues and contradictions, one that problematises the very categories with which sex and gender are constructed.[75]

While their subject matter is more recent, and Woolf is not positioning herself self-consciously within a 'lesbian' genre, the connection is useful. In her essay 'Modern Fiction' Woolf makes a comparison between the demands of literary convention and the demands of fashion when she states that:

> The writer seems constrained, not by his own free will but by some powerful and unscrupulous tyrant who has him in thrall, to provide a plot, to provide comedy, tragedy, love interest, and an air of probability embalming the whole so impeccable that if all his figures were to come to life they would find themselves dressed down to the last button of their coats in the fashion of the hour.[76]

Fashion (particularly feminine) and fiction demand adherence to a kind of formula, both of which Woolf resists. She tests the limits of the genre and undertakes a 'jettisoning of [heterosexual] generic structures' in order to contest categories of sex, gender and sexuality.[77] The novel does indulge in an interest in the feminised topic of dress but it also employs cross-dressing to open up possibilities for non-heteronormative desires and refuses to shut them down, refuses to clothe its characters in the 'correct' costumes. Woolf stalls moments of confession where the sex of a cross-dressed figure is exposed, and rather than serving to confirm heterosexual binaries, as they often do in mainstream historical romance, these moments becomes crises of desire. If desire is divorced from biological sex, if it is autonomous and constant, then it is not a particular sex or gender that we desire, but bodies and people. Sexuality, the novel seems to suggest, is therefore as false a construction as gender, performatively constituted through compulsive social acts.

The refusal of the genre's restrictions is epitomised by Orlando's choice of pearls at key moments throughout the text. As she emerges from her sex-altering coma, Orlando adopts androgynous Turkish garb and arms herself with a pair of pistols and several strings of emeralds and pearls to fund her adventures (p. 128). Later, as a Victorian woman, she wraps pearls around her neck and uses them as a visual assurance to herself and others (such as nosey park-keepers) of her feminine and heteronormative identity (p. 168 and p. 256). However, the modern and androgynous Orlando, whose multiple identities seem to coalesce as the novel emerges into the present moment of 1928, and who has found a way of manipulating the spirit of the age so that she may write freely, again dons pearls to act as a beacon for her returning husband. She bares her breast to the moon 'so that her pearls glowed like the eggs of some vast moon-spider. [. . .] Her pearls burnt like a phosphorescent flare in the darkness' (p. 295). By this stage her pearls have abandoned any gender marker. They were once the currency of male adventure and then the reassuring symbol of female passivity, but they now transform into a thoroughly modern and almost supernatural accessory that welcomes back an equally androgynous mate.

The cross-dressed figure of 1920s historical romance would ultimately abandon her transgressive costume for clothes and behaviour deemed more appropriate for her sex. However, in the final pages Orlando makes one final and significant change of clothes: returning home from a shopping expedition to London, she changes her skirt 'for a pair of whipcord breeches and leather jacket, which she did in less than three minutes' (p. 283). Orlando teams the traditionally masculine trousers with the feminine pearls, but the suggestion seems to be not that she is adopting the dress of another gender, or entering into disguise, but that those binaries have, in this modern and modernist moment, dissolved.[78] The modern woman can change her costume as she desires and without motive, and she can also marry her androgynous mate (whose sex is never unequivocally confirmed), with whom she has a very unconventional romance, without compromising her identity or her writing. Therefore while Woolf employs the conventional trajectory of the romance narrative embedded within a historical context, it is delivered in a reworked form as an optimistic, and in some senses futuristic, vision of what sexual and gender identity could be if given a chance.

NOTES

1. Woolf (1882–1941) has become integral to, if not synonymous with, scholarly and populist ideas of bohemian Bloomsbury. Although Woolf published essays, literary criticism and journalism from the early twentieth century onwards, she is foremost known as a novelist and short story writer (with her first novel, *The Voyage Out*, published in 1915) whose innovative body of work is now considered a mainstay of the modernist aesthetic movement, early twentieth-century women's writing and literary feminism. From an intellectual and artistic family, Woolf lived comfortably on a legacy left to her by her father's sister, Caroline Emelia Stephen, after her death in 1909. Although she married Leonard Woolf in 1912, with whom she set up The Hogarth Press and through which she published many of her own works, much has been written about her relationships with women and in particular with Sackville-West (who inspired the writing of *Orlando*). Scholarship on Woolf has benefited not only from her extensive corpus but also the publication of her diaries, letters and reading notebooks which has, as with Stein and Barney, placed the critical emphasis upon her biography as well as her art.
2. Woolf, 'Middlebrow', in *Collected Essays Volume Two*, pp. 196–203 (pp. 198–9). Subsequent references are noted in parenthesis.
3. Rose, *The Intellectual Life*, p. 393. Carey has also written on this topic in *The Intellectuals and the Masses*.
4. Bourdieu, *The Field of Cultural Production*, p. 75.
5. Ibid. p. 75.
6. Bourdieu discusses this point in *The Field of Cultural Production*, pp. 67–8.
7. On modernism and cultural elitism, see Latham, 'Am I a Snob?'.
8. Humble, for instance, comments on the sway exerted by institutions such as book clubs and lending libraries over the popularity of certain titles through promotion and recommendation. *The Feminine Middlebrow*, pp. 43–4.
9. See Beauman, *A Very Great Profession*, Humble, *The Feminine Middlebrow*, and Brown and Grover (eds), *Middlebrow Literary Cultures*.
10. Humble highlights these institutions as crucial in the formation of the middlebrow. *The Feminine Middlebrow*, p. 43.
11. Ibid. p. 11.
12. Latham, 'Am I a Snob?', p. 107. Woolf notes details of these sales figures in her diary. See Woolf, 18 December 1928, *Diary Volume 3*, pp. 211–14 (p. 212).
13. Ibid. p. 108.
14. Woolf is included in Bloom's survey of popular fiction, *Bestsellers*, pp. 204–5.
15. Marcus, 'Virginia Woolf and the Hogarth Press', p. 142.
16. Nicholson calls *Orlando* an 'elaborate love-letter' in 'Introduction', *A Change of Perspective*, p. xxii. For the latter approach to *Orlando* see Meese, *(Sem)erotics*, and Hankins, '*Orlando*: "A Precipice Marked V"'.
17. Latham comments upon the irony of this disparity and the anxiety that Woolf experienced because of the novel's wide readership. 'Am I a Snob?', p. 109.

18. Woolf, *Orlando*, p. 250. Subsequent references are noted in parenthesis.
19. Woolf, 18 December 1928, *Diary Volume 3*, p. 212.
20. Ibid. p. 212.
21. It might also be productive to think about Woolf's involvement in the marketplace in terms of her success as a publisher at The Hogarth Press. On this see, for instance, Marcus, 'Woolf and the Hogarth Press'.
22. Dubino suggests that due to financial motivations Woolf was not selective in this stage of her career. See Dubino, 'Virginia Woolf', p. 26.
23. Dubino's categorisation of these essays is of course dependent on a subjective distinction of literary value, which she admits is problematic. She bases this on how seriously the writer was taken by the highbrow literary establishment at the time. Dubino, 'Virginia Woolf', pp. 35–6.
24. Ibid. p. 37.
25. Woolf, 'Sir Walter Scott', in *Collected Essays Volume One*, pp. 134–43 (p. 139).
26. Woolf, 'Phases of Fiction' [1929], in *Granite and Rainbow*, pp. 93–145 (p. 108).
27. In *Charleston Past and Present*, the authors recall Woolf and Vanessa's love of Yonge's novels. Bell et al, *Charleston Past and Present*, p. 156. It is also worth noting that at the time of *Orlando*'s publication, Woolf wrote to Hugh Walpole regarding the submission of a book on the historical novel for The Hogarth Lectures on Literature series. Walpole's book was announced as forthcoming in 1930 but it never appeared. Woolf, '4 November 1928', *A Change of Perspective*, p. 556.
28. Woolf, 'Impressions of Sir Leslie Stephen', in *The Essays of Virginia Woolf: Volume I*, pp. 127–30 (pp. 127–8).
29. Stephen, 'Sir Walter Scott', in *Hours in a Library*, pp. 137–68 (p. 143).
30. Ibid. p. 156.
31. Ibid. p. 155. In other instances Stephen condemns Scott's attempts to 'amuse us with mere contrasts of costume, which will lose their interest when the swallow-tail is as obsolete as the buff-coat' and derides one of Scott's characters because he is 'made chiefly of plumes and jackboots'. See p. 143 and p. 156 respectively.
32. Ibid. p. 149.
33. Wallace, *The Woman's Historical Novel*, p. 21.
34. See Huyssen on the alliance between mass culture and femininity. Huyssen, *After the Great Divide*.
35. Bernbaum, 'The Views of the Great Critics on the Historical Novel', p. 431.
36. For critical work on Woolf's relationship with dress see, for instance: Edson, 'Kicking off her Knickers'; Gilbert, 'Costumes of the Mind'; Hartley, 'Clothes and Uniform in the Theatre of Fascism'; Holmes, 'Clothing and The Body'; and Koppen, *Virginia Woolf, Fashion and Literary Modernity*.
37. See Humm, *Snapshots of Bloomsbury*. Koppen also notes the popularity of Bloomsbury costume parties around this time in *Virginia Woolf, Fashion and Literary Modernity*, p. 26.
38. The Dreadnought Hoax took place on 7 February 1910 and involved Adrian Stephen, Duncan Grant and three male friends, with Woolf included at the last minute. Posing as the Emperor of Abyssinia and his royal party, the group received a tour of the Dreadnought warship. Their unsuspecting hosts were oblivious to any deception and the hoax was only discovered when one participant (Horace Cole) informed both the press and the Foreign Office, causing great embarrassment and scandal, not least to Woolf as the only woman involved. As Lee suggests: 'The hoax combined all possible forms of subversion: ridicule of empire, infiltration of the nation's defences, mockery of bureaucratic procedures, cross-dressing and sexual ambiguity (Adrian and Duncan became lovers at about this time, though

the Navy didn't know *that*; but the fact that one of the Abyssinians was a woman was the greatest source of indignation).' Lee, *Virginia Woolf*, p. 283. On details of Woolf's green dress see Koppen, *Virginia Woolf, Fashion and Literary Modernity*, p. 11, and Woolf, 'A Sketch of the Past', in *Moments of Being*, p. 153. For Woolf's article in *Vogue*, see 'A Professor of Life'.
39. Woolf, 'A Society', in *The Complete Shorter Fiction of Virginia Woolf*. Other short stories which tackle the subject of clothing are 'Ancestors', 'Mrs Dalloway in Bond Street', and 'The New Dress'. Woolf also explores the significance of clothing and in particular uniform in *Three Guineas* (1938) and *Between the Acts* (1941).
40. Fletcher discusses this shift to the subject of romance in *Historical Romance Fiction*, p. 49.
41. Ibid. p. 49.
42. Writing on the historical romance, Hughes argues that 'the "disguise" motif is perhaps the most frequent and important', and Wallace concurs when she suggests that the cross-dressed heroine is as significant a figure in historical fiction as the tragic queen. Hughes, *The Historical Romance*, p. 15, and Wallace, *The Woman's Historical Novel*, p. 21. Fletcher also explores the importance of cross-dressing for the historical romance in *Historical Romance Fiction*, p. 50.
43. On this topic see Oram, *Her Husband Was a Woman!*
44. For instances of this trope one could look to *The Recess* by Sophia Lee (1783), Vernon Lee's play *Ariadne in Mantua: A Romance in Five Acts* (1903), Marjorie Bowen's *The Viper of Milan: A Romance of Lombardy* (1906) and *Black Magic: A Tale of the Rise and Fall of the Antichrist* (1909), Edith M. Dell's *Charles, Rex* (1922), D. K. Broster's *Mr Rowl* (1924), Georgette Heyer's *These Old Shades* (1926), *The Masqueraders* (1928) and *The Corinthian* (1940), Sheila Kay Smith's *Superstition Corner* (1934), Nora Purtscher-Wydenbruck's *Woman Astride* (1934), Margaret Goldsmith's *Christina of Sweden: A Psychological Biography* (1933), Elisabeth Augustin's *Outcasts: A Novel* (1937), Vita Sackville West's *Joan of Arc* (1936), Daphne du Maurier's *Frenchman's Creek* (1941), Magdalen King Hall's *The Life and Death of the Wicked Lady Skelton* (1944), Doris Leslie's *Polonaise* (1942) and *The Peverills* (1946), and H. F. M. Prescott's *The Man on a Donkey* (1952).
45. See Woolf, 'The "Movie" Novel' [1918], in *The Essays of Virginia Woolf: Volume II*, pp. 288–91.
46. Orel, *Popular Fiction in England*, pp. 98–9.
47. On lesbian interpretations of this film see Villarejo, *Lesbian Rule*.
48. Bowen, *The Viper of Milan*, p. 171
49. On female cross-dressers on the Renaissance stage see Straub, 'The Guilty Pleasures of Female Theatrical Cross-Dressing'. On the homoerotic implications of cross-dressing in Renaissance romance prose see Schleiner, 'Male Cross-Dressing and Transvestism in Renaissance Romances', and Jardine, *Still Harping on Daughters*, p.25. On the Renaissance and cross-dressing more generally, see Mirkin, 'The Portrait of Elizabeth Cary in the Ashmolean Museum: "cross-dressing" in the English Renaissance', and Bray, *Homosexuality in Renaissance England*. Interestingly, Bryher wrote an article in 1920 on 'The Girl-Page in Elizabethan Literature' in which it is clear that she understands its appeal to be in the liberty it allows both writers and their female characters. Bryher, 'The Girl-Page in Elizabeth Literature'.
50. Wallace, *The Woman's Historical Novel*, p. 42.
51. Ibid. p. 42.
52. Heyer, *The Masqueraders*, pp. 99–100.
53. Heyer, *These Old Shades*, p. 88.

54. On *Orlando* as a modernist historical novel see Fleishman, *The English Historical Novel*, p. 233; Maxwell, 'Historical Novel', p. 546; Wilt, 'Steamboat Surfacing: Scott and the English Novelists', p. 476; Miller, *Historical Dictionary of Lesbian Literature*, p. 89.
55. Woolf, *The Voyage Out*, p. 231.
56. Riviere, 'Womanliness as a Masquerade'.
57. Schleiner, 'Male Cross-Dressing and Transvestism in Renaissance Romances', p. 615.
58. Woolf, Letter to Lady Cecil, 28 October 1928, *A Change of Perspective*, p. 553.
59. Gilbert, 'Costumes of the Mind', pp. 404–5. On this subject, see also Gubar, 'Blessings in Disguise'.
60. The question of the relationship between dress and identity is, as we can see from the European medieval and Renaissance sumptuary laws, partly a historical one. See Garber, *Vested Interests*, p. 25. One might also point to the relationship between clothes-reform and the suffrage movement to understand the importance of dress for the politicisation of identity.

    Koppen has also suggested the possibility that Woolf may have been influenced by other works on the psychology and philosophy of dress, namely Thomas Carlyle's *Sartor Resartus* (first published serially in 1833–4) and J. C. Flügel's 1930 *The Psychology of Clothes*. As Koppen explains, Flügel's theories were published in papers in the late 1920s and delivered in a series of BBC talks in 1928. Woolf's Hogarth Press went on to publish Flügel's work in 1930. See Koppen, *Virginia Woolf, Fashion and Literary Modernity*, p. 44 and p. 59.
61. Garber, *Vested Interests*, p. 135.
62. Ibid. p. 132.
63. Ibid. p. 133.
64. Taylor, *Women, Writing, and Fetishism*, p. 22.
65. Shakespeare, *The Tempest*, I. 2. 402, p. 3076.
66. Fletcher, *Historical Romance Fiction*, p. 49.
67. Ibid. p. 49.
68. Pacteau, 'The Impossible Referent', p. 78.
69. On transvestism as a 'third', see Garber, *Vested Interests*, p. 133.
70. Rado, 'Would the Real Virginia Woolf Please Stand Up?', p. 153.
71. Fletcher, *Historical Romance Fiction*, p. 49.
72. A thunder clap drowns out Orlando's vows (p. 236) and the birth of Orlando's son is announced without any prior knowledge of a pregnancy (p. 266).
73. Woolf quoted in Laing, 'Addressing Femininity in the Twenties', p. 66. On the idea that Woolf's enjoyment of fashion was tainted, see Laing, 'Addressing Femininity in the Twenties', p. 66 and p. 69. Koppen's *Virginia Woolf, Fashion and Literary Modernity* also tackles the complexities of Woolf's interest in dress.
74. Bowlby, *Feminist Destinations*, p. 43.
75. Doan and Waters, 'Making up Lost Time', p. 25.
76. Woolf, 'Modern Fiction' [1925], in *The Essays of Virginia Woolf: Volume IV*, pp. 157–65 (p. 160).
77. Doan and Waters, 'Making up Lost Time', p. 25.
78. It is worth noting that in 1928 it was not commonplace for women to wear trousers. Sackville-West was known to do so in certain circumstances, but this would have been controversial in public. Glendinning's biography of Sackville-West, for instance, notes that as late as 1954/55, Harold Nicholson would not allow Sackville-West to wear 'breeches' on holiday. Glendinning also notes that Sackville-West was known to wear a strange assortment of clothes, including trousers, much as Orlando does in the final pages. See Glendinning, *Vita*, p. 281 and p. 381.

PART III
CRIME

It tends to be assumed that the Golden Age of detective fiction – the period understood to traverse the interwar years – represents a conservative and reactionary epoch in the history of the genre.[1] Certainly, a cursory reading of an archetypal Golden Age novel might support this interpretation. Often taking place in a classic country house setting, seemingly abstract from the outside world, these are the realms of the white, patriarchal and middle to upper-classes, and they depict a vision of Englishness tinged with patriotic nostalgia and motivated by a desire for postwar escapism.[2] As we see from the following statement taken from G. K. Chesterton's 1901 essay 'A Defence of Detective Stories', the crime story articulates society's fear of the enemy within, whose affinity for social disturbance is often located in sexual, class, racial and gender differences:

> By dealing with the unsleeping sentinels who guard the outposts of society, it tends to remind us that we live in an armed camp, making war with a chaotic world, and that the criminals, the children of chaos, are nothing but the traitors within our gates. When the detective in a police romance stands alone [. . .] it does certainly serve to make us remember that it is the agent of social justice who is the original and poetic figure[3]

What occurs within the confines of a detective story, then, is a microcosmic battle between the homogenised core of society and its aberrant elements, most often represented by the criminal but, at times, also by the victim (whose fate can be a result of their chequered past returning to haunt them). As Gill Plain argues, '[c]rime fiction in general, and detective fiction in particular, is about confronting and taming the monstrous. It is a literature of containment, a narrative that "makes safe"'.[4] In part, the enjoyment derived from reading detective fiction is found in the encounter with such transgressive, even forbidden, elements of society, safe in the knowledge that 'social justice' and order will ultimately be reinstated.[5]

Chesterton was merely one of a number of writers at this time reflecting on the nature of the genre. The Detection Club, founded in 1928 by Anthony Berkeley and presided over by Chesterton, epitomised the formal, ritualistic nature of detective fiction. The Club admitted members by election only and required the swearing of an oath to abide by the 'rules' of the form. One such rule required the members to:

> observe a seemly moderation in the use of Gangs, Conspiracies, Death-Rays, Ghosts, Hypnotism, Trap-Doors, Chinamen, Super-Criminals and Lunatics; and utterly and for ever to foreswear Mysterious Poisons unknown to Science[6]

Other conditions, such as promising never to conceal a vital clue and honouring the 'King's English', are indicative of the conservative and patriotic tone of much crime writing at this time.[7] The aim of this creative regulation appears to have been the maintenance of a sense of believability and 'fair play' for the reader, but what emerges from such standardisation is a highly self-conscious and stylised body of writing, formulaic and heavily codified in its choice of conventions.

However, claims of the genre's conservatism have been exaggerated, in part because of the practice of reading meaning solely from the crime novel's resolution. Plain instead insists that 'the genre's transgressive "potential" is not to be found in its conclusions: rather, it finds expression in the writing *before* the ending – in the body of the text – which demands that we return anew to these deceptively familiar fictions'.[8] As Plain suggests, crime fiction is replete with 'gendered and sexualised bodies' that throw into question heteronormative states of being and evoke 'unexpected pockets of resistance'.[9] This shift in reading methodology reinvigorates our understanding of Golden Age detective fiction by women, which is arguably rife with such subversive 'pockets'. One such example of this is the figure of the lesbian criminal. Often wreaking havoc in enclosed female communities such as the school, college, hostel or hospital, the lesbian criminal is depicted as predatory, cunning, intelligent, and often a professional or working woman. Her sexuality is inextricably woven into the violence of the text, and her 'perverse' sexual desires are implicated in her disrespect for the law. Anthony Slide cites the inauguration of the homosexual villain (and victim) to be with Gladys Mitchell's 1929 *Speedy Death*, a novel in which a woman murders her cross-dressing fiancé upon discovering the truth of her beloved's identity.[10] However, this overlooks Dorothy L. Sayers' *Unnatural Death*, which precedes Mitchell's novel by two years and features both a lesbian murderess and murder victim. Indeed, the crime writers Mitchell and Sayers were not alone in their coupling of violence and lesbianism. The American writer Hilda Lawrence's *Death of a Doll* (1947) features a psychotic lesbian murderess in a hostel for working women. In Josephine Tey's *Miss Pym Disposes* (1946), set in a girls' physical-training school, infatuations and over-zealous favouritism lead to the death of an innocent student. Nancy Spain's comic detective novel *Poison for Teacher* (1949), set in the girls' school 'Radclyff Hall [sic]', similarly exploits the supposed connection between same-sex desire and violence to camp effect.

Slide laments the prevalence of this Golden Age trope, but consoles us with the fact that by the 1980s it is replaced by more affirmative representations.[11] Scholars of lesbian crime fiction would agree with this historicisation of the genre in the sense that the 1980s is seen as the decade in which the lesbian crime novel emerges to develop into an established and strongly marketed sub-genre.[12] It is, in part, the emergence of the lesbian detective, self-consciously engaging with her own sexual identity and her place within the establishment, that allows for this categorisation to occur. But we should be wary of imposing such an evolutionary narrative onto the genre because, as Rosalind Coward and Linda Semple state, 'it is inaccurate to drive a wedge between earlier women detective novelists and the new, progressive wave'.[13] I pose the idea, then, that women's Golden Age detective fiction lent itself to the discussion of sexual identity, and in the chapters that follow I examine the delicate balance between seeming compliance with and resistance to the established heteronormative order as it is explored through this figure of the lesbian criminal.

The alliance between lesbianism and violence may be codified and crystallised into the stock presence of the lesbian criminal in detective fiction, but it was not limited to this genre. The abundance of this trope elsewhere demonstrates that, as Florence Tamagne argues, the psychopathic and criminal lesbian comes into vogue during the interwar years in Europe.[14] In fact, the lesbian has long been afforded these associations in legal and medical discourses, if not in the popular imagination. In Linda Hart's study of the relationship between lesbianism and aggression, she investigates how the combined efforts of sexology, criminal anthropology and psychoanalysis have worked to historically configure lesbian identity as bound up with deviancy, criminality and violence, so dovetailing the lesbian with the female offender:

> Lesbian identity has served many functions, among them as a site where women's aggression has been displaced. It is commonly understood that the pathological model superseded the criminalization of homosexuality, the 'sickness' replaced 'sinfulness.' But history is not so linear. Both

models continue to operate. And what is particularly pertinent for lesbian historians and theorists to remember is that the female invert's *aggressiveness* was what marked her as deviant and therefore dangerous, *not* her object choice.[15]

It is the lesbian's gender transgression, her ability to behave as a man might be expected to, aggressively rather than passively, that constructs her both as medical aberration, consumed with sickness, and as a threat to society. As the sexologist Ellis states in his 1890 work *The Criminal*:

> The strongest barrier of all against criminality in women is maternity. [. . .] Crime is simply a word to signify the extreme anti-social instincts of human beings; the life led most closely in harmony with the social ends of existence must be the most free from crime.[16]

A woman avoids decline into criminal existence, then, by committing to the heterosexual gender economy and fulfilling the 'social ends of [her] existence' as a wife and mother.

The congenital female invert is estranged from these socially assigned roles of wife and mother, and consequently, it follows from Ellis's logic, tragically susceptible to delinquency. It is therefore unsurprising that many of the case histories employed by Ellis in his study of sexual inversion feature women who commit acts of violence.[17] Ellis remarks that:

> a remarkably large proportion of the cases in which homosexuality had led to crimes of violence, or otherwise under medicolegal observation, has been among women. It is well known that the part taken by women generally in open criminality, and especially in crimes of violence, is small compared with men. In the homosexual field, as we might have anticipated, the conditions are to some extent reversed. Inverted men, in whom a more or less feminine temperament is so often found, are rarely impelled to acts of aggressive violence, though they frequently commit suicide. Inverted women, who may retain their feminine emotionality combined with some degree of infantile impulsiveness and masculine energy, present a favourable soil for the seeds of passional crime, under those conditions of jealousy and allied emotions which must so often enter into the invert's life.[18]

If it is masculinity that is most closely associated with criminal tendencies, the homosexual woman, whose sexual preference is defined under sexology's scheme as an inversion of gender characteristics, is inevitably associated with criminality by mere virtue of her object-choice. Ellis's examples of this connection between violence and lesbianism all involve sexual jealousy, homicidal intentions and a history of insanity.[19] In the case of Alice Mitchell, who cut her lover's throat when plans to adopt a male persona and marry her were thwarted, we are told that her family had a history of mental illness, that her habits and behaviour were masculine, and that her body (specifically her 'unsymmetrical' and unusually youthful face) was evidence of her social and sexual difference.[20] This makes her, Ellis states, 'a typical invert of a very pronounced kind'.[21]

What takes place, then, within Golden Age detective fiction is the reification and codification of this historical association into the stock character of the lesbian criminal, whose capacity for violent unlawful acts is dependent on both her non-heteronormative sexual identity and rejection of conventional gender roles. While the lesbian criminal is indeed a pathologised and demonised figure, and her inclusion an ostensibly homophobic narrative act, there is far more at stake in her deployment than has heretofore been acknowledged. Far from embodying the reactionary and homophobic politics associated with this period of the genre, I suggest that the lesbian criminal is a potentially productive and, at times, subversive generic convention that provides an avenue for heterodoxy within the ostensibly orthodox and formulaic text. She produces fissures where the boundaries between 'normal' and 'abnormal', man and woman, heterosexual and homosexual, criminal and legal, are blurred and sometimes broken down altogether.

The frequency with which the lesbian criminal is invoked in this period is telling because, as Hilary Neroni states:

> when depictions of the violent woman appear in large numbers and in similar roles [...] they tell us about the functioning of ideology. [...] The violent woman appears at moments of ideological crisis, when the antagonisms present with the social order – antagonisms that ideology attempts to elide – become manifest. [...] Such an ideological crisis occurs when strictly defined gender roles – roles that give a logic and a sense to sexual difference – break down.[22]

In many of the texts discussed here, the lesbian criminal is recurrently construed as the paradigm of sexual and gender modernity. Representing progressive womanhood, she rejects hackneyed gender roles and familial duties in favour of an independent existence, and takes advantage of newly won opportunities available to middle-class women. That is to say, in her relation to loaded social and cultural markers such as fashion, education, profession and marital status, she evokes a mesh of anxieties coalescing around the changing roles of women and represents the increasingly diverse range of choices that the contemporary woman faced.

In Chapter 5, I examine the appearance of the lesbian criminal in select works by Sayers, Mitchell and Tey, to explore how her violence is motivated by desire and a declaration of modern identity. More specifically, this chapter is interested in the mimesis that forms between female detective and lesbian criminal and the way in which the latter woman acts as a dynamo for the detective's own muted homoerotic desires. In these instances, the lesbian criminal is used to dredge up a nexus of contemporary anxieties surrounding the modernity of single middle-class women. In Chapter 6, I examine Gertrude Stein's foray into detective fiction, commonly thought of as a response to a modernist aesthetic crisis. I instead suggest that Stein invokes the lesbian criminal Lizzie Borden as an awe-inspiring totem to preside over her detective fiction. Borden represents, I suggest, the belief that the female body is under threat from the structures of heterosexuality and ultimately faces the choice between aggressor and victim. In these readings, I intentionally neglect the lesbian criminal's bleak fate and instead consider the disruption that she provokes in the body of the text and the residue that she leaves behind once she is forcibly expelled.

Notes

1. Symons believes that the Golden Age is marked by right-wing politics and an ignorance of certain aspects of life, including sexuality. Kaplan argues a number of Queens of the Golden Age 'celebrate normative heterosexuality'. Symons, *Bloody Murder*, p. 21 and p. 96. Kaplan, 'An Unsuitable Genre for a Feminist?', p. 18.
2. Coward and Semple explain that 'Golden Age' is traditionally used to refer to writing from Agatha Christie's first novel (*The Mysterious Affair at Styles*, 1920) to Dorothy L. Sayers' last (*Busman's Honeymoon*, 1937). However, Knight suggests that stylistic traits of this 'classic' form are exhibited in texts produced after 1940 by both fledgling and established writers. Coward and Semple, 'Tracking Down the Past', p. 39. Knight, 'The Golden Age', p. 77. There are also numerous studies that attempt to define and theorise crime fiction. See, for instance, Knight, *Form and Ideology in Crime Fiction*; Munt, *Murder by the Book?*; Plain, *Twentieth-Century Crime Fiction*; Rzepka, *Detective Fiction*; Symons, *Bloody Murder*; Todorov, 'The Typology of Detective Fiction'.
3. Chesterton, 'A Defence of Detective Stories', p. 6.
4. Plain, *Twentieth-Century Crime Fiction*, p. 3.
5. Ibid. p. 6.
6. The Detection Club, 'The Detection Club Oath', p. 198.
7. Ibid. p. 198. Other writers such as S. S. Van Dine and Ronald A. Knox similarly apostrophised on the genre, outlining specifically what could and could not form a 'detective story'. See Knox, 'Detective Story Decalogue'; Knox, 'Introduction', in *The Best Detective Stories of the Year 1928*; and Van Dine, 'Twenty Rules for Writing Detective Stories'.
8. Plain, *Twentieth-Century Crime Fiction*, p. 6.
9. Plain, *Twentieth-Century Crime Fiction*, p. 5 and p. 11. Coward and Semple similarly argue that it is important to remember that detective fiction is 'about the breaking of the law' as much as its restoration. Coward and Semple, 'Tracking Down the Past', p. 51.
10. Slide, *Gay and Lesbian Characters and Themes in Mystery Novels*, pp. 5–6.
11. Ibid. pp. 5–6.
12. Munt, for instance, believes that the lesbian crime novel originates from pulp fiction of the 1950s and 1960s, citing the first as M. F. Beal's *Angel Dance* in 1977. Donoghue's recent study of lesbian literature counters this somewhat by

situating Golden Age novels as part of a tradition of 'lesbian detection'. Munt, *Murder by the Book?*, pp. 121–2; and Donoghue, *Inseparable*, p. 266. On lesbian crime fiction as a recent development see Reddy, 'Women Detectives', p. 200, and Palmer, 'The Lesbian Feminist Thriller and Detective Novel'.
13. Coward and Semple, 'Tracking Down the Past', p. 45.
14. Tamagne, *A History of Homosexuality*, p. 61.
15. Hart, *Fatal Women*, p. 9. On lesbian violence see also Duggan, *Sapphic Slashers*.
16. Ellis, 'The Criminal', p. 19.
17. Hart also makes this point in *Fatal Women*, p. 10.
18. Ellis, *Studies in the Psychology of Sex*, pp. 200–1.
19. For further examples of violent inverts see Ellis, *Studies in the Psychology of Sex*, pp. 201–3.
20. For details of the Alice Mitchell case see Ellis, *Studies in the Psychology of Sex*, p. 201. For a more recent account see Katz, *Gay American History*, pp. 53–8.
21. Ellis, *Studies in the Psychology of Sex*, p. 201. Surprisingly the association between the lesbian and violence still has social and cultural currency. For instance, when Ian Rankin, the contemporary crime writer, was asked his opinion on the increasingly violent content of crime fiction, he commented that he believed women writers to be responsible for the most graphic novels, and moreover, confessed 'I will tell you that they are mostly lesbians as well, which I find interesting'. Rankin's comments sparked controversy, not least from lesbian crime writer Val McDermid who suggested in response that this was more an issue of gender than of sexuality and that it was the incorporation of aggression in women's writing, and how this contravened gender expectations, that disturbed critics such as Rankin. For Rankin's comment see Kean, 'Ian Rankin: The Singing Detective' and for McDermid's response see 'Woman's Hour'.
22. Neroni, *The Violent Woman*, p. 18.

5

'MURDER IS A QUEER CRIME': THE LESBIAN CRIMINAL AND FEMALE COMMUNITIES IN DETECTIVE FICTION

SPINSTERS AND DETECTIVES

Upon arriving to investigate the mysterious death of Everard Mountjoy in Mitchell's *Speedy Death* (1929), Chief Constable Sir Joseph observes that '[m]urder is a queer crime'.[1] This is merely one instance in the novel of a persistent use of the word queer to describe the events taking place and the characters central to them, and so it would appear that 'queer' is simply the only appropriate term to address the tenor of this plot.[2] The reliance on this adjective may simply be a creative quirk, or evidence of an inexperienced writer – this was, after all, both Mitchell's first published novel and attempt at detective fiction – or it might be an intentional narrative act which cumulatively produces the sense that murder is indeed 'queer' or that in this literary context it is both a sexualised and homoerotic crime.[3]

Taking Mitchell's linguistic idiosyncrasy as a starting point, this chapter explores the idea that where the lesbian criminal (as earlier discussed) is featured in women's detective novels of the period, murder is both queer and queering in the sense that it both stands in for and inspires lesbian desire. In the chapter that follows I examine how the lesbian criminal's acts of murder and violence – most often directed towards other women, and more specifically other lesbians – double as acts of passion and declarations of modern identity. More interesting, however, is the mimesis that forms between the female detective and the lesbian criminal. The latter is a dynamo for the inspiration of the detective's own muted homoerotic desires, and the act of detection itself functions as a way of sublimating those tabooed sexual forces and unconsciously navigating the complexities of her own sexual and gender identity. What emerges from this relationship is evidence that incriminates the female detective and suggests that she is an accessory to the lesbian criminal's own aberrant, and 'illegal', sexual and gender stance. This is particularly obvious when crime is set within the environment of an enclosed female community, as it is in two of the novels I discuss. In these instances, the lesbian criminal is used to dredge up a nexus of contemporary anxieties surrounding the modernity of single middle-class women, an increasing number of whom were taking advantage of newly won rights to education and embarking on careers at the expense of marriage and motherhood.

This chapter focuses on two classic country house crime novels of the 1920s – Sayers' *Unnatural Death* (1927) and Mitchell's *Speedy Death* (1929) – and two detective fictions set in female collegial communities – Sayers' *Gaudy Night* (1936) and Tey's *Miss Pym Disposes* (1946). Although Sayers' (1893–1957) reputation has fared better, in part because her life has received significant attention from biographers, all three women were remarkably popular writers of their time. Sayers' career was varied and successful, and included time spent in publishing, advertising and teaching; as a novelist, playwright, translator, essayist and poet, her creative work was similarly prolific and diverse. Her first published novel, the 1923 *Whose Body*, introduced Lord Peter Wimsey who became Sayers' staple detective, featuring in eleven novels and several short stories. Mitchell's (1901–83) biography is somewhat less well documented, although details about her life are available. As well as working as a schoolteacher, Mitchell was a prolific writer who penned over sixty crime novels featuring her detective Mrs Bradley. She also wrote mystery novels under the name Malcolm Torrie, historical novels under the name Stephen Hockaby, as well as children's fiction and short stories. There seems to be much informal speculation on the topic of Mitchell's sexuality, but what is known is that she shared a home with fellow writer Winifred Blazey, who Nicholas Fuller describes as her companion in an introduction to a collection of Mitchell's work.[4] Like Mitchell, the Scottish Elizabeth Mackintosh (1896–1952) worked as a teacher for the early part of her career until she returned to her family to care for her mother and her father. It was at this point that Mackintosh embarked on a career as a writer, publishing fiction and the Alan Grant Mystery series under the pseudonym Josephine Tey. She also found success as a playwright, working under the name Gordon Daviot, and is particularly remembered for her play *Richard of Bordeaux*.[5]

That the original title of Sayers' *Unnatural Death* was 'The Singular Case of the Three Spinsters' speaks of the way that the lesbian criminal is put to use by each of these writers because she is distinguished by signifiers of gender modernity, independence and masculinity in a way that links her capacity for violence with her progressive womanhood.[6] Given that the spinster was often conflated with the lesbian around this time, at least in the public imagination, I suggest that for Sayers this term (as well as other indicators of gender independence) operates as a coded synonym for women who love women, therefore implying that this is a novel concerned with the lives and choices of 'Three Lesbians', who we might assume to be the three pivotal characters of victim (Agatha Dawson), detective (Miss Climpson), and criminal (Mary Whittaker).[7] Mary is described as a 'well-educated, capable girl, with a great deal more brain than her aunt. Self-reliant, cool [. . .] Quite the modern type', and when Miss Climpson meets her for the first time she notes that:[8]

> With her handsome, strongly-marked features and quiet air of authority, she was of the type that 'does well' in City offices. She had a pleasant and self-possessed manner, and was beautifully tailored – not mannishly, and yet with severe fineness of outline that negatived the appeal of a beautiful figure. (p. 45)

Her intelligence and grasp of legal matters is similarly admired as 'an almost masculine understanding' (p. 186). The modish, assertive and distinctly androgynous Mary is marked out as an ambitious, intelligent, professional woman at ease in the progressive urban environment. Indeed, Mary's ability to forge her own career as a nurse informs and supports her violent activities since she possesses the skills that enable her to commit murder without immediate detection and she uses her knowledge of medicine to poison her victims in later attacks. A self-sufficient existence is similarly conceived as the ultimate goal of her criminal endeavours in that Mary and her unwitting accomplice and lover, Vera Findlater, intend to leave their village lives behind and build an existence elsewhere as farmers, 'interested in things, not in men', or so Vera claims (p. 169). The sincerity of this idyll is questionable (potentially it is merely a ruse to manipulate Vera) but it would appear that dreams of lesbian domesticity and independent industry both facilitate Mary's criminal plan and are its ultimate reward. Indeed, it is the actions of this nurse that undermine the authority and tarnish the reputation of a local male doctor when he raises suspicion over the seemingly natural death of his elderly patient, Agatha. When the autopsy finds nothing untoward the local residents are resentful of the doctor's interference and, as a consequence, his business dwindles. The amateur detective Lord Peter Wimsey encounters the doctor one day and feels compelled to investigate the matter further. It soon becomes apparent that the culprit is Mary, the deceased's niece who had abandoned a nursing career in London to care for her dying aunt and so all that remains is to prove how and why Mary murdered a relative from whom she was already due to inherit a fortune. The investigation takes a turn for the worse when Wimsey's interference provokes Mary to obscure evidence of her original deed by committing further violent attacks, including the brutal murder of her lover Vera. It finally emerges that, fearful of an impending change in the law that would disinherit her from Agatha's fortune, Mary hastens events by administering an empty syringe to her victim, thereby injecting air into her bloodstream and causing heart failure.

It is Miss Climpson that is first sent to investigate the crime in a chapter entitled 'A Use for Spinsters' and introduced with an epigraph commenting on the number of surplus women in England (p. 19).[9] Indeed, this middle-aged spinster is employed by Wimsey as an inquiry agent for the very reason that 'old maids [. . . are] simply bursting with energy' and make the least conspicuous of detectives (p. 28). Like Mary she is a professional woman who supports herself through employment and who has, for unspecified reasons, remained unmarried. However, in contrast to the fashionable and androgynous Mary, Miss Climpson is physically hemmed in by the uniform and démodé quality of her spinsterish dress:

> the door was opened by a thin, middle-aged woman, with a sharp, sallow face and very vivacious manner. She wore a neat, dark coat and skirt, a high-necked blouse and a long gold neck-chain with a variety of small ornaments dangling from it at intervals, and her iron-grey hair was dressed under a net, in the style fashionable in the reign of the late King Edward. (p. 23)

Although financially independent, her choices in life have been heavily influenced by her father. We are told, for instance, that she might have been a lawyer had he not been averse to female education (p. 26). The conflation of gender independence and non-heteronormative sexuality is nowhere more evident than in Miss Climpson's observation that the murderess is 'not of the marrying sort. She is a professional woman by nature' (p. 167). In contrast to this, the unmarried Miss Climpson pronounces herself to be 'a spinster made and not born – a perfectly womanly woman' who likes a 'masterful' man (p. 167). Miss Climpson's rationale is nonsensical given that neither spinsters nor professional woman are 'born' 'naturally' with the disinclination to marry or the ambition to pursue a career. In these instances, she arguably employs the terms 'spinster' and 'professional woman' as coded synonyms for sexual identification, a censorship that is necessary on a personal, psychical level, and possibly on a textual level as well.

For Catherine Kenney, Miss Climpson is 'similar to most of the great male detectives, who tend to be either asexual [. . .] or at least do not mix romance with detection', but this belies the complexity of Miss Climpson's response to the lesbian criminal, which reveals an internal conflict of desire and repression and, essentially, an inability to acknowledge her own sexual history.[10] Writing to Wimsey to relay her progress, she explains that:

> I *really think* she [Mary] means to set up farming *with Miss Findlater*, though what Miss Whittaker can see in that gushing and really *silly* young woman I cannot think. However, Miss Findlater has evidently quite a 'pash' (as we used to call it at school) for Miss Whittaker, and I am afraid none of us are above being *flattered* by such outspoken admiration. I must say, I think it rather *unhealthy* – you may remember Miss Clemence Dane's *very clever book* on the subject? – I have seen so *much* of that kind of thing in my rather WOMAN-RIDDEN existence! (pp. 76–7)

Turning to Clemence Dane's 1917 lesbian novel *Regiment of Women* as a cultural reference point, Miss Climpson situates Mary and Vera's alliance as romantic and erotic, but her evident jealousy also indicates that Miss Climpson is herself located within this female-orientated continuum. Convinced that Vera is being 'preyed upon' by the '[b]eastly, blood-sucking woman', the spinster detective imagines Mary as an evil seductress, akin to the predatory teacher of Dane's book (p. 167 and p. 239). Yet she is relieved when it appears that Mary has been kidnapped (a scene that has been staged by Mary) and when the evidence suggests that the murders were in fact committed by a distant relative, the West-Indian Reverend Hallelujah Dawson. Deciding that a mysterious man is most likely responsible for these acts, and that Agatha's death might, after all, have been natural, she forms 'a nightmare image of him in her mind – blood-boltered, sinister, and – most horrible of all – an associate and employer of debauched and brutal black assassins' (p. 244). Her keenness to absolve Mary of guilt speaks of the psychologically freighted relationship between the detective and lesbian criminal. The former is beleaguered by the clichés and antiquated stereotypes of lesbian identity (and as respite from those she falls back upon similar sexualised racial constructs), but this act of figuring Mary as demonic lesbian also functions as an erotic imaginative process and a method of projecting desire which cannot be otherwise fathomed.

As part of her investigation, Miss Climpson almost obsessively invokes her own experiences of what she terms a 'woman-ridden existence' as a lens through which to comprehend the psyche of the lesbian criminal (p. 77). After her first meeting with Mary she assesses her suspect:

> With her long and melancholy experience of frustrated womanhood, observed in a dreary succession of cheap boarding-houses, Miss Climpson was able to dismiss one theory which had vaguely formed in her mind. This was no passionate nature, cramped by association with an old woman and eager to be free to mate before youth should depart. [. . .] But meeting Mary Whittaker's clear, light eyes under their well-shaped brows, she was struck by a sudden sense of familiarity. She had seen that look before, though the where and the when escaped her. (p. 45)

Arguably, this uncanny sense of familiarity is an unacknowledged affinity, but Miss Climpson is unable to read either her own desire for, or identification with, Mary.[11] Similarly, after Mary's murder of her lover, Vera, the detective stumbles upon the latter's confession sheet in the village church and analyses its contents:

> From these few fossil bones, Miss Climpson had little difficulty in reconstructing one of those hateful and passionate 'scenes' of slighted jealousy with which a woman-ridden life had made her only too familiar. 'I do everything for you – you don't care a bit for me – you treat me cruelly – you're simply sick of me, that's what it is!' [. . .] Humiliating, degrading, exhausting, beastly scenes. Girls' school, boarding-house, Bloomsbury-flat scenes. [. . .] Silly *schwärmerei* swamping all decent self-respect. Barren quarrels ending in shame and hatred. (p. 239)

As Emma Donoghue states, this passage is a 'strange excess', or outpouring of emotion, 'in a book which is otherwise witty and worldly', and it effectively tells the reader 'less about Mary and Vera than about what Miss Climpson herself may have endured'.[12] What Miss Climpson resurrects from these 'fossil bones' are the lesbian scenes of Mary's life, but in conjuring up female environments in which intimacy may flourish, she simultaneously provides a parallel narration of her own romantic history.

Mary's specific acts of violence (the murder of Agatha and Vera and the attempted murder of Miss Climpson) might, then, be read as symbolic attacks upon other, and perhaps démodé, models of lesbian living. Mary's aunt, Agatha, spends the majority of her adult life building a home and business with her companion Clara, with whom she formed a friendship when they were schoolgirls. Perceived in their community as simply 'a remarkable pair of old ladies' or 'devoted friend[s]' (p. 125 and p. 6), their union is one in which they appropriate conventional marital roles. Agatha is described as the '"domestic" partner' and confines her activities to the house, while Clara is said to have cropped her hair and set herself up in business as a horse breeder (p. 77). It is Clara's *'revolutionary'* activities as a businesswoman, rather than any radical sexual lifestyle, that attracts opposition (pp. 77–8). Miss Climpson is to some extent an exemplar of sexual repression, beleaguered by ideas of what is 'natural' and 'proper'. Haunted by her father's edict, she is controlled by unspoken patriarchal law and, as a detective, is the literal representative of a legal system governed by men. Mary, in contrast to both women, is transgressive to her last moment. Her actions are illegal, but they also challenge the authority of a male medical establishment and question the validity and fairness of the law itself, which threatens to disinherit her in favour of an unknown male cousin. Indeed, it could be said that this is a plot in which men strive to protect male interests over the claims of women: Wimsey is motivated to investigate the death of Agatha after hearing of the doctor's reputation; he ensures that Reverend Hallelujah Dawson receives a significant share of Agatha's money; and the inheritance is eventually settled on a male first cousin according to the law's, and not Agatha's, wishes (p. 263). Even as Mary exits the text she refuses the jurisdiction of the law by hanging herself before her punishment can be meted out, so retaining possession, albeit through death, of her own body and its destiny.

Unlike her aunt or Miss Climpson, there is nothing innocuous or repressed about Mary's own sexuality. Indeed, it is clear that active desire forms an integral part of who she is and the violent acts that she commits, as is evident when she attempts to seduce and murder Wimsey. Feeling the investigation closing in, she lures Wimsey to her flat and offers him a laced drink. It is here that her criminal machinations come undone because something about her strikes Wimsey as uncanny and surreal:

> For all her make-up and her somewhat outspoken costume, she struck him as spinsterish – even epicene. [. . .] He felt her body stiffen as he slipped his arm round her, but she gave a little sigh of relief. He pulled her suddenly and violently to him, and kissed her mouth with a practised exaggeration of passion. He knew then. No one who has ever encountered it can ever again mistake that awful shrinking, that uncontrollable revulsion of the flesh against a caress that is nauseous. He thought for a moment that she was going to be actually sick. (pp. 163–4)

Mary is disguised at this moment as her alias, Mrs Forrest, a character who with her overwhelming perfume, bleached hair, brash make-up, and heavy jewellery is excessively feminine (p. 66). Garber has pointed out that '[c]ross-dressing is a classic strategy of disappearance in detective fiction', used most often by criminal figures.[13] Although Mary is not cross-dressed in the usual sense, given the way that sexual and gender differences are mapped onto one another in this text, we might plausibly think of this disguise as a form of sexual cross-dressing or an attempt, and failure, to pass as heterosexual. Mary's revulsion arguably makes the point that the lesbian woman cannot be adequately accounted for with the theory of romantic friendship (as with Agatha and perhaps Vera), nor with the cliché of the surplus spinster (as with Miss Climpson), because she is driven by innate corporeal urges which cannot be simply suppressed or papered over.

Mitchell's *Speedy Death* is not as finely tuned or sophisticated a work as Sayers', but it does employ the lesbian criminal to similar effect. The novel opens on a note of conjugal bliss with two couples engaged to be married – Garde to Dorothy, and Eleanor (Garde's sister) to Everard Mountjoy. Within a few pages Mountjoy is discovered lifeless in the bath and at the same time is revealed to be a woman who has been 'masquerading as a man' (p. 19).

Luckily, Mrs Lestrange Bradley (Mitchell's serial detective), a psychoanalyst and guest at the house, is on hand to investigate these strange events. The other characters believe that Eleanor has committed the murder after discovering Mountjoy's secret, and this assumption is supported by Eleanor's increasingly erratic and dangerous behaviour as well as her desperate bid to attract the only other eligible bachelor in the house, Bertie. Two attacks are made on Eleanor's life in an attempt to protect her potential victims, first by Bertie and then by Mrs Bradley. The latter's attack, elaborately and nonchalantly carried out, is successful, and the novel closes with Mrs Bradley's prosecution and acquittal for Eleanor's murder.

Like Sayers' novel this text is replete with transgressive figures and, moreover, characters that blur the boundaries between innocence and criminality. Mountjoy, found drowned, has passed as a man for a significant period and forged a career as a professional explorer and archaeologist whose expert opinion is valued by 'scientists of two continents' (p. 19). Known to be taken by 'working fit[s]' which keep him to his room, Mountjoy has chosen an alternative gender identity to gain freedom and access to a realm otherwise barred to him (p. 52). While able to comprehend that a woman would desire to adopt the privileges of the male sex, the house party cannot conceive of Mountjoy's masquerade as being motivated by sexual orientation, either in terms of lesbian or transvestite pleasure, nor by transgender identity. Trying to establish why Mountjoy would allow herself to become engaged to another woman, Mrs Bradley is the only character to contemplate the possibility of same-sex desire or what she deems 'sexual perversion', when she explains that 'Mountjoy may have formed a very real and [. . .] a very strong attachment to Eleanor' (p. 105). Mountjoy's lover and murderer, Eleanor, is a curious, silent figure (as with most lesbian criminals, she is denied a voice) and she possesses many of the characteristics typical to the lesbian villain, driven to madness and violence through sexual 'aberrance'. She is seemingly prim, but during episodes of violence she is transformed into an animalistic and vulgar criminal, as her attack on a female rival demonstrates:

> Eleanor stopped short, and listened with a kind of ferocious intentness. Gone were her puritanical expression and prim demeanour; gone her faintly derisive smile and her neat Victorian coiffure. This was Fury incarnate which stood before them [. . .] – wild-eyed, streaming-haired Fury loosed from hell! [. . .] Eleanor, beholding the empty bed and knowing herself foiled of her prey, slashed and slashed again at the bedclothes, ripped open the eiderdown, cut and sawed the blankets, and tore the sheets into strips with the knife and her own cruel strong hands. [. . .] Eleanor fought and struggled, while from the lips which were accustomed to employ the most trite and correct of expressions there poured

forth a stream of the most foul and abominable filth which ever disgraced the name of language. (p. 135)

As I explore in the latter part of this chapter, the spinster's life was often perceived as a potential breeding ground for repressed desires that might become twisted and ultimately lead to violence, madness and the betrayal of appropriate gender behaviour. While not explicitly signalled as homosexual, her violence is certainly connected to her sexuality, or rather, her lack of seemingly heteronormative impulses. Upon hearing the news of Eleanor's engagement to Mountjoy, Dorothy declares such a thing as highly unlikely:

I have *never* seen anything so – so wildly improbable as Eleanor's behaviour with young, youngish, and middle-aged men. She might as well go straight to a nunnery and have done with it. (p. 9)

Similarly, it is initially deemed laughable that Eleanor could have murdered Mountjoy because 'she's such a prim sort of young woman she'd hardly like to *think* about people with no clothes on, never mind coming in where they were and murdering 'em!' (p. 123). But Mrs Bradley recognises Eleanor as a woman motivated by 'repressed desires [. . . and] unsatisfied cravings for enjoyment and for freedom' (p. 103). Her decision to incorporate Eleanor as a case study in her '*Handbook to Psycho-Analysis*' effectively pathologises her violence and sexual difference, as does her choice to kill Eleanor with 'a queer drug' commonly used to treat nymphomaniacs and homicidal maniacs (p. 107 and p. 160). In the aftermath of Eleanor's death, and before Mrs Bradley's guilt is discovered, this detective insists that Eleanor could not have committed suicide and 'talked a lot of psychological stuff about Eleanor not being the type that does away with itself, and quoted books and things, mostly by American and German authors' (p. 144). We might assume that the books Mrs Bradley refers to here are works of sexology – Ellis, for instance, believed that male inverts tended towards suicide, while female inverts were inclined towards 'passional crime'.[14] Mrs Bradley, then, makes every effort to incorporate Eleanor into medical discourse (and to financially profit from it by publishing her research), and as the ultimate pathologising act, she poisons her with a drug used to control those socially inappropriate desires and instincts.

What rescues Mitchell's novel and characters from a flat interpretation in which we read the lesbian criminal as simply that, is the last-minute introduction of Eleanor's diary as evidence. In the time since the murders, Garde and Dorothy, now married, have discovered Eleanor's diary but 'can't make anything out of it' (p. 162). Carstairs, returning to the scene of the crime in search of evidence to use for Mrs Bradley's defence (by this point she is on trial for Eleanor's murder), inspects this new material. The implanted text of Eleanor's diary provides her with a posthumous voice with which she describes how she is 'curiously attracted' to Mountjoy (p. 164):

> It is torture [. . .] to be with my dear Everard as much as I am, and to know that he has no desire to caress me. One should be content, I suppose [. . .] with his beautiful platonic love, but sometimes strange desires come into my mind. I scarcely like to confess them, even to myself. I said to him something about leaving his tennis-shirt open at the neck like Garde and Bertie do, but he mumbled something, and kept it fast buttoned. [. . .] I want Everard to be manly and sunburnt. (p. 165)

Considering that Eleanor is said to be unmoved by men, it is interesting that it is Mountjoy, who is earlier described to be 'a little, slim, clean-shaven, shy sort of fellow', that inspires 'strange' and 'curious', or perhaps 'queer', desires in Eleanor (p. 9 and pp. 164–5). Despite Mountjoy's feminine appearance, Eleanor wishes him to perform what she perceives to be a version of masculinity, suggesting that it is the transgendered nature of his/her body that holds the most erotic potential for her. She emerges, then, from this palimpsestic text not as a woman driven mad by unsatisfied longing, but rather as passionate, thoughtful and complex. She is able to recognise her own desires (although not necessarily the extent of their transgression) but is also prepared to content herself with 'beautiful platonic love' if she must (p. 165).

The violence that Eleanor commits against Mountjoy – if, indeed, we are to believe that she is the murderer – could therefore be seen as an act of what Patricia Juliana Smith terms 'lesbian panic':

> the disruptive action or reaction that occurs when a character – or, conceivably, an author – is either unable or unwilling to confront or reveal her own lesbianism or lesbian desire. Typically, a female character, fearing discovery of her covert or unarticulated desires – whether by the object of her desires, by other characters, or even by herself – and motivated by any of the factors previously described, lashes out directly or indirectly at another woman, resulting in emotional or physical harm to herself or others.[15]

Looking beyond the realm of crime fiction, one might cite Nella Larsen's *Passing* (1929) which concludes with Irene Redfield pushing Clare Kendry from an apartment window, or Molly Keane's *Devoted Ladies* (1934) which similarly culminates with the repressed Piggy Browne driving herself and her lesbian passenger over a cliff and to their deaths, as examples of such panic. Murder can be figured in this sense as a substitute for the enactment and satisfaction of desire that cannot be otherwise articulated. The crime scene, with Mountjoy naked in the bath, feasibly doubles as one of erotic confrontation and suggests that Eleanor's violence is motivated by a psychical refusal to recognise the nature of her attraction.

The idea that murder functions as lesbian panic is made more potent by the transformation of Mrs Bradley from detective into criminal.[16] If murder is deemed to be a 'queer crime', as it so often is in this novel, then by positioning herself as a killer, Mrs Bradley 'queers' her own identity. Furthermore, if sexual difference is shown to make a woman violent, then surely Mrs Bradley's nonchalant destruction of Eleanor's life raises suspicions about her own sexual identity. Like the lesbian criminal, then, she is positioned by Mitchell as a figure of alterity. Although not a spinster (she has married more than once and has a son), she has much in common with the spinster detective in that she is a lone figure, eccentric in dress and manner, and is thought to be fairly innocuous and consequently inconspicuous. However, she is also depicted as threatening and frequently described in animalistic terms, as is Eleanor in her moments of aggression. Predicting that Eleanor will make an attempt on Dorothy's life as she sleeps, Mrs Bradley secretly takes the latter into her room. The scene is somewhat charged as Mrs Bradley pulls their beds close together 'so that if you feel lonely you have only to stretch out an arm and I'll wake up' (p. 79). Waking to the sound of a terrifying scream, they decide to investigate, but Mrs Bradley, 'eyeing Dorothy's silk pyjamas with admiration', decides that she should first wrap her attractive body in an eiderdown (p. 80). The particularly sinister relish which Mrs Bradley takes in murdering Eleanor also hints at deeper motivations. Although Mrs Bradley kills Eleanor in her bed by exchanging a sleeping draught for poison, she unnecessarily embellishes the deed by hiding her dead body in the wardrobe, taking Eleanor's place in her bed, and then staging her dead, presumably unclothed, body in the bath, so replicating Eleanor's original act of violence. The female body is again exposed (but this time needlessly) and put on display, and the original scene of lesbian eros (between Mountjoy and Eleanor) replicated while Mrs Bradley literally assumes the identity of the lesbian criminal by taking her place in bed. Carla T. Kungl points out that Mrs Bradley is also responsible for the death of the female criminal in *The Saltmarsh Murders* (1932), but she believes that with this 'Mrs. Bradley sympathetically takes care of the women perpetrators in what she feels is a more humane way'.[17] With capital punishment still in effect at this time, all detectives effectively become 'murderers' when they bring the criminal to justice and to the gallows, but Mrs Bradley's murder of Eleanor seems too elaborate, and too easy, an act to be humane. The fact that she is capable of murder indicates that she is also capable of 'other' desires and that she is as transgressive as Mountjoy or Eleanor, because she dissolves the boundary between legitimate and criminal behaviour, as well as heterosexual and homosexual identification.

If Mrs Bradley's murder of Eleanor, and in particular her reconstruction of the original murder scene, are acts of lesbian panic, she also compensates for these desires by staunchly defending the structure of the hetero-patriarchal system. She rationalises the killing of Eleanor with the strange eugenic philosophy that 'I merely erased her, as it were, from an otherwise fair page of the Bing family chronicle' (p. 183). It is also mentioned that Mrs Bradley is known to the Bing family because she has previously helped Garde to escape 'police-court proceedings on the night of the Oxford and Cambridge boat race', which involved a situation with 'that tobacconist's young woman' (p. 103 and p. 69). In contrast, Eleanor's diary reveals her to be a perceptive critic of the system that Mrs Bradley endorses. The diary divulges the dullness of Eleanor's existence, dominated by housekeeping until Mountjoy's arrival, but it also declares her repulsion at the sexual morals of her brother and father. She documents the latter's affair with a servant, that woman's consequent pregnancy, and her father's determination for his mistress to remain in the house. Eleanor is aware that Garde is little better, having been rescued by Mrs Bradley from the police and punishment for some kind of 'scrape' (p. 164). Eleanor surmises that 'I feel that it is pollution to be in the same house with them', and while it is perhaps too generous to attribute feminist principles to this lesbian criminal (she is fairly unsympathetic to the plight of the pregnant and exploited servant girl), the heteronormative conditions of her family disgust her and marriage to the androgynous Mountjoy poses as an appealing escape route (p. 163).

In their collusion to silence and eliminate Eleanor, the characters that represent the heterosexual hegemony are also shown to be quite as capable of murderous machinations. Bertie's attempt to kill Eleanor is overlooked by friends and the authorities because he is deemed to be 'perfectly harmless' (p. 151). This nonchalance can no doubt be attributed to the police's own strange level of malice towards Eleanor: the Chief Constable claims to detest her and the Inspector can sympathise with a desire to kill her because 'there's some young women that are past all bearing, and [. . .] would be better out of the way' (p. 154 and p. 95). Similarly, Carstairs is so embarrassed by the frankness of Eleanor's diary that he burns it, obscuring the possibility of lesbianism and any evidence that paints Eleanor in a more positive light (p. 165). Thus the evidence of Eleanor's diary is misread and her posthumous voice silenced, and although Eleanor's family and friends know Mrs Bradley to be guilty of her murder, they obscure that fact. Mitchell makes a statement about the wider forces at work here. It is evident that those who represent the heterosexual and patriarchal hegemony collude to destroy or contain transgressive elements of society and are themselves as guilty of violence and criminal acts as the supposed villains.

Alma Mater and Murder

Given that the lesbian criminal is associated with modernity and her access to a profession (in the case of both Mary and Mrs Bradley) it is unsurprising that a number of female crime novelists at this time were drawn to enclosed female communities for the setting of their narratives. Lawrence turns to a New York City hostel for working women as the backdrop to murder in *Death of a Doll* (1947), while Christianna Brand's *Green for Danger* (1945) takes its murder suspects from a group of nurses. A more popular setting for crime was a school or college. Mitchell was particularly fond of academe (*Laurels are Poison* (1942) and *Spotted Hemlock* (1958) are set respectively in women's physical training and agricultural colleges), as was Sayers (*Gaudy Night*, 1936), Tey (*Miss Pym Disposes*, 1947), Spain (*Poison for Teacher*, 1949) and Christie (*Cat Among the Pigeons*, 1959). As Alison Hennegan comments in her introduction to Spain's reissued *Poison for Teacher*:

> There are two things that every foreigner used to know about the English. The first is that they are obsessed by their school- and college-days. The second is that Englishwomen write the best detective stories of all. To combine the two – *Alma Mater* and murder – makes supreme good sense.[18]

For women writers, the academic crime novel made 'good sense' because women's education was an important talking point at that time.[19] It was a particularly sensitive topic for the reason that hostile associations were forming, in the minds of the popular press and the public at least, between female educational environments and lesbianism. Oram's work on the spinster teacher in interwar Britain builds a portrait of this increasing hostility in which 'the perceived image of the spinster teacher suffered an increasingly negative change, resulting in the stereotype of an embittered, thwarted, sexually frustrated or deviant woman'.[20] As she points out, because the majority of Local Education Authorities adopted the policy that women should resign on marriage, the dominant number of women employed as female teachers were inevitably single.[21] The teaching profession therefore became associated with those who had opted out, for reasons no doubt including sexual preference, of the heterosexual economy. Oram clarifies that although attacks on unmarried teachers were primarily framed as attacks on spinsters rather than lesbians, they reached their most vilifying when associated with sexuality, as a press report of an educational conference in 1935 demonstrates:

> Dr Williams had [...] said that games such as hockey and lacrosse develop that part of the suprarenal gland which presides over the combative element of a person's character. 'You cannot confine the desire and aptitude for combat to cricket and football,' he said. 'They inevitably appear in the whole character, and what was originally a gentle, feminine girl becomes harsh and bellicose in all relations to life. The women who have the responsibility of teaching these girls are, many of them themselves *embittered, sexless or homosexual* hoydens who try to mould the

girls into their own pattern. And far too often they succeed.' Dr Williams declared that girls who have no desire to play combative games are cajoled and coerced into taking part by 'these thin-lipped, flat-chested, sadistic creatures.'²² [my emphasis]

It is the traverse of the gender divide that proves most troubling to these commentators. The teacher who encourages girls to jeopardise their femininity is herself devoid of feminine features (plump lips and an ample chest) and is perceived as 'sadistic', which again speaks of the persistent association between masculine female identities, non-heteronormative desire and violence. Accusations and suspicions of lesbianism were seemingly beginning to coalesce around the unmarried teacher, and the single-sex educational community was increasingly perceived as a context where the innocent, feminine and heterosexual girl might by perverted into a masculine, homosexual monstrosity.

In higher education, a similar atmosphere of suspicion was brewing. Jennifer Fitzgerald's biographical study of the historian Maude Violet Clarke and her time at Oxford's Somerville College provides an insight into the vulnerability of female educators in this period.²³ Shortly before 1920, the principle of Somerville, Emily Penrose, received a complaint from female students of a lesbian relationship conducted between two of their peers.²⁴ As Fitzgerald concludes, 'women-only spaces, suspected of being able to dispense with men, were effectively policed by homophobia'.²⁵ Ellis draws a similar thread between education, professional women and lesbianism in *Studies in the Psychology of Sex* when he argues that sexual inversion 'has been found, under certain conditions, to abound among women in colleges and convents and prisons'.²⁶ Furthermore, Ellis associates sexual inversion and masculine identification with higher intellect and access to privileges reserved for men:

> inversion is as likely to be accompanied by a high intellectual ability in a woman as in a man. The importance of a clear conception of inversion is indeed in some respects, under present social conditions, really even greater in the case of women than of men. For if, as has sometimes been said of our civilisation, 'this is a man's world,' the large proportion of able women inverts, whose masculine qualities render it comparatively easy for them to adopt masculine avocations, becomes a highly significant fact.²⁷

Ellis is less condemnatory than Dr Williams, but he nevertheless constructs a causal chain between female education and the emergence of lesbian passions. It is the intelligent woman or the woman who wishes to participate in a 'man's world', and therefore the woman who would turn to education, who is predisposed to inverted sexual desires. For Ellis, and for more damning commentators of the period, there is an evident slippage between the woman who shirks her duty to marriage and motherhood in favour of a profession and autonomous existence and the woman who is erotically or emotionally attached to those of her own sex.[28]

It is evident that these connective threads were partly woven in the wake of anxieties surrounding women's increasing independence and access to male professions through the province of education. Vicinus makes the point that the schoolgirl rave and collegial romantic friendship were tolerated only so far as they did not threaten the established gender order, and that once this began to occur, their status, and that of women's education, altered:

> one of the natural results of the new educators' emphasis on careers for women, public responsibilities, and professional behavior was a blurring of the clear distinctions between the domestic, female world and the male, public world. As women gained a voice in the public sphere, their single-sex institutions came under attack.[29]

The all-female settings chosen in these crime novels come ready-inscribed with homoerotic resonances, then, and dredge up contemporary anxieties surrounding the modernity of the single middle-class woman and her relationship to education.

Given that Sayers achieved first class honours from Somerville College, Oxford, and was among the first women to be awarded degrees when she graduated in 1920 with a Master's, her choice to set *Gaudy Night* in an Oxford University college is apt. The novel opens with the famous mystery novelist Harriet Vane returning to her former college, the fictional Shrewsbury, for the first time since her graduation and on the request of an infirm friend, to attend the annual Gaudy Night celebration. Initially hesitant about revisiting her past, not least because she has since been accused of the murder of her lover (as told in *Strong Poison*, 1930), she is soon absorbed back into the comforting fold of the sororal academic world. At the time of her arrival, the college is blighted by a series of malicious and violent crimes against the staff and students: what begins as merely vandalism and poison-pen letters soon escalates to acts of mental and physical brutality (the attempted murders of Harriet and the new faculty member, Miss de Vine). Harriet is convinced that the criminal is a member of the academic body who has become psychologically warped by repressed desires, but despite her presence at Shrewsbury for almost an academic year she is unable to ascertain the identity of the perpetrator. As the situation becomes more serious, Harriet summons reinforcements in the form of Lord Peter Wimsey who discovers within the space of a week that the criminal is in fact a maid at the college, Annie, determined to avenge the humiliation of her scholar husband, who took his own life after Miss de Vine exposed his thesis as fraudulent.

From the moment that the mysterious vandal strikes, her crimes are read through her supposed sexual deviance and her actions are blamed upon an over-exerted intelligence and a cloistered female educational environment. Harriet contemplates why a member of the college would harm her fellow academics and assumes that:

> The warped and repressed mind is apt enough to turn and wound itself. 'Soured virginity' – 'unnatural life' – 'semi-demented spinsters' – 'starved appetites and suppressed impulses' – 'unwholesome atmosphere' – she could think of whole sets of epithets, ready-minted for circulation.[30]

Harriet relies on a set of stock responses and clichéd phrases, most likely lifted verbatim from a scaremongering press article such as that mentioned earlier, and she assumes that the culprit is 'demented', and it is implied lesbian, by her same-sex environment. Suspicious of her friends and colleagues, Harriet considers the nature of the advice that she must seek in order to catch the criminal:

> There were plenty of people in London – both men and women – to whom the discussion of sexual abnormalities was a commonplace; but most of them were very little to be trusted. They cultivated normality till it stood out of them all over in knobs, like the muscles upon professional strong men, and scarcely looked normal at all. [. . .] 'The fact is,' said Harriet to the telephone, 'I don't know whether I want a doctor or a detective.' (p. 287)

Despite her understanding that sexuality, or rather sexual normativity, is a cultivated state, which in its artificiality can at times appear grotesque, she promotes the belief that lesbian identity is a sickness. The lesbian criminal can only be understood through medico-legal discourses, as a transgressor of either sexual norms or the law, to be cured or punished respectively.

Despite Harriet's career as a mystery novelist, and her experience writing her own textual clues, she consistently misreads those in this real life crime drama.[31] As Wimsey comments upon his arrival:

> do all those facts taken together suggest nothing to you beyond a general notion of sex repression? [. . .] I wish you could clear this personal preoccupation out of your mind. My dear, what are you afraid of? The two great dangers of the celibate life are a forced choice and a vacant mind. Energies bombinating in a vacuum breed chimaeras. But *you* are in no danger. If you want to set up your everlasting rest, you are far more likely to find it in the life of the mind than the life of the heart. (p. 324)

Wimsey's incredulity of Harriet's theory and the questions he poses are telling. The crimes themselves do not overtly suggest a sexual motive but Harriet is so absorbed by this notion of lesbian criminality that she misinterprets the facts. Marya McFadden tackles this point in her reading of homoerotic desire in

Gaudy Night by arguing that Harriet fears the emergence of her own female-oriented desire and therefore 'displaces her own passions onto the poison pen culprit and consequently presumes her to be motivated by repressed homoeroticism'.[32] McFadden also believes that the generic convention of violence is used 'as a pretense for exploring the homoerotic desires and fears that surface' and that this creates 'a work in which gender and sexuality are deconstructed to unleash a play of polymorphously perverse possibilities', or effectively, what McFadden deems a 'queer' text.[33]

Yet, I would suggest that more is at stake in Harriet's conjuring up of the lesbian criminal than simply her own suppressed desires. While detection is derailed in *Unnatural Death* by a sublimation of desire and a disguised mimesis between detective and criminal, the lesbian criminal in *Gaudy Night* more forcefully evokes the choice, as Wimsey defines it, between a 'life of the mind' and a 'life of the heart', that is a career and independence or marriage, commitment, and the sacrifice of autonomy (p. 324). The violence in the text does project Harriet's inarticulate sexuality but more explicitly it is also a platform on which to exhibit the choices that Harriet, and other contemporary middle-class women, face. Harriet assumes that the criminal's decision to define herself as a professional woman has made her unstable, and the choice that Harriet faces at this juncture in her life between the professional (her career as a mystery novelist and the possibility of a life in female academe) and the personal (the prospect of marriage to Wimsey) promotes the fear that if she chooses the former she too will be at risk of mental and sexual derangement. Harriet might become the very criminal that she seeks to expose, and indeed, having been accused and tried for the murder of her lover in *Strong Poison*, she is already in some sense a criminal, or at least tainted with that association. With her own rather masculine features ('black brows fronting squarely either side of a strong nose, a little too broad for beauty', p. 8), profession as a writer and interest in academia, there is arguably a strong resemblance. But while Miss Climpson struggles to recognise the similarity between herself and the lesbian criminal, Harriet is all too aware of the affinity. In a remark that seems to evoke Ellis's own view that '[t]he strongest barrier of all against criminality in women is maternity', Harriet worries that one will inevitably become 'potty' from a life in the confines of a female college, since 'that seems to be what happens to one if one keeps out of the way of love and marriage and all the rest of the muddle' (p. 393).[34]

Harriet believes heterosexuality to be the most effective insurance against insanity and criminality, and ultimately she chooses to marry Wimsey and risk compromising her independent lifestyle and feminist principles. But as McFadden points out, there is something 'queer' about the pairing, in that it both lacks the expected sexual chemistry and affects a sense of camp.[35] While Harriet's appearance is distinguished by her slightly masculine features,

Wimsey is distinctly dapper and effete, and as the true criminal Annie makes clear, it is Wimsey's version of masculinity that has helped to construct the society that she so abhors:

> It's men like you that make women like this. You don't know how to do anything but talk. What do you know about life, with your title and your money and your clothes and motor-cars? [. . .] You're fit for nothing but to keep your hands white and father other men's children. (p. 488)

He is perhaps an apt match for Harriet, who similarly refuses to comply with societal expectations. This odd pairing is epitomised by a strange scene between Wimsey and Harriet, in which he tries to prepare her for a possible attack by mimicking her strangulation:

> 'You have a nice throat for it,' pursued his lordship, thoughtfully. 'It has a kind of arum-lily quality that is in itself a temptation to violence. [. . . I]f you will kindly step aside with me into this convenient field, it will give me great pleasure to strangle you scientifically in several positions.' (p. 413)

Wimsey completes this innuendo-laden scene by purchasing a dog collar for Harriet to wear as protection (p. 417), which McFadden reads as 'a stylized, mock sadomasochistic ritual', again implying that acts of violence and murder can be highly sexually charged.[36] The element of play involved here suggests that despite Harriet's submission to marriage, neither wife nor husband will fulfil the standard expectations of a conventional heterosexual dynamic.

As a rebuttal to *Unnatural Death*, this more sophisticated and knowing novel comes to the conclusion that the lesbian criminal is merely apparitional, a chimerical product of social psychology, and that the women's collegial environment is unfairly victimised. The revelation that Annie is to blame for these events emphasises that it is the system of conventional heterosexual relations that produces women, and presumably men, of such hypertrophied gender proportions that it perverts or dements the mind. With her belief that '[a] woman's job is to look after a husband and children', Annie is in fact a caricature of the good wife, and her hope that her daughters will be 'good girls [. . .] and good wives and mothers' instead of the professional and independent women that they dream of becoming – interestingly, in this case, mechanics – again acts out the choice that many women in the novel are faced with (pp. 485–6 and p. 246). But, as Virginia B. Morris points out:

> Annie never recognizes that she has become exactly what she despises: a woman who is doing a man's job. She is breadwinner by necessity, first when her husband cannot keep a job and then after he commits suicide. And when she chooses a method to commit murder, she chooses and

nearly succeeds at strangling her victim – an extremely rare method for a woman either in real life or in fiction.[37]

Indeed, those characters who encounter the vandal report her to be 'unfeminine', exceptionally strong, with a 'horrid voice, like glue' and a propensity for obscene language (p. 464 and p. 222). Her behaviour is therefore characterised by her transgression of appropriate feminine behaviour, despite the fact that this kind of gender transgression is the target of her violence. When discovered, Annie (as with Mary in *Unnatural Death* and Eleanor in *Speedy Death*) degenerates into 'half dreadful and half grotesque' hysteria (p. 488):

> You'd destroy your own husbands, if you had any, for an old book or bit of writing . . . I loved my husband and you broke his heart. If he'd been a thief or a murderer, I'd have loved him and stuck to him. He didn't mean to steal that old bit of paper – he only put it away. It made no difference to anybody. It wouldn't have helped a single man or woman or child in the world [. . .] but you killed him for it. [. . .] I wanted to see you thrown out to starve, like us. I wanted to see you all dragged in the gutter. I wanted to see you – you – sneered at and trampled on and degraded and despised as we were. It would do you good to learn to scrub floors for a living as I've done, and use your hands for something, and say 'madam' to a lot of scum. (pp. 486–7)

Annie is motivated by perverse heterosexual loyalties both to a dead husband who never really cared for her and to a system which prescribes such relationships as the norm, although her argument is not without merit or reason given that it highlights the inequalities of class, the privilege of educated women, and her own vulnerability as a working-class woman left alone to support her family. Annie's speech also exposes the violent and demented lesbian criminal for what she really is – a construct fuelled by societal anxieties over the role of the modern professional and educated woman, her transgression of proper gender roles, and her usurpation of men's jobs and privileges. Her husband's demise is, after all, the result of his failure as an academic in comparison to a new generation of more capable female scholars. As such, it is significant that it is Annie, and not the lesbian criminal, that is ultimately ushered out of the text and 'medically dealt with', so reversing the usual process of pathologising the sexual other (p. 494).

As Shrewsbury is for Harriet Vane, so Leys Physical Training College is for Miss Pym a space in which intimate female friendships become the norm and female passions can flourish. Tey's *Miss Pym Disposes* opens with Lucy Pym, a famous but informally trained psychologist who has distinguished herself by breaking away from 'Freud and Company', embarking upon a lecture visit to Leys Physical Training College, where her old friend and former school rave, Henrietta, is now Principal.[38] Her visit is extended well beyond the intended one night as she is drawn into collegial life and friendships with the senior schoolgirls. As the end of term, exams, and the search for employment approaches, Henrietta erroneously assigns the prize job to her favourite, but by no means most elite, student. Her nepotism incites uproar amongst student and staff bodies until the favoured student, known as Rouse, is involved in an accident and dies. Miss Pym's suspicions are aroused when she notices wet footprints and a discarded shoe ornament in the vicinity of the crime scene. It transpires that Miss Pym's 'beloved Beau' (her new schoolgirl rave), furious that her own friend, Innes, should be overlooked for the choice position arranges Rouse's accident to temporarily incapacitate her and clear the way (p. 225).

Harriet Vane and Miss Pym are fairly ineffectual and reluctant detectives for the reason that they are both distracted by desires that arise on their return to the enclosed female community. Harriet is unconsciously determined to misread the evidence because of her own psychological demons, while Miss Pym makes the conscious decision to shun her responsibilities and, in effect, enter into an unspoken alliance with the murderer herself. Leys is rife with raves and romantic friendships, with the only clearly signalled heterosexual character, Teresa Desterro, in the minority and on the margins of the community. Teresa deems attachments between women to be a particularly English trait and one which is not wholly healthy, and she describes the relationship between her fellow students Innes and Beau as '[n]ice, of course, [...] quite irreproachable. But normal, no' (p. 36). As contemporary critics of female educators and education were wont to do, Teresa makes a connection between sexual 'abnormality' and the physical and mental exertion of learning, claiming that '[i]t would be difficult to go through their years of training here and be quite normal in their last term' (p. 36). But Miss Pym rejects this theory in the sense that she 'doubts whether as a specimen a Physical Training Student is likely to be psychologically interesting' since they seem to be 'too normal and too nice' (p. 36). Unlike Mitchell's Mrs Bradley or Sayers' Harriet Vane, Miss Pym firmly refuses to pathologise these college women.

Miss Pym's loyalties are swayed by her own investment in such friendships and her enjoyment of a context where homoerotic intimate relationships are at home. As she reasons when she is inadvertently observed bathing by a student, 'the gaffe was less important in these surroundings than it would have been elsewhere' (p. 28). Miss Pym's impressions of the head girl, the aptly named Beau, are similarly inflected with desire:

> A goddess with golden hair, a bright blue linen tunic, sea-blue eyes, and the most enviable pair of legs. Lucy always noticed other women's legs, her own being a sad disappointment to her. (p. 20)

Beau reciprocates this voyeuristic admiration with a kind of fetishistic focus on Lucy's 'very feminine, very thriftless, very feathery' shoes that lie discarded on the floor (p. 21). While Beau is Miss Pym's favourite, her time at the school is generally punctuated by moments of admiration for the women and girls around her, such as when she relates a blazon of the exotic Teresa's charms: '[e]verything about her was smooth and fluid: her voice, her drawling speech, her body, her movements, her dark hair, her honey-brown eyes' (pp. 32–3). However, she is also united with these collegial women by a common rejection of marriage in favour of a life of independent and professional industry. As she recounts, her one potential male partner, Alan, was ultimately rejected because she found his Adam's apple repulsive, and because, on reflection, she realised that as his 'cherished' wife she would have to display equal devotion and inevitably 'mend socks' (p. 68). Miss Pym's rather comedic, nightmarish vision of heterosexual domesticity (and one could add, of the male body) suggests that it is not only erotic attachment that links her to the women of Leys but a common goal and lifestyle choice. The schoolgirls plan to become teachers or even doctors, and like Miss Pym they will shun marriage in favour of professional satisfaction and female comradeship. Female bonds formed in collegial environments are thus portrayed as potentially fruitful, both in terms of securing a vocation and an alternative familial arrangement.

Tey, in a manner, does confirm the belief that schools and colleges breed lesbian bonds and that these passions can hold real dangers. It is the college principal's affection for her favourite student that leads to her unfair promotion and ultimately her death, and it is Beau's love and loyalty to her friend Innes that prompts her to orchestrate Rouse's accident. Furthermore, Miss Pym's loyalties to the girls force her to withhold evidence of a murder:

> she wished very heartily that the Deity had found another instrument. She had always hated responsibility; and a responsibility of this magnitude was something that she could not deal with at all. She wished that she could throw away the little rosette – toss it out of the window now and pretend that she had never seen it. [. . .] She was seriously considering keeping back evidence in a capital charge. Becoming an accessory after the fact. A criminal. [. . .] Of course she had no choice in the matter at all. Who disposed or did not dispose was no concern of hers. This was a matter of public inquiry, and she had a duty to do. A duty to civilisation, to the State, to herself. Her private emotions had nothing to do with it. However unequal and wrong-headed the Law might be, she could not suppress evidence. (pp. 215–17)

The 'duty' of which she speaks here is also textual because as a detective in a crime novel she has a narrative responsibility to 'dispose' of the criminal and so ensure the stability and containment of the wider community. Her loyalty to the women around her, her 'private emotions' and desires, and inherent suspicion of the authority of the law, eventually prevent her from disclosing the evidence that would convict Beau of murder, so making her complicit in the girl's criminality (p. 216). Instead she 'disposes' in the sense that she determines the course of events or decides, when she has no formal authority to, who should and should not be punished for their crimes. This is significant in several respects because like the lesbian criminal, Miss Pym challenges the authority of the law and becomes a woman thrown into a criminal life because of the relationships she has formed. Miss Pym (and, by implication, Tey) therefore refuses to play detective fiction's game or to abide by its codes. In the same way that she steps outside of the medical establishment (away from formal training and Freud's theories), she renounces the responsibilities and loyalties of the traditional and masculine detective. Miss Pym initially believes that Innes is responsible for Rouse's accident and agrees to let her mete out her own private penance (p. 221), but as she prepares to leave the college it becomes apparent that Innes has falsely confessed to protect the true criminal, Beau. Miss Pym responds to this disturbing development by resolving to give up her career as an expert of psychology and return to the anonymity of the city:

> She wondered why she had never noticed before how cold those blue eyes were. Brilliant and cold and shallow. [. . .] In London was her own, safe, nice, calm, collected existence, and in future she would be content with it. She would even give up lecturing on psychology. What did she know about psychology anyhow? [. . .] She could write a book about character as betrayed by facial characteristics. [. . .] Yes, she would write a book about face-reading. (pp. 233–5)

Thus, she has chosen twice over to protect the criminal because her judgement has been clouded by her attraction and loyalty to those women involved. Despite the fact that Miss Pym's reasoning is rather misguided, since her impressions of fellow women have been belied by their physical and facial attributes, what results from these experiences is a surprising renewal of her position as a professional woman of independent means and a reinforcement of her resolve against heterosexual domesticity.

Unlike Sayers, Tey does not employ the lesbian criminal for keenly ideological or precisely thought out ends. She exploits the connection between women's education and homoeroticism to provide an environment where desire between women can flourish, but to what extent these are discussions of lesbian identity and desire in their own right is questionable. However, both Tey and Sayers do have a keen sense of the lesbian criminal as the product of smoke and mirrors. *Miss Pym Disposes* makes a clear stand against medical discourses that might demonise the lesbian, and in the final pages we are reassured that Beau's nonchalant capacity for violence is not a symptom of her sexual proclivity but of her class difference and privileged lifestyle (p. 234). Similarly, in *Gaudy Night* the lesbian criminal is a mere spectre and scapegoat for the real societal villain. In some respects, then, the lesbian criminal in all of these texts is used to foster a debate that might be applied equally to both homosexual and heterosexual women in that it reflects on shifting gender and sexual roles. These authors recognise that the creation of the lesbian criminal as a demonised cultural figure is rooted in anxieties surrounding the widening scope of choices for women and the turn away from marriage towards profession and vocation. Sayers, in particular, deconstructs heterosexual normativity to reveal that the criminal truly does lie within 'us', or within what is deemed to be 'normal' and 'safe', and that the lesbian criminal is a psychological construction that distils fears and anxieties regarding socially 'deviant' modern women.

If the lesbian criminal is essentially a social renegade who must be controlled, so too is the female detective, although she might struggle with or be unable to fully acknowledge this as her role. As the object of pursuit the lesbian criminal represents all that the female detective could be in other circumstances or all that she is but cannot admit to. It is this mimetic relationship that holds the real potential for ideological resistance in these texts, since if the 'agent of social justice', as Chesterton has called the detective, is even unconsciously invested in lesbian criminality, then while the lesbian criminal might be expelled from the text, the 'lesbian' detective remains behind as a forceful presence.[39] If she is there to mete out 'social justice' and restore order, she does so ineffectively and in a way that does not always, if at all, serve the interests of mainstream society. Detective fiction is a genre with conservative tendencies because its narrative is, essentially, based on the battle between right and wrong, or good and evil, but these women writers use the trope of the lesbian criminal to destabilise and throw into question such moral and sexual certainties and dichotomies. It is therefore through the nuanced negotiation with ostensibly conservative generic conventions that these texts take on a deeper significance than they might at first claim to. By showing that there is more at stake in acts of murder and acts of detection than merely the transgression of the law or the catching of a criminal, the lesbian criminal is, to some extent, exonerated of her crimes.

Notes

1. Mitchell, *Speedy Death*, p. 58. Subsequent references are noted in parenthesis.
2. Mrs Bradley deems that there is 'something [v]ery queer about this house' (p. 37); Carstairs suggests that 'the fact that Mountjoy turned out to be a woman is the queerest thing about it' to which Mrs Bradley concurs '[y]es, that was queer' (p. 49); Carstairs later interprets the mysterious events to be 'a very queer business' to which Mrs Bradley echoes again 'very queer' (p. 84); Mrs Bradley further surmises that '[m]ad people do such queer things' (p. 106); Carstairs explains that the

drug used to kill Eleanor is 'a queer drug for a lay murderer to procure' (p. 160). For other instances of 'queer' see p. 16, p. 19, p. 37 and p. 65.
3. Although the term's common usage still indicated something that was strange, it would by this point have been in circulation as a marker of sexuality. Faderman posits that by the 1920s 'queer' was in use in America as a reference to male and female homosexuality. See Faderman, *Odd Girls*, p. 66. On this point see also McFadden, 'Queerness at Shrewsbury', p. 361.
4. Fuller, 'Introduction' to *Sleuth's Alchemy*, p. 8.
5. For details of Tey's life, see Aird, 'Josephine Tey, The Person', pp. 69–71.
6. Sayers, MS 'The Singular Case of the Three Spinsters'.
7. Kenney discusses the significance of the novel's original title and comes to a similar conclusion regarding this tripartite split, although she does not make an explicit connection between the spinster and lesbian. Kenney, 'Detecting a Novel Use for Spinsters', pp. 123–4. On these titles, see also Donoghue, *Inseparable*, p. 153. On the conflation of the terms lesbian and spinster see Doan, 'Introduction', in *Old Maids to Radical Spinsters*, pp. 4–5.
8. Sayers, *Unnatural Death*, p. 7. Subsequent references are noted in parenthesis.
9. On the topic of the spinster detective see, for instance, Kenney, 'Detecting a Novel Use for Spinsters' and Warthling Roberts, 'Amelia Butterworth: The Spinster Detective'.
10. Kenney, 'Detecting a Novel Use for Spinsters', p. 129.
11. Miss Climpson, much later, assigns this look of familiarity to her experience with a young man who gave her a cheque that could not be honoured (p. 248).
12. Donoghue, *Inseparable*, p. 153.
13. Garber, *Vested Interests*, p. 186.
14. Ellis, *Studies in the Psychology of Sex*, p. 201.
15. Smith, *Lesbian Panic*, p. 2.
16. This contradicts S. S. Van Dine's 'Twenty Rules for Writing Detective Stories' in which he specifically states that '[t]he detective himself, or one of the official investigators, should never turn out to be the culprit'. Van Dine, 'Twenty Rules', p. 190.
17. Kungl, *Creating the Fictional Female Detective*, p. 109.
18. Hennegan, 'Introduction' to Spain, *Poison for Teacher*, p. ix.
19. Other scholars discuss the academic crime novel, although their focus is often on more recent fiction. Marchino cites Sayers' *Gaudy Night* as the first novel to set crime in this way. See Marchino, 'The Female Sleuth in Academe', p. 94, as well as Leonardi, 'Murders Academic'.
20. Oram, 'Embittered, Sexless or Homosexual', p. 99.
21. Oram provides figures to demonstrate this trend: 'The censuses of 1921 and 1931 show that around 85 per cent of all women teachers (in all types of school) were unmarried. Separate figures for elementary schools confirm this pattern, while for secondary schools the figure was probably higher. The actual number of spinster teachers working in state schools was about 150,000 throughout the period.' See Oram, 'Embittered, Sexless or Homosexual', p. 100.
22. Oram does point out that this is a particularly extreme example, but it demonstrates that a connection was being made between the spinster teacher and the lesbian. Quote from the *Daily Herald*, 5 September 1935, Oram, 'Embittered, Sexless or Homosexual', pp. 105–6.
23. Fitzgerald, 'Persephone Come Back From the Dead'.
24. Ibid. p. 383.
25. Ibid. p. 383.
26. Ellis, *Studies in the Psychology of Sex*, p. 195.
27. Ibid. p. 196.

28. Iwan Bloch, another key figure in sexological studies, makes a similar connection: 'there is no doubt that in the "women's movement" – that is, in the movement directed towards the acquirement by women of all the attainments of masculine culture – homosexual women have played a notable part. Indeed according to one author, the "Women's Question" is mainly the question regarding the destiny of virile homosexual women'. Quoted in Jeffreys, *The Spinster and Her Enemies*, p. 108.
29. Vicinus, 'Distance and Desire', p. 618.
30. Sayers, *Gaudy Night*, pp. 77–8. Subsequent references are noted in parenthesis.
31. Brody provides an interesting discussion of the misreading of signs in *Gaudy Night* in 'The Haunting of *Gaudy Night*'.
32. McFadden, 'Queerness at Shrewsbury', p. 365.
33. Ibid. p. 356.
34. Ellis, 'The Criminal', p. 19.
35. McFadden, 'Queerness at Shrewsbury', p. 373.
36. Ibid. p. 372.
37. Morris, 'Arsenic and Blue Lace', p. 493.
38. Tey, *Miss Pym Disposes*, p. 14. Subsequent references are noted in parenthesis.
39. Chesterton, 'A Defence of Detective Stories', p. 6.

6

'LIZZIE BORDEN TOOK AN AXE': REPETITION AND HETEROSEXUAL CRIME IN GERTRUDE STEIN'S DETECTIVE FICTION

A 'Gertrude Stein' Detective Story

Introducing a collection of the best detective stories from 1928, the crime writer Ronald Knox commented that:

> You cannot write a Gertrude Stein detective story. For the detective story is a game between two players, the author of the one part and the reader of the other part. The reader has scored if, say, half way through the book he has laid his hand on the right person as the criminal, or has inferred the exact method by which the crime was perpetrated, in defiance of the author's mystifications. The author on his side counts the victory, if he succeeds in keeping the reader in a state of suspended judgment over the criminal, or complete mystification over the method, right up to the last chapter; and yet can show the reader how he ought to have solved the mystery with the light given him.[1]

That Knox should single out Stein as antithetical to detective fiction is intriguing, but presumably his reason can be found in the lack of transparency to, and unpredictable nature of, her writing. While her reader must indeed become an investigator and search for clues to decipher her meaning, unlike the plots of detective fiction she offers no easy or clear-cut answers. If detective fiction is a game of two halves, as Knox sees it, Stein's writing, in its complexity and contested meanings, might be deemed a one-sided, or unequal, pursuit.

Knox's ideals, and his belief that detective fiction should be governed by rules are typical of the Golden Age. S. S. Van Dine's 'Twenty Rules for Writing Detective Stories', originally published in 1928, set out similar instructions, including the claim that:

> A detective novel should contain no long descriptive passages, no literary dallying with side-issues, no subtly worked-out character analyses, no 'atmospheric' preoccupations. Such matters have no vital place in a record of crime and deduction. They hold up the action, and introduce issues irrelevant to the main purpose, which is to state a problem, analyze it, and bring it to a successful conclusion.[2]

In this sense, Golden Age detective fiction makes no claim to newness or innovation but rather determines its success by how well it follows the rules and meets the reader's expectations. And like Knox, Van Dine sets up the 'literary', or perhaps modernist, work as anathema to detective stories. As Marcus states, detective fiction has often been thought of as a 'reaction against modernist narrative', in part because '[w]hile high literature represented a world threatening to reason, detective fiction reassures through its rationalism'.[3] No doubt, then, that in making his comment Knox also rails against Stein's writing as paradigmatic of the esoteric and inaccessible avant-garde, the supposed counterpart to the body of popular culture to which detective fiction belongs. His comments are also symptomatic of the belief that the high and low cannot mix, that the experimental cannot be generic, nor the generic experimental, although unusually his is a voice speaking in favour of the formulaic, rather than the avant-garde, text.

Whether Stein was aware of the inadvertent challenge posed by Knox in 1929 remains to be seen. Nevertheless, a few years later her novella *Blood on the Dining-Room Floor* (written in 1933 and published in 1948) and her two short pieces 'Is Dead' and 'A Water-fall and a Piano' (both written in 1933 but published in 1936 and 1937 respectively), set about proving that a detective story conducted in a 'Stein' fashion is indeed possible.[4] But Stein's love of detective fiction and interest in crime began much earlier than this, as the somewhat impenetrable 'Subject-Cases: The Background of a Detective Story', written in 1923, suggests.[5] And as an avid reader of detective novels (she particularly admired the work of Dashiell Hammett and Edgar Wallace) her appetite was voracious:[6]

> if you want to read one a day well not one a day but one every other day, say three a week and if you are willing to read over and over a lot of them even then there are not enough to go around. ('Why I Like Detective Stories', p. 148)

Stein's comments speak of the fact that detective fiction is contingent upon readerly pleasure for its success and that this is a form of literature written for quick and eager consumption. But her particular enjoyment of detective fiction, what exactly she found 'soothing', stemmed from the genre's specific narrative structure ('Why I Like Detective Stories', p. 147). Opening as it often does with a crime, the detective story quickly turns its focus to investigation, which leaves you 'free to enjoy yourself', as Stein saw it ('Why I Like Detective Stories', p. 147). For Stein, this marks the distinction between 'real' crime and the crime story because the former is, naturally, concerned with the deed or crime itself, while the latter is focused on the process of detection. Yet in both real and textual life, Stein favours the unsolved variety of crime, as she makes evident in the essay 'American Crimes and How They Matter' when she states that '[e]verybody remembers a crime when nobody finds out anything about who did it and particularly where the person mixed up with it goes on living'.[7] Stein's professed enjoyment of detective fiction is therefore somewhat paradoxical in its contradiction of the genre's conventions. She complains that in 'crime stories knowing the answer spoils it. [. . .T]he answer is a let down from the interest', but given that most crime stories, and the characters within them, endeavour to discover and reveal this very answer, Stein's textual pleasure seems bound to be frustrated every time.[8] In a similarly contrary fashion, she laments the repetitive nature of the form, its return to the selfsame premise, and uniform narrative structure:

> detective fiction [. . .] progresses by a continuous beginning and ending and once more therefore destroys itself into not existing. It is too bad because it might have been yes it might have been something but always beginning and ending is as destructive to existing as never beginning and ending. (*Narration*, p. 44)

Stein's comments are indicative of the thought she gave to the patterns of detective fiction, as well as the fact that in her own experiments she manipulates these very conventions to her own ends. With no detective and very little overt detection, no explicit crimes, no answers given or punishment doled out, Stein discards many of the traditions to which we are accustomed. 'They had a country house. A house in the country is not the same as a country house' (p. 1), *Blood on the Dining-Room Floor* begins by telling us, and Stein ensures that the reader is absorbing the vital information by explaining 'Has everybody got it straight. So far we have two families and besides a country house. We have three times crime' (p. 1 and p. 17). The epigraph opening 'A Water-fall and a Piano' even establishes Stein's own idiosyncratic rules for the genre:

> There are so many ways in which there is no crime.
> A goat comes into this story too.
> There is always coincidence in crime.[9]

In one sense, then, Stein clearly flouts, or even mocks, more conventional renderings of the form as well as those writers who zealously promoted its idealist principles, and she instead offers her own revised generic paradigm.

What critical work there is on Stein's detective fiction has tended to treat *Blood on the Dining-Room Floor* as an enquiry into creativity and a response to the writer's block she experienced after the unprecedented success of *The Autobiography of Alice B. Toklas*, which again promotes the idea that a 'Gertrude Stein detective story' is impossible. Franziska Gygax, for instance, reads *Blood on the Dining-Room Floor* as 'more about the mystery of writing than about the mystery of crime(s), [although] crime and death occur'.[10] Certainly, Stein was concerned with questions of creativity and identity during this period of her life, as we see in *Everybody's Autobiography* (1937) when she recalls the summer of 1933:

> All this time I did no writing. I had written and was writing nothing. Nothing inside me needed to be written. [. . .] I began to worry about identity. I had always been I because I had words that had to be written inside me and now any word I had inside could be spoken it did not need to be written. I am I because my little dog knows me. But was I I when I had no written word inside me.[11]

Her choice of a heavily encoded and formulaic genre fiction could, on the one hand, be seen as a form of aesthetic therapy in the sense that Stein escapes her creative stagnancy by learning to write once again with the aid of a formula. Certainly, the artistic inhibition that she experienced was also largely tied up with a fresh sense of her work as a commodity and herself as pandering to the reading public. Her newly found fame provoked questions surrounding her identity as a writer: would she now be writing for others as opposed to herself; would this affect the nature or quality of her writing; would the publicity of being 'Gertrude Stein' the personality alter Gertrude Stein the artist and self-proclaimed genius? This is the view put forward by Janet Malcolm's biographical study in which she suggests that Stein 'felt she had to atone for [. . .] the crisp linear narrative of *The Autobiography of Alice B. Toklas*, which she had adopted merely in order to woo the conventional reading public'.[12] Malcolm goes on to suggest that such atonement was achieved when Stein resumed her enigmatic style with *Everybody's Autobiography*.[13] One could reason, then, that Stein's detective fiction was a more immediate response to this mainstream triumph. If Stein believed that she had somehow compromised her modernist aesthetic with *The Autobiography of Alice B. Toklas*, *Blood on the Dining-Room Floor* could be seen as Stein shamefacedly labelling herself as a generic, mainstream, and commercially motivated author – the supposed antithesis of the literary and experimental modernist. As she anxiously states in *Everybody's Autobiography*, 'somehow if my writing was worth money then it was not what it had been' (p. 67).

However, to read Stein's detective pieces as serving a grander aesthetic purpose – as a route to trace her way back to the avant-garde – rather than as experiments with the form for their own sake, is to be complicit with the cultural dichotomisation that I discussed in the Introduction, and this approach to Stein tends to ignore what Marcus terms the 'relationship of reciprocity between popular and "metaphysical" detective stories', or the bleeding between the high and the low.[14] It also neglects the importance of the actual crimes and overlooks Stein's obsessive return, across her corpus, to the series of suspicious events that inspired this detective fiction. It was during the summer of 1933, which Stein and Alice B. Toklas spent in their country house in the French village Bilignin, that the women became embroiled in a series of real-life crimes and mysterious events. Along with a number of problems with troublesome servants and seemingly motiveless acts of vandalism to their property, two women with whom Stein was familiar were found dead. Mme Pernollet, who ran a local hotel with her husband, fell from a window (or so it was assumed), while an English woman living with Stein's neighbour, Mme Caesar, was found shot, or as it was suggested, having shot herself, twice in the head. The deaths, although highly suspicious, were quickly dismissed by the villagers and the authorities as either accidents or suicides.[15] Stein's work is littered with references to these mysterious events, but their most substantial narration takes place in the three pieces of detective fiction and *Everybody's Autobiography*. How exactly these real-life events form the narrative of the detective pieces is hard to say since there is no coherent plot, as such, to any of them. A cross-textual investigation becomes necessary, then, to read meaning into the slippages and shifts of each rendering. In this respect, Stein rails against what she perceived to be the continuous 'beginning' and 'ending' endemic to detective fiction and transforms the contained detective story into a regenerative, self-sustaining investigative process. She maintains the pleasure of the genre, which spills out from each text and into another telling, as we are forced to seek answers elsewhere in her corpus. The critical interest in Stein's use of repetition has tended to concentrate on its linguistic significance, but in these texts we see a repetition that owes a debt to its parent genre, detective fiction, and its conventions. Stein's return to the same premise or story, the woman's death, allows her to mourn that loss and others like it. With this in mind, I continue my discussion of the lesbian criminal by highlighting Stein's invocation of the alleged murderess Lizzie Borden. *Blood on the Dining-Room Floor* is haunted by the presence of a figure named 'Lizzie', a reader or listener who Stein appeals to for attention and empathy and who oversees the detective proceedings. Scholarly work has paid little attention to this 'Lizzie', seeing her, as Brooks Landon does, as merely 'a personified or dramatized audience' who probably received her name from Toklas.[16] But it seems likely that, as John Herbert Gill suggests, there is a connection between this fictional 'Lizzie' and the infamous Lizzie Borden, the woman at the centre of the Fall River murder case.[17] If this is the case, Stein's invocation of Borden is a freighted narrative act that should not be overlooked. Given her association with rebellion against familial hegemony (she was accused of murdering her parents) and rumoured passion for women, we might think of her in the same vein as we do the fictional Mary Whitaker and Eleanor Bing, as a lesbian criminal. But rather than fear or demonise her, Stein reveres Borden and uses her to articulate a passionate critique of heterosexual familial dynamics.

The Causes Which Were Almost a Poem

On 4 August 1892, Borden found the bodies of her father and stepmother, Andrew and Abby, hacked to beyond recognition with an axe. Evidence pointed towards her involvement: a local pharmacy reported that she had tried to buy prussic acid the day before the murders; a family friend staying with Borden claimed to have seen her burning a dress supposedly stained by paint; and Borden's version of the events and her whereabouts that day were confused. Arguably, her potential motive was not insignificant given that the relationship between Borden and her stepmother had been strained for some time and bad feeling had built up amongst the family over the financial support given to Abby Borden's sisters. Borden also appeared to have a problematic relationship with her frugal and domineering father and it is often noted in accounts of the murders that Andrew Borden had killed a flock of pigeons for which his daughter had been caring.[18] Tried but acquitted for the killings the following year, Borden's defence was successful, recent commentators have suggested, partly because it played upon common assumptions about gender identity. Borden was prone to tears and fainting fits during the trial, and this behaviour encouraged the belief that such a conventionally feminine woman, in particular of her class, was incapable of committing brutal acts of patricide and matricide.[19] Although Borden would never escape her association with the crime, her parents' deaths did in fact afford her independence, wealth and freedom.[20]

Borden and the Fall River murders have held a firm place in the American cultural imagination ever since and the bare facts have merged with myth to create various theories of the events. It has been speculated, for instance, that Borden had suffered sexual abuse at the hands of her father; that Andrew Borden was murdered by a vengeful, illegitimate son; and that the mistreated maid of the house, Bridget Sullivan, lashed out against her oppressive employers. The legend of Borden has therefore achieved cult status, and she has been appropriated in culturally diverse ways (rhymes such as the one referenced in the title to this chapter, as well as songs, novels, societies, plays, opera etc.), which have sometimes paid attention to her sexual identity. While there is no reliable evidence of Borden's erotic or romantic relationships with women, it has been rumoured that she may have been involved with the actress Nance O'Neil and that this perhaps led to a rift with her sister.[21] Other studies and creative interpretations of Borden have also put forward this theory, although its origin is unclear. Victoria Lincoln's study, based on her experiences growing up in Fall River and living alongside Borden after the murders, recalls that:

> There were a handful of dirty-minded old puritans in Fall River who saw Lizzie's association with Nance as a blatantly flaunted homosexual affair; they were the ones who whispered, and a few ancient survivors still do. I think that they were wrong – in any overt sense, at least. Young, Lizzie had crushes on school teachers that she talked about freely; her closer friendships had always been slightly overcharged and demanding; she was sentimental, and sexually immature. But I doubt that she was capable of any kind of love affair. I see the Nance business only as another instance of the same nature that led Lizzie to bury her pets in the local pet cemetery around a central monument that bore the tender inscription *Sleeping Awhile* – in other words, as the sort of sentimentality to which my mother used to refer mildly as 'sort of sickening.'[22]

While this is obviously problematic evidence – Lincoln's assertions are merely conjecture and the association which she makes between lesbianism and arrested mental development renders her opinion highly suspect – her comment is useful as an indication that Borden was believed to have been engaged in relationships with women. Ann Jones situates Borden in a similar fashion:

> just after World War II, when women liberated by wartime jobs and independence were shoved back into the sculleries and bedrooms of America, antifeminists [. . . pried] Lizzie Borden free of her own history and resurrect[ed] her as a 'feminist vigilante,' a lesbian marching out of the kitchen with a bloody ax[23]

Precisely when Borden becomes understood in these sexualised terms it is not possible to say, although Lincoln would have us believe that it was during her lifetime and therefore before the writing of Stein's detective fiction. Rumours and suspicions about Borden's sexuality, and the connection (made after the Second World War if not, most likely, earlier) between her relationships with women and capacity for violence, are important because they suggest that she may have been understood or available to Stein on these terms, that is essentially as a lesbian criminal.[24]

Certainly, Stein was intrigued by the Borden case, perhaps particularly so because, as Gill points out, the murders took place only a year after her own father's death.[25] Indeed, as Souhami mentions in her biographical study of Stein, the writer had a complicated and remote relationship with her own parents.[26] Borden's case is considered in more depth by Stein in 'American Crimes and How They Matter':

> I know I was perfectly astonished to know that even the present generation knew the name of Lizzie Borden and that she had gone on living. [... S]he held back nothing she never lied but she never told anybody anything, that is integrity and is very American. The whole case was so American, the orchard was American the surrounding family was American the person who had the pig farm and had something to say but never said anything, it was all so American, the causes which were there which were almost a poem and at the same time filled with evil meaning (p. 103)

Although Stein confuses the Fall River murder case with another here, the admiration and empathy in this passage are palpable, and although she assumes that Borden is guilty, she deems her behaviour laudable and almost patriotic. We can only guess at Borden's 'causes', and more so at Stein's meaning when she refers to them as 'poetic', since the latter is not easy to define when deployed by as vanguard a poet as Stein, but we might assume that Borden's motivation is the rebellion against patriarchal (and matriarchal) familial oppression and the struggle for the female body to survive, and for Stein it is this that poses as a lyrical and rarefied cause. Certainly, in *Blood on the Dining-Room Floor* there does seem to be certain sympathy with those who endeavour to liberate themselves from domineering, abusive or parasitical parents. Alexander, a rather suspicious character implicated in many of the crimes, 'got rid of the father', Stein tells us, with the help of a wealthy old woman:

> The father was using up everything and was getting fatter and the eight of them with a very bony mother who wore a wig, bowed and ran hither and thither and were not getting but were thinner. (p. 19)

As Stein later confides, '[a]nybody could be just as angry as pleased about Alexander' (p. 43).

Borden's presence, and by implication her crimes, constantly bubble through *Blood on the Dining-Room Floor*, often threatening to become unruly and dangerous. While this spectre is denied an actual voice in the piece, Stein does engage in dialogue with her and responds to questions that 'Lizzie' puts forward but to which we are not privy. This means that Stein, as detective, creates a sense of affinity with the lesbian criminal – the latter 'understands' how things can come to murder and how the gender and sexual politics of a family, a community or society can lead to violence and crime. At one point, a woman named 'Edith' joins this disembodied community and Stein asks them both 'do you do you really understand' (p. 72). Gill believes that this refers to the poet Edith Sitwell, who Stein knew well, and whose father was reportedly physically and psychologically abusive.[27] 'Lizzie' and 'Edith', then, are allied as women who understand how murder and crime can come to be both inflicted upon and by the female body. Stein's invocation of Borden as a spectre-like totem overseeing her detective fiction implies that the women of this text are victims of comparable familial patterns and abuses. Even Stein's formulaic, and somewhat tongue-in-cheek, title *Blood on the Dining-Room Floor* indicates that the crimes within this text are those of a domestic nature.[28] Despite the disparity between the nineteenth-century American murderess and the inhabitants of this French village, Stein suggests that these crimes are in some way related, for they are all born of heterosexual and conventional familial ideology. Thus, *Blood on the Dining-Room Floor* operates as Stein's rendering of Borden's, and by extension the French women's, 'causes'.

The foremost crime that occurs in *Blood on the Dining-Room Floor* is the death of Mme Pernollet. We are told that '[s]he fell upon the pavement of cement in the court and broke her back but did not die nor did she know why. In five days she was dead' (p. 5). As a poor woman married to a wealthy hotelier, Mme Pernollet's life is one of monotonous industry, childbearing and dutiful service to the family business:

> She would be occupied with every little thing that she ever saw. She would know about clean linen, about peaches and little cakes, as few as possible of each, and yet always enough. [. . .] She was always very nearly perfect when she stood. She never sat. [. . .] Every day and every day she had to see that everything came out from where it was put away and that everything again was put away. [. . .]
> He was busy every day. (p. 7, p. 8 and p. 10)

Harriet Scott Chessman reads the repetition that distinguishes her life as a positive and feminine force, a 'domestic movement, which has seemed to fill the hotel with a kind of sensual and mutual dance'.[29] But *Everybody's Autobiography* offers us a different perspective:

> Once in a while she [Mme Pernollet] said to us, well she did not say it, but once in a while she did say it as if it was, not the work, but something was overwhelming, not the not going out, that was not overwhelming not her children, she had three boys and a little girl, well anyway they did go on as they always had done. (p. 40)

Although the bond is unspoken, Stein sympathises with Mme Pernollet and portrays her not as a woman who relishes her role in her home's 'domestic movement' but rather as someone who is overwhelmed by unhappiness and crushed by domestic burden. Her routine and pointless rearrangement of household objects (compared to her husband's status as simply 'busy') characterises Mme Pernollet as more of an automaton than a dancer, unable to pinpoint the reason for her unhappiness.

Her life continues in this way until her husband's affair with a woman working in the hotel is discovered. On discovery of this relationship, Mme Pernollet can only falteringly continue with her daily routine:

> She tried and once when she tried, do you remember once when she tried she cried. She could not try and not cry. She could smile and take things in and take things out. But if she were to try she would be obliged to cry. (*Blood on the Dining-Room Floor*, p. 11)

This recollection of her distress suggests where Stein's sympathies lie, as well as, ultimately, attributing guilt for the woman's death. As Stein tells us, '[n]ow you see what there is to see' or, rather, how Mme Pernollet comes to be dead (*Blood on the Dining-Room Floor*, p. 11). Numerous possibilities are hinted at, some relatively innocuous, others more menacing. It is possible that she chose to end her life, or that, as one local suggests, she had been sleepwalking and fell. Stein provokes the reader to self-consciously take the part of detective by making the necessary investigative questions explicit: 'Had she walked in her sleep. Who had walked in her sleep. Where did she walk. And whose was it that she walked. Whose was it.'[30] Here, the emphasis seems to be on foul play and the possibility that someone else was indeed involved in that final walk. Numerous possible motivations for her murder emerge: her husband is eager to have a new wife and 'did not say he did not want another even if she tried and died' (p. 5); his mistress is keen to exert her control; and it is the mistress's brother, Alexander, who rather suspiciously puts forward the unlikely explanation of sleepwalking (p. 18). Yet it is the absence of grief and the collusion to forget the dead woman and return to life, and business, as usual that affect Stein most deeply:

> It was wonderful the way they covered it up and went on. [. . .] Do you see how the whole place was ready, not for anybody to be dead but for anybody not to be interested in anything that was said. (*Blood on the Dining-Room Floor*, p. 17 and p. 36)

Stein describes the funeral service in more detail in *Everybody's Autobiography*:

> I went to the church, and in the French way went up to shake hands with the husband and the father and the two sons and the hotel keeper who had been a very little fat man became a very thin one and [. . .] all his sons came to be with him in the hotel business and he went out from time to time and whether they will pay for the new piece of hotel or not is not anybody's business. (p. 40)

The daughter is notably absent or excluded from the service, perhaps on account of her age, and Stein pays her condolences to what feels like a procession, or perhaps even divine trinity, of men. This is now a firmly homosocial family with matters of business at the forefront of their minds. Having given birth to a further generation of hotelkeepers, Mme Pernollet is evidently expendable.

The story of this woman's demise is retold in various pieces by Stein, but critical approaches to her experimental detective fiction underplay this textual recycling. She explains her need to retell the story in *Everybody's Autobiography*:

> It was a funny thing that summer so many things happened and they had nothing to do with me or writing. I have so often wanted to make a story of them a detective story of everything happening that summer and here I am trying to do it again. I have never wanted to write about any other summer, because every other summer was a natural one for me to be living, but that summer that first summer after the Autobiography was not a natural summer and so it is a thing to be written. Once more and yet again. It is funny about how often I have tried to tell the story of that summer, I have tried to tell it again and again. (p. 38)

The events of that summer were as important, and as haunting, for Stein as her unprecedented aesthetic crisis, and so she compulsively returns to and repeats her rendering of the narrative '[o]nce more and yet again'. But Stein did not believe in repetition, at least not in terms of her own work, as she explains in 'How Writing is Written':

> there is no such thing as repetition. [. . .] Everybody is telling the story in the same way. But if you listen carefully, you will see that not all the story is the same. There is always a slight variation. Somebody comes in and you tell the story over again. Every time you tell the story it is told slightly differently. [. . .] If I had repeated, nobody would listen. Nobody could be in the room with a person who said the same thing over and over and over. [. . .] I conceived the idea of building this thing up. It was all based upon this thing of everybody's slightly building this thing up.[31]

What Stein addresses here is the meaning of her creative circuitousness. The reader may feel, at times, as if they are trapped with someone who says the 'same thing over and over', suffocated by cyclical narrative, reproduced and truncated sentences, but Stein's repetition builds meaning gradually and slightly, layering and adjusting understanding with each new utterance. Her urge to tell, and then tell again, the story of that summer can be understood in much the same way, and here Stein directs us towards the appropriate interpretative approach. Each new rendition contains slight slippages or shifts, so forcing the reader into a prolonged detective process, rather than a single act, thus building across time an understanding of these crimes. Stein's theory and practice of repetition is thus remarkable in its resemblance to the narrative structures of detective fiction, in that it employs the selfsame process of layering knowledge and building a case. And the reader, consuming the same formula time and again with each novel, must read meaning into the slight shifts and differences of plot.

Stein's choice of genre, then, suddenly takes on new weight and import. In her hands, detective fiction, with its corpse conventionally situated at the beginning of the narrative, evolves into a generic ritual of bereavement and a vehicle to mourn the loss of a woman over time. Stein believed that she had excised the corpse from her detective fiction ('Why I Like Detective Stories', p. 148) but, at the same time, by repeating this story Stein never allows her reader (or herself) to forget the cold, victimised body of the housewife. In this respect, she challenges and subverts the usual conventions of this generic form, and in particular of the Golden Age, which work towards the re-establishment of order through the disposal of the corpse and the punishment/death of the criminal. Stein refuses to do either of these things in that the criminal is not identified or punished (in part because those responsible for this woman's death are many) and Mme Pernollet, far from forgotten, is exhumed time and time again. Refusing the containment typical to the genre, Stein forces an open and endless detective process to reinstate the significance of the female body. If, as Miriam Brody has stated, '[d]etective fiction is prototypically semiotic' and relies upon the detective's eventually correct and final interpretation of a series of signs, Stein refuses to provide any definitive reading, meaning that the detective story and its accompanying signs are never shut down.[32]

Stein's use of genre fiction in this way is arguably born from a concern with the marginal, and in particular female, body. In 'American Crimes and How They Matter', she recalls accompanying a Chicago police car on patrol, during which the policeman tells her about the recent death of a 'negro' in the area:

> he was an old man he had no money he had no family, no story, [. . .] he was peaceable he was just nothing and then one night quite early just on the street corner he was shot down dead, nobody saw it, nobody heard anything, nobody is interested, nobody will find out anything about it because it is of no importance to anybody. (p. 101)

As a black man at this time, his death is perceived as unimportant, and his victimisation meets with only indifference. Stein's earlier fiction *Three Lives* (1909) is similarly concerned for the vulnerable and victimised body, and its three stories, 'The Good Anna', 'Melanctha' and 'The Gentle Lena', each reveal that the conventional narrative of self-sacrifice, passivity and sexual morality damage and ultimately kill each of these women. As wives, mothers and lovers, the women after who these stories are named sacrifice their bodies to concepts of feminine goodness and heterosexual propriety. Notably, upon Lena's death during childbirth, her husband finds himself 'very happy, very gentle, very quiet, very well content alone with his three children'.[33] The resemblance between this scene and the portrait of M. Pernollet at his wife's funeral is significant. As Stein cuttingly remarks in *Everybody's Autobiography*: 'It is funny the two things most men are proudest of is the thing that any man can do and doing does in the same way, that is being drunk and being the father of their son' (p. 52). Mme Pernollet and Lena, amongst other women in Stein's collection, are expendable, used up and discarded once they have served their purpose.

Malcolm's biographical study of Stein examines the monolithic *The Making of Americans* and reads the treatment of the mother Fanny Hersland as an expression of Stein's suppressed grief for the loss of own mother years ago:

> In Stein's oblique telling of her story of unacceptable loss, she achieves an extraordinary level of expressiveness. The refrain about the mother's unimportance has the effect, of course, of implying the opposite. Stein breaks through the hard shell of her child's self-protectiveness, and allows herself to mourn her mother.[34]

Malcolm quotes one particular passage from *The Making of Americans* that bears further scrutiny:

> [Fanny Hersland] was lost among them and mostly they forgot about her, now she died away among them and they never thought about her, sometimes they would be good to her, mostly for them she had no existence in her and then she died away and the gentle scared little woman was all that they ever after remembered of her.[35]

Fanny Hersland, then, barely exists even when alive and is only remembered in vague terms when she is gone.[36] Versions of Fanny Hersland – women nonplussed by their existence, bled dry by service to the family, but barely acknowledged or remembered – exist throughout Stein's writing. The women that inhabit Stein's detective fiction, and in particular Mme Pernollet, might be seen as surrogate mother figures for Stein, and the generic experiment as a working through of the loss she never acknowledged or grieved for. The focus on the victim of crime – the wife and mother – allows for a desire to enact the trauma and loss associated with the mother's death, bringing to the fore repressed psychical material. Freud's understanding of mourning as a long and drawn out experience and a battle between reality and the ego is useful here:

> Reality-testing has shown that the loved object no longer exists, and it proceeds to demand that all libido shall be withdrawn from its attachments to that object. [...] Reality's orders] are carried out bit by bit, at great expense of time and cathectic energy, and in the meantime the existence of the lost object is psychically prolonged.[37]

Stein's circuitous detective process doubles as psychical compulsion. By recycling the story again and again through the use of generic repetition, Stein mourns the loss of the mother and the mother surrogate 'bit by bit', refusing to withdraw attachment.

But Mme Pernollet is not the only casualty of heteronormativity in *Blood on the Dining-Room Floor*. Three young women – Helen, Mabel and a third who remains unnamed – fall prey to crimes of a sort. Two of the women are married to the sons of a local elderly woman:

> The eldest one was married to some one who was not able to live continuously in a city as she had an absolute need for a private life. In between she stayed with her own mother, her own father and her own aunt. She might have married a rich man if her father had not lost his money in South America [. . .]
>
> The second son was a rich man as long as it was rich to have a lot of money in everything, and then and alas and all of a sudden it was no longer rich, not any longer rich to have money, in everything. He had married a beautiful and young little girl and her name was Mabel. Mabel with her face against the pane looking out upon the rain. [. . .] But Mabel who had loved her old husband who was deaf and wore a monocle now that everything was not the same did not love him any more. If she could she would have gone to the bad. (p. 23)

Both of these wives long for something other than their lot – a private or independent life, a life of sexual satisfaction, a life in the 'bad'. Stein sympathises with these married women and later explains how each is drawn into an affair with Alexander, the local gardener who is implicated in the death of Mme Pernollet. The rumours about Alexander's extra-marital adventures (circulated by the fearsome mother-in-law) provide him with a 'great reputation' while his married lovers are shamed by the talk, 'about which they do cry' (p. 24). Again, Stein asks us to consider what crimes have been committed: 'It makes no difference how often it is said that everybody can go to bed. [. . .] Can you see crime. No not I' (p. 40). Stein can see no crime in sexual pleasure, but these women are condemned by society while Alexander is lauded for his prowess. Stein reinforces this point with her references to a fairytale-like Garden of Eden, since Alexander's family 'lived in a garden and they lived off the garden' (p. 14). Alexander, as Adam, represents Edenic sexual pleasure, but the allusion is also indicative of the gendered blame assigned to original sin and at work in this scenario.

Strange Women

However, Alexander's control does not extend to all of the women in the locale and it is this that leads to the next series of sexualised crimes, only marginally dealt with, but intriguing nonetheless. Stein informs the reader that:

> A goat comes into this story too. Somewhere some one had two beautiful dogs that were big. One of them was a male and the other was a female, they were to have puppies, their owner, a woman, wealthy and careful too, always wore carpenter's trousers and carpenter's shirts and loved to work. She said when the puppies came there would be nine and they would need more milk than their mother had. [. . .] So she said she would buy a goat. (*Blood on the Dining-Room Floor*, p. 35)

Having paid for the goat, Alexander unexplainably refuses to deliver the animal to the woman (p. 36). This incident, and the above passage, are remarkable for several reasons, but most of all for their suggestion of alternative forms of domesticity. From the details in *Everybody's Autobiography* we can identify this woman as Mme Caesar, a neighbour of Stein's, who lived with Mme Steiner and later an unnamed Englishwoman (p. 63). Stein's pointed clues in the above passage – the masculine attire and love of work – imply that there is more to Mme Caesar than meets the eye. Her use of goat's milk for the puppies – a kind of cross-species wet nursing that importantly aims to take the burden off the 'mother' – also maps the animal onto the human to suggest that these women defy the 'natural' or conventional order to construct alternative forms of familial arrangement for themselves. In *Everybody's Autobiography*, Mme Caesar is depicted as a woman beyond Alexander's powers of manipulation:

> Well Madame Caesar had not really known very intimately the man who was very important to everybody and who was a sort of agent and gardener for everybody. He now says he has always known her father. That probably is not so, that her father had been a great influence in his life that too is probably not so. (*Everybody's Autobiography*, p. 64)

She declines to know him 'intimately', or sexually, and is impervious to claims of familial allegiance. Stein summarises the dynamic of Alexander's relationships with the local women quite logically: 'He asked and they went with him, strange if they had not been with him, strange women.' (*Blood on the Dining-Room Floor*, p. 69). Stein includes herself amongst these odd women, for she is also determined that 'he will not be intimate not with all of them particularly not with the subject of servants' (*Blood on the Dining-Room Floor*, p. 58). Considering that Stein was preoccupied with unruly servants that summer, it is likely that she refers to herself here and her frustration of Alexander's attempts to gain her confidence. The mystery of the goat is suddenly clarified: Alexander's act is both a refusal to co-operate with women who will not respond to his advances, as well as a stand against those who are sexually unconventional.

Initially these peripheral events might seem to indicate that these 'strange' women, abstract from the heterosexual system and having formed their own communities, are sheltered from crime, but the death of the Englishwoman, referred to only elliptically in *Blood on the Dining-Room Floor*, insists that nobody is safe:

> How often could I add so many cases to as many more. But she said if I add will anybody hover as they do hover from cover to cover [...]
> Not as strange as in case that there too somebody was killed only he did not die. [...] If they are all secretly that is secret in shooting and one is shot, they will not die not officially of course not. (*Blood on the Dining-Room Floor*, pp. 53–4)

Stein, or perhaps, more accurately, the 'she' that is most likely Toklas, is conscious of the demands of detective fiction and its reliance on the appetite of the reader – an additional crime story might satiate that hunger all too quickly so defusing the desire to 'hover from cover to cover'. This brief reference to the second death that summer in Bilignin where 'they are all secretly that is secret in shooting' suggests a calculated collusion to dispose of the Englishwoman. This secondary crime story becomes interesting, then, through its absence in *Blood on the Dining-Room Floor*, which forces the reader to look elsewhere to solve this mystery. Turning to Stein's 1936 piece 'A Waterfall and a Piano', it is apparent that the Englishwoman's sexuality played a part in her demise:

> There are many places where every one is married even in the country, some of them are not. Think of it even in the country some of them are not.
> The Englishwoman was not. She was not married. The French women either had been or were going to be, but the Englishwoman never had been nor was going to be. (p. 32)

The Englishwoman rejects the institution of marriage and comes to an alternative domestic arrangement with Mme Caesar and Mme Steiner:

> Madame Caesar and Madame Steiner lived there together and Madame Steiner worried about her. [...] Madame Steiner managed to worry about her and little by little the Englishwoman came to stay there and she worried about her too. (*Everybody's Autobiography*, p. 63)

What it actually means to 'worry' about Mme Caesar, and whether Stein intends for this to encode another erotic or loving act, is an important point, but certainly this triadic relationship is romantic and the domestic arrangements by which they live are depicted as legitimate.

Stein, however, has her suspicions about Mme Caesar and when she learns that the Englishwoman has given all of her money to her lover, this 'made me at that time not want to see Madame Caesar again, [...] I do get frightened about it again and again' (*Everybody's Autobiography*, p. 63). Stein seems to worry that she, and her wealth, might also be vulnerable to the French woman's attentions. Shortly after the Englishwoman returns from a holiday she is found dead ('A Water-fall and a Piano', p. 32), and Stein is again appalled by the general nonchalance and all-too-ready willingness to leave this death unexplained:

> The police disturbed her they had no business to, the protestant pastor buried her he had no business to, because nobody had been told what had happened to her. ('A Water-fall and a Piano', p. 32)

In much the same manner that Alexander dismissed Mme Pernollet's death as an accident, a nameless 'officer' claims that it is possible to shoot oneself in the head twice, allowing for a verdict of suicide ('A Water-fall and a Piano', p. 32). Again, a suspicious and peripheral masculine figure puts forward a theory of female self-harm. By withholding evidence about this crime from the reader of *Blood on the Dining-Room Floor*, Stein breaks the rules of popular, mainstream detective fiction. 'A Water-fall and a Piano' hints at Mme Caesar's involvement in the Englishwoman's death, in that after this event her 'character' is 'changed and remained changed ever after' (p. 32). The Englishwoman is also swiftly replaced by an American 'but she has not come to be dead', suggesting the danger involved in a liaison with Mme Caesar (p. 32). *Everybody's Autobiography* also mentions that the Englishwoman financially supports her lover and that both she and Mme Steiner are unofficially employed as workers on her farm (*Everybody's Autobiography*, p. 63), so commenting further on the potentially exploitative nature of the dynamic between Mme Caesar and the women surrounding her. The odd scene at Mme Caesar's house immediately after the death – at which Stein, an American woman, a local man who installs electric heaters, his wife and her mother are present – is also omitted from 'A Water-fall and a Piano' but included in *Everybody's Autobiography* (p. 65). Curiously, Stein also tells us that 'in a little while although she [Mme Caesar] was always there nobody was there with her that is to say Madame Steiner never was there any more and the wife of the electric installer was' (*Everybody's Autobiography*, p. 66). Again, some kind of collusion seems hinted at here and implies the ease with which one exploited lover can be replaced by another. In light of this, Mme Caesar is transformed into a somewhat threatening figure, and the American woman is arguably in great danger of one day becoming as defunct as her predecessor. That Stein decides to obscure information, or at least to downplay what seems to be an obvious implication of guilt on Mme Caesar's part, works to more heavily implicate heterosexuality in this series of crimes. It is when faced with this material that a potentially neat interpretation of Stein's detective fiction breaks down. Although she might try to obscure the connection between lesbian criminality and violence in *Blood on the Dining-Room Floor*, it is evident that all forms of domesticity hold the potential for danger and that the female body can be used up, discarded and replaced under any sexual scheme.

To return once more to Knox's assertion that '[y]ou cannot write a Gertrude Stein detective story', it is evident that *Blood on the Dining-Room Floor* defies that claim. Stein embarks on Knox's precious reader/author game but she refuses to allow either of the players a clear victory, and the reader's guess is as good as the author's when it comes to the elusive answer. Partly, this stems from the fact that Stein's pleasure is rooted in the process of investigation and the joy of mystery, both ideally prolonged as long as possible. But it is also grounded in the need to grieve for the women whose deaths are barely acknowledged or regretted in real life. Yet what drives Stein to employ this particular form of genre fiction is the very thing she believed she had excluded – the corpse. Both the emotional and physical corpses of the women she has encountered litter the text: Mme Pernollet, the Englishwoman, the beautiful but unsatisfied wives of the rich old men, and the skeletal mother of Alexander, amongst others. Stein's detective fiction acknowledges the damage done to these female bodies. In this respect, Stein's rendering of the detective genre is not dissimilar from Knox's ideal. There are indeed criminals to be sniffed out, and it would appear that they are heterosexuality and the family. Their dynamics force both men and women into conventional and dangerous roles that lead to a proliferation of 'crimes': adultery, social ostracism, insanity, and even murder. In contrast to these women is the continual presence of Borden, a woman who, as some theories and rumours would have it, experienced a similar emotional, mental and physical abuse. But unlike the victims in these pieces – insane, exploited and murdered women – Borden became the murderer herself. Stein recognises that 'Lizzie' 'always want[ed] something else but not that but not that yes' (*Blood on the Dining-Room Floor*, p. 71): this 'something else' is not specified, but one might speculate that it is either a female-centred form of sexual satisfaction or perhaps freedom from familial chains. Stein's crime story suggests that the female body must struggle for 'something else', not heterosexual or familial ties, but independence and freedom. It must struggle to metaphorically, and perhaps in some extreme cases literally, murder those that oppress it or else it will itself be destroyed.

Notes

1. Knox, 'Introduction', in *The Best Detective Stories of the Year*, p. x.
2. Van Dine, 'Twenty Rules', pp. 191–2.
3. Marcus, 'Detective and Literary Fiction', p. 249.
4. Landon notes that *Blood on the Dining-Room Floor* was written in the summer of 1933. Landon, 'Not Solve It But Be In It', p. 490. The dates of the shorter pieces are established in Dydo and Rice, *Gertrude Stein*, p. 564.
5. Stein, 'Subject-Cases: The Background of a Detective Story', pp. 3–32.

6. Stein notes recommending Wallace's novels in 'Why I Like Detective Stories'. She also wanted to meet Hammett when on a visit to the United States in 1934–5. Stein, 'Why I Like Detective Stories', p. 146. Subsequent references are noted in parenthesis. For details regarding Hammett see Hobhouse's introduction to Stein, *Blood on the Dining-Room Floor* (1985), p. xii. Subsequent references are noted in parenthesis.
7. Stein, 'American Crimes', pp. 102–3. Subsequent references are noted in parenthesis.
8. Stein, *Narration*, p. 40.
9. Stein, 'A Water-fall and a Piano', p. 31. Subsequent references are noted in parenthesis.
10. Gygax, *Gender and Genre*, p. 94. Hobhouse makes a similar claim in her introduction to *Blood on the Dining-Room Floor*, p. xii. For other interpretations see Chessman, *The Public is Invited to Dance*; Landon, 'Not Solve It But Be In It'; Rohr, 'Everybody sees, and everybody says they do'; Levay, 'Remaining a Mystery'.
11. Stein, *Everybody's Autobiography*, pp. 49–50. Subsequent references are noted in parenthesis.
12. Malcolm, *Two Lives*, pp. 16–17.
13. Ibid. pp. 16–17.
14. Marcus, 'Detective and Literary Fiction', p. 252.
15. Details from Gill's Introduction to Stein, *Blood on the Dining-Room Floor* (2008).
16. Landon, 'Not Solve It But Be In It', p. 494.
17. Gill, Introduction to Stein, *Blood on the Dining-Room Floor*, p. xv.
18. Gill, *Detecting Gertrude Stein*, p. 154.
19. Several scholars have commented upon this aspect of Lizzie's trial. See for instance Neroni, *The Violent Woman*, p. 65.
20. Gill points out that although she remained in the Fall River area, she relocated to a more affluent neighbourhood. She also, he tells us, spent her time enjoying the theatres and concert halls of Boston and New York. Gill, *Detecting Gertrude Stein*, p. 158.
21. Ibid. p. 158.
22. Lincoln, *A Private Disgrace*, p. 309.
23. Jones, *Women Who Kill*, p. 251.
24. On Lizzie's rumoured lesbianism see also Charles and Louise Samuels's fictional piece *The Girl in the House of Hate*.
25. Gill, *Detecting Gertrude Stein*, p. 152. One might further note that *Blood on the Dining-Room Floor* was written only a few years after Lizzie's own death in 1927.
26. Souhami sketches an interesting portrait of Stein's relationship with her parents in 'Gertrude's Early Years', *Gertrude and Alice*.
27. Gill, *Detecting Gertrude Stein*, p. 47. It is worth noting that another Edith, Edith Wharton, was also interested in Lizzie Borden. She toyed with the idea of turning Lizzie's story into a play titled *Kate Spain*, but in the end used the material as the basis for her 1936 story 'Confession'. However, this might be a merely coincidental connection to Stein's work. For details on Wharton see Lee, *Edith Wharton*, p. 639.
28. It is worth noting that Alice B. Toklas's 1954 cookery book includes an entry entitled 'Murder in the Kitchen', again prompting thoughts of the intersection between violence and domesticity. Toklas, *The Alice B. Toklas Cook Book*.
29. Chessman, *The Public is Invited to Dance*, p. 163.
30. Stein, 'Is Dead', p. 36.
31. Stein, 'How Writing is Written', pp. 158–9.
32. Brody, 'The Haunting of *Gaudy Night*', p. 94.

33. Stein, *Three Lives*, p. 200.
34. Malcolm, *Two Lives*, p. 119.
35. Stein, *The Making of Americans*, p. 114.
36. Souhami paints a similar portrait of Stein's own mother. Souhami, 'Gertrude's Early Years', *Gertrude and Alice*.
37. Freud, 'Mourning and Melancholia', pp. 244–5.

CODA

I began this book by sketching out the impact of censorship on the cultural landscape of the 1920s and 1930s, in order to establish an understanding of the context in which lesbian fiction was produced and to stress that after *The Well of Loneliness*'s ban, the question of how to represent sexuality was an urgent one. Drawing on archival material from government records, I suggested that 'serious' and 'frank' literature was particularly vulnerable to attack while light, escapist fiction was perceived as less threatening. Unfortunately, few of the authors examined here are as outspoken about their creative choices, or bestow on us such documentation, as Mitchison who tells the reader of her memoir that when faced with censorship she rejected realism in favour of historical fiction.[1] Even without such evidence of intent, the work examined here affirms the idea that genre fiction offered women a viable alternative to realism and experimental modernism, that is a resource and a countermeasure to the effects of censorship. Inevitably, this selective study does not produce a seamless narrative, since the response to this scenario took on diverse forms to varied and often conflicted effects. Burdekin's, Goldsmith's and Gordon's works are perhaps the most distinct examples of genre fiction being put to use as a vehicle for sexual content. As is evident from the unpublished material in Burdekin's archive, her attempt to publish a realist narrative about sexual inversion in 1928 was frustrated, while in her published speculative fiction the invert masquerades as the utopian figure belonging to another era – the time-travelling monk, the highly evolved Person, the revolutionary artist Grania

– allowing Burdekin to freely explore the topics of sexual and gender identity. Goldsmith and Gordon frame the lesbian woman in similarly anachronistic ways, summoning up historical figures and presenting them as pioneers, ancestors and role models to which the modern lesbian can look for inspiration. But this is not to say that the structures of genre fiction are merely a guise for these writers or that they encode content that can simply be decrypted. For Burdekin, the choice of speculative fiction embodies her understanding of lesbian identity (and more widely the identity of the invert) as existing in a state of flux, involved in a sustained process of striving towards something finer, or utopian. For Goldsmith and Gordon also, biography is essentially a project in historiography, a challenge to the traditional narration and definition of history. For these two writers, history is not merely a subject but also a practice, in the sense that they turn to the past to constitute a present sense of self, both communal and individual. Other texts in this study are less ideologically determined but their use of genre fiction nonetheless provides opportunities for the expression of lesbian eroticism. Barney is one of a number of lesbian women who felt an affinity with the occult, in fact and fiction, and who conceived of relationships with women in spiritual terms. *The One Who is Legion* turns to supernatural fiction and finds stimulation in the spiritual union with the spectral lover, presenting the erotic but incorporeal relationship as an ideal if contradictory romantic bond. For Woolf, *Orlando* employs conventions of the historical romance to create moments of heightened homoeroticism, but she resists the genre's eventual containment by introducing false moments of closure (for instance, the revelation of the cross-dressed body or the instigation of the heterosexual romance plot), thus maintaining the presence of lesbian desire while discrediting the supposed certainty of sexuality intrinsic to historical romance. Stein also embraces and yet resists the formula of detective fiction and in particular its tendency towards closure and the reinstatement of social order. In part, this is done to rebuff the genre's potential for conservatism, but in refusing containment Stein further insists that we should not forget the female victims of this crime story.

On the one hand, Stein's and Woolf's resistance to genre fiction's rules seems to confirm the assumption that, as Jean Radford puts it:

> Literature is seen as operating transformatively on ideology, producing a 'knowledge' of it, whereas popular fiction merely reproduces and transmits that ideology. [. . .] In the realm of Literature, the text's internal operations guarantee to some extent the deconstruction of the ideological, whereas the formulaic structures of popular fiction naturalise the ideological discourses they contain[2]

It might seem that it is only Stein and Woolf who use genre fiction self-consciously, but the crime novels by Mitchell, Sayers and Tey demonstrate that mainstream fictions do not necessarily deploy conventions blindly or without interrogation. For these writers, the lesbian criminal is a locus for questions of what it means to be a white middle-class woman in early twentieth-century Britain, and in this respect these novels present a confluence between the feminist and lesbian. Like Stein, who privileges the lesbian criminal in order to disclose the dangers of the nuclear heteronormative family, Mitchell, Sayers and Tey depict her as both a product of patriarchal abuse and a threat to its monopoly of power. This figure also takes on a narrative role as the catalyst for homoerotic desires, and while she may disappear as the novel comes to a close, what we are left with, most radically of all, is a newly framed lesbian detective.

What does it mean to alter, adapt or negotiate with generic fictional forms in this way? Genre fiction operates on the premise that the reader can know what to expect. These codes with which we are so familiar arguably naturalise the association between the presence of a set of conventions and the reader's textual pleasure (a reader might, for instance, be disappointed were the criminal to evade capture). That is to say, the reader's enjoyment of encoded works is dependent on the text meeting their expectations. If popular fiction is commonly thought to reproduce or serve the purposes of the status quo, then the ritual of genre fiction might be said to induce the reader to comply with its reactionary motivations, since enjoyment becomes dependent upon encountering a certain kind of experience. Following this line of thought, the refusal to deploy conventions or to follow genre fiction's rules, as we know them at least, can be read as a dramatically significant textual act that interferes with the causal chain between the reader's pleasure, the generic codes, and its ideology. What is essentially at stake, then, in each of the texts in this study is a manipulation of genre fiction's rules for the writer's own ends, although these are not uncomplicated, homogenous, or necessarily always subversive. Indeed, what emerges from my readings of these texts is their delicate balance between compliance and resistance to sexual and gender hegemonies. One might look to Burdekin, for instance, with her stoical approach to passion, or Goldsmith and her excessive pathologisation of homosexuality.[3] Such texts as these, in their resistance to avowedly affirmative readings of sexuality, do not make for a neat account of either lesbian literature or lesbian modernism. However, this is where their value lies and it is important to find a place for such narratives not despite, but because of, their ideological conflicts. It is significant, for instance, that Burdekin believes in a form of love that is platonic and spiritual, that Goldsmith becomes tangled up in a intellectually discursive net, and that the ostensibly homophobic figure of the lesbian criminal can raise interesting questions about what it 'means' to be a woman and a lesbian. By taking account of ideological complexities and nuances, we can begin to move towards a more holistic understanding of the relationship between sexuality and textuality in the period.

My reading of modernists and mainstream writers as analogous in their deployment of genre fiction suggests that modernism is potentially not as autonomous as both it, and critics, have believed it to be. The few modernist writers examined here demonstrate a dependence on the structures of popular fiction and imply that one form bleeds into the other. Both Woolf and Stein feared becoming generic through success, and Barney seemingly wrote in a way that declined interaction with the market, but all three rely on the traditions and codes of popular fiction. My examination of both modernist and mainstream writers has been necessarily selective, but those texts that I have attended to imply the need to rethink lesbian modernism as a category of literature. These mainstream texts are not experimental in form and thus I do not make a case for their inclusion under those terms. However, their comparison against canonical works suggests that it might be productive to think of modernism as about content as much as style.[4] Marshall Berman defines modernism as 'any attempt by modern men and women to become subjects as well as objects of modernization, to get a grip on the modern world and make themselves at home in it'.[5] One way in which we understand lesbian modernism is as an engagement with the lesbian as a modern subject and as a textual exploration of her desires.[6] It is also defined, as Winning suggests, by the 'sets of discourses' and the context that influences it.[7] Thus, I suggest that it is on these terms that genre fiction also has a part to play in the aesthetic project that is modernism. What is striking about this range of texts is the lack of homogeneity: produced from a myriad of influences (scientific and cultural), what each of these writers understands the modern lesbian subject to mean is contested and diverse. For writers such as Burdekin and Barney, lesbianism is a spiritual endeavour, but while the former is informed by sexological and mystical discourses the latter's work comes to this conclusion via the sadomasochist eroticisation of death and the ghostly beloved. For writers such as Mitchell, Sayers, Stein and Tey, there is a marked slippage between lesbian and feminist identity and they each evoke the sense that the lesbian is defined in part by her rejection of patriarchal control and heteronormativity. While Gordon by no means excludes the somatic, she similarly makes this confluence and conjures up a historical continuum of female-oriented women. Like Burdekin, Goldsmith is bound by sexological and psychoanalytic theories of female sexuality but to such an extent that lesbianism is excessively pathological – a position that she adjusts and softens in her later historical biographies. Woolf, in contrast to all of these positions, insists upon the idea that '[s]ometimes women do like women' but resists promoting a stable concept of sexuality, thus throwing the very category of 'lesbian' into doubt.[8] All of these writers in their various ways, and with differing conclusions, arguably explore the meaning of modern lesbian subjectivity and thus deserve consideration under the rubric of lesbian modernism.

Dollimore states that '[t]o take art seriously – to recognize its potential – must be to recognize that there might be reasonable grounds for wanting to control it. [. . .] We accord it the seriousness it deserves by trusting it less'.[9] My study has shown that we must place less trust in genre fiction. While genre fiction does not neatly encode sexual content that is unequivocally radical or subversive, what might be drawn from the sample of works on offer here is the idea that although seemingly escapist and light reading, it had a role to play in the complex depiction of modern lesbian sexuality by both experimental and mainstream modernists in an era when 'honest' and 'serious' realist narratives were vulnerable to attack. With this in mind, I propose that we need to continue to explore and rethink how genre fictions work and what they are capable of at any specific cultural moment.

NOTES

1. Mitchison, *You May Well Ask*, p. 179.
2. Radford, 'Introduction', in *The Progress of Romance*, p. 6.
3. In a similar vein, Fletcher talks about the 'dual impulse' of the romance genre in *Historical Romance Fiction* (pp. 4–5).
4. Elliott and Wallace also comment upon the critical assumption that '[r]adical experimentation with form [. . .] is "modernist" while radical experimentation with content is not'. Elliott and Wallace, *Women Artists and Writers*, p. 15.
5. Berman, *All That is Solid*, p. 5.
6. I have drawn on Winning's definition of lesbian modernism in *The Pilgrimage of Dorothy Richardson*, p. 4. Doan and Garrity discuss the alliance of modernity and sapphism in their 'Introduction' to *Sapphic Modernities*.
7. Winning, 'Writing by the Light of *The Well*', p. 374.
8. Woolf, *A Room of One's Own*, p. 87.
9. Dollimore, *Sex, Literature and Censorship*, p. 97.

BIBLIOGRAPHY

PRIMARY SOURCES

Barney, Natalie Clifford, *In Memory of Dorothy Ierne Wilde: 'Oscaria'* [1951], New Edition (Dijon: privately printed, 1952).

——, *The One Who is Legion or A.D.'s After-life* [1930] (Orono, ME: National Poetry Foundation, 1987).

Bell, Quentin, Angelica Garnett, Henrietta Garnett, and Richard Shone, *Charleston Past and Present* [1987], 2nd edn (London: The Hogarth Press, 1993).

Bernbaum, Ernest, 'The Views of the Great Critics on the Historical Novel', *PMLA*, 41.2 (1926), 424–41.

Borden, Mary, 'Man, The Master. An Illusion', in *Man, Proud Man*, ed. Mabel Ulrich (London: Hamish Hamilton, 1932), pp. 11–38.

Bowen, Marjorie, *Black Magic: A Tale of the Rise and Fall of the Antichrist* (London: Alston Rivers, 1909).

——, *The Glen o' Weeping* (London: Alston Rivers, 1907).

——, *The Viper of Milan: A Romance of Lombardy* [1906] (Harmondsworth: Penguin, 1963).

Bryher, Winifred, 'The Girl-Page in Elizabeth Literature', *The Fortnightly Review*, 107 (1920), 442–52.

Burdekin, Katharine, The Archive of Katharine Burdekin, New York City, The Dobkin Family Collection of Feminism.

——, TS 'Dolly', The Archive of Katharine Burdekin, New York City, The Dobkin Family Collection of Feminism.
——, *The End of This Day's Business*, Afterword by Daphne Patai (New York: The Feminist Press, 1989).
——, 'The Power of Merlin' [as Murray Constantine], *Life and Letters To-Day*, 13.1 (1935), 134–42.
——, *Proud Man* [1934 as Murray Constantine], Foreword and Afterword by Daphne Patai (New York: The Feminist Press, 1993).
——, *The Rebel Passion* [as Kay Burdekin] (New York: William Morrow, 1929).
——, TS 'The Stars Shine in Daylight', The Archive of Katharine Burdekin, New York City, The Dobkin Family Collection of Feminism.
——, *Swastika Night* [1937 as Murray Constantine], intro. Daphne Patai (New York: The Feminist Press, 1985).
——, TS 'Two in a Sack' [as galley proofs], The Archive of Katharine Burdekin, New York City, The Dobkin Family Collection of Feminism.
——, TS 'Walking to Mark', The Archive of Katharine Burdekin, New York City, The Dobkin Family Collection of Feminism.
Burdekin, Katharine [as Murray Constantine], and Margaret Goldsmith, *Venus in Scorpio: A Romance of Versailles, 1770–1793* (London: John Lane, 1940).
Butler, Lady Eleanor, Sarah Ponsonby and Caroline Hamilton, *The Hamwood Papers of the Ladies of Llangollen*, ed. Mrs G. H. Bell (London: Macmillan, 1930).
Carpenter, Edward, *Civilisation: Its Cause and its Cure, and Other Essays* (London: Swan Sonnenschein, 1889).
——, *The Intermediate Sex: A Study of Some Transitional Types of Men and Women* (London: Swan Sonnenschein, 1908).
——, *Intermediate Types Among Primitive Folk: A Study in Social Evolution* [1914], 2nd edn (London: Allen & Unwin, 1919).
——, *Love's Coming-of-Age: A Series of Papers on the Relations of the Sexes* [1896] (London: Swan Sonnenschein, 1906).
Chesterton, G. K., 'A Defence of Detective Stories' [1901], in *The Art of the Mystery Story: A Collection of Critical Essays*, ed. Howard Haycraft (New York: Grosset & Dunlap, 1961), pp. 3–6.
Cukor, George (dir.), *Sylvia Scarlett* (RKO Radio Pictures, 1935).
Dehan, Richard, *The Lovers of the Market-Place* (London: Thornton Butterworth, 1928).
The Detection Club, 'The Detection Club Oath', in *The Art of the Mystery Story: A Collection of Critical Essays*, ed. Howard Haycraft (New York: Grosset & Dunlap, 1961), pp. 197–9.
Ellis, Havelock, 'The Criminal' [1890], in *Sexology Uncensored: The Documents*

of *Sexual Science*, ed. Lucy Bland and Laura Doan (Cambridge: Polity, 1998), pp. 17–20.

——, *Studies in the Psychology of Sex Volume II Sexual Inversion* [1897], 3rd edn (Philadelphia: F. A. Davis, 1917).

Freud, Sigmund, 'Creative Writers and Day-Dreaming' [1908], in *Art and Literature: Jensen's* Gradiva, *Leonardo Da Vinci and Other Works*, trans. under the general editorship of James Strachey, ed. Albert Dickinson (Harmondsworth: Penguin, 1990), pp. 129–41.

——, 'Dreams and Occultism', in *New Introductory Lectures on Psychoanalysis* [1933], authorised trans. W. J. H. Sprott (London: The Hogarth Press, 1957), pp. 45–77.

——, 'Mourning and Melancholia' [1917], in *The Standard Edition of the Complete Psychological Works of Sigmund Freud: Volume 14, 1914–1916 On the History of the Psycho-analytic Movement, Papers on Metapsychology, and Other Works*, trans. under the general editorship of James Strachey in collaboration with Anna Freud (London: The Hogarth Press, 1957), pp. 237–58.

Friedman, Susan Stanford (ed.), *Analyzing Freud: Letters of H.D., Bryher, and Their Circle* (New York: New Directions, 2002).

Goldsmith, Margaret, *Christina of Sweden: A Psychological Biography* (London: Arthur Barker, 1933).

——, *Sappho of Lesbos: A Psychological Reconstruction of her Life* (London: Rich & Cowan, 1938).

Gordon, Mary, *Chase of the Wild Goose: The Story of Lady Eleanor Butler and Miss Sarah Ponsonby, Known as the Ladies of Llangollen* (London: The Hogarth Press, 1936).

Graves, Robert, and Alan Hodge, 'The Long Weekend: A Social History of Great Britain 1918–1939' [1940], in *The Long Weekend and The Reader over Your Shoulder*, intro. Jane Aitken Hodge (Manchester: Carcanet, 2006).

Hall, Radclyffe, 'Miss Ogilvy Finds Herself', in *Miss Ogilvy Finds Herself* (Leipzig: Bernhard Tauchnitz, 1934).

——, *The Well of Loneliness*, with a commentary by Havelock Ellis (London: Jonathan Cape, 1928).

Hall, Radclyffe, and Una Troubridge, 'On a Series of Sittings with Mrs. Osborne Leonard', *Proceedings of the Society for Psychical Research*, 78 (1919), 339–554

——, 'A Veridical Apparition', *Journal of the Society for Psychical Research*, 20 (1921), 78–88.

H.D., YCAL MSS 24 Box 9 f.298, H.D. Papers, Beinecke Rare Book and Manuscript Library, Yale University.

Herring, Robert and Petrie Townshend, 'Editorial', *Life and Letters To-Day*, 13.1 (1935), 1–2.

Heyer, Georgette, *The Masqueraders* [1928] (London: Mandarin, 1991).
——, *These Old Shades* [1926] (London: Mandarin, 1993).
James, Norah C., *Sleeveless Errand* (Paris: Henry Babou and Jack Kahane, 1929).
Jameson, Storm, 'Man the Helpmate', in *Man, Proud Man*, ed. Mabel Ulrich (London: Hamish Hamilton, 1932), pp. 105–36.
Knox, Ronald A., 'Detective Story Decalogue' [1929], in *The Art of the Mystery Story: A Collection of Critical Essays*, ed. Howard Haycraft (New York: Grosset & Dunlap, 1961), pp. 194–6.
——, 'Introduction', *The Best Detective Stories of the Year 1928* (London: Faber & Gwyer, 1929), pp. vii–xxiii.
Knox, Ronald, and H. Harrington (eds), *The Best Detective Stories of the Year, 1928* (London: Faber & Gwyer, 1929).
Krafft-Ebing, Richard von, *Psychopathia Sexualis, with Especial Reference to the Antipathic Sexual Instinct: A Medico-Forensic Study* [1886], 12th edn, trans. F. J. Rebman (New York: Medical Art Agency, 1922).
Mackenzie, Compton, *The Early Life and Adventures of Sylvia Scarlett* (London: Martin Secker, 1918).
——, *Extraordinary Women: Themes and Variations* (London: Martin Secker, 1928).
——, *Sinister Street*, 2 vols (London: Martin Secker, 1913–14).
Mitchell, Gladys, *Speedy Death* [1929] (London: Penguin, 1943).
Mitchison, Naomi, *You May Well Ask: A Memoir 1920–1940* [1979] (London: Flamingo, 1986).
Moberly, C. Anne E. and Eleanor F. Jourdain, *An Adventure* [1911], 4th edn, Preface by Edith Olivier, Note by J. W. Dunne (London: Faber & Faber, 1931).
The National Archives, CUST 49/2134 Indecent publications: list of books to be seized, 1936.
——, DPP 1/92 Partridge, EH Offence: Obscene publication Sleeveless Errand, 1929.
——, HO 45/15139 Publications (including indecent publications): Books and other literature: questions on obscenity, 1927–33.
——, HO 45/15727 Publications (including indecent publications): 'Extraordinary Women': book by Compton Mackenzie. Legal and political opinions regarding possible ban due to lesbian themes; decision not to ban publication, 1928–9.
——, HO 45/23588 Publications: interception of indecent books in the post: *My Life* by Frank Harris and *Lysistrata* by Aristophanes. Importation of indecent books for use as evidence in divorce proceedings: Home Office permission, 1927–8.

——, HO 45/24939 Publications (including indecent publications): Indecent Literature: various cases involving public protest, 1932–4.
——, HO 144/14042 Publications: Suppression of indecent literature, 1929–31.
——, HO 144/22430 Publications: Indecent Literature: various causes and correspondence, 1934–6
——, HO 144/22547 Publications: *The Well of Loneliness* by Miss Radclyffe Hall: obscene publication; order by Chief Magistrate for destruction 16 November 1928. Includes many newspaper cuttings, 1928–46.
——, MEPO 3/383 Obscene Books: report on method of destruction of the books by police, following criticism by 'The New Statesman', 1929.
Renault, Mary, 'Notes on *The King Must Die*', in *Afterwords: Novelists on their Novels*, ed. Thomas McCormack (New York: Harper & Row, 1969), pp. 80–7.
——, *Purposes of Love* [1939] (Harmondsworth: Penguin, 1986).
Riviere, Joan, 'Womanliness as a Masquerade', *The International Journal of Psycho-analysis*, 10 (1929), 303–13.
Sackville-West, Vita, 'The Unborn Visitant: An Edwardian Story', in *Thirty Clocks Strike the Hour and Other Stories* (Garden City, NY: Doubleday Doran, 1932), pp. 283–304.
Sayers, Dorothy L., *Gaudy Night* [1936] (New York: HarperTorch, 2006).
——, 'Gaudy Night' [1937], in *The Art of the Mystery Story: A Collection of Critical Essays*, ed. Howard Haycraft (New York: Grosset & Dunlap, 1961), pp. 208–21
——, 'Introduction', in *Great Short Stories of Detection, Mystery, and Horror* (London: Victor Gollancz, 1928), pp. 9–47.
——, MS 'The Singular Case of the Three Spinsters', DLS/MS-185, Wheaton: Marion E. Wade Center, Wheaton College, <www.wheaton.edu/wade-center/collection/manuscripts/sayersms.pdf> [accessed 2 August 2010].
——, *Unnatural Death* [1927] (New York: HarperCollins, 1995).
Shakespeare, William, *The Tempest, The Norton Shakespeare Based on the Oxford Edition*, 2nd edn, ed. Stephen Greenblatt (New York: Norton, 2008).
Spain, Nancy, *Poison for Teacher* [1949], intro. Alison Hennegan (London: Virago, 1994).
Stein, Gertrude, 'American Crimes and How they Matter' [1935], in *How Writing is Written: Volume II of the Previously Uncollected Writings of Gertrude Stein*, ed. Robert Bartlett Haas (Los Angeles: Black Sparrow Press, 1974), pp. 100–5.
——, *The Autobiography of Alice B. Toklas* (London: John Lane, 1933).
——, *Blood on the Dining-Room Floor* [1948], intro. Janet Hobhouse (London: Virago, 1985).

——, *Blood on the Dining-Room Floor: a Murder Mystery* [1948], with an introduction and afterword by John Herbert Gill (Mineola, NY: Dover, 2008).
——, *Everybody's Autobiography* [1937], intro. Janet Hobhouse (London: Virago, 1985).
——, 'How Writing is Written' [1935], in *How Writing is Written: Volume II of the Previously Uncollected Writings of Gertrude Stein*, ed. Robert Bartlett Haas (Los Angeles: Black Sparrow Press, 1974), pp. 151–60.
——, 'Is Dead' [1936], in *How Writing is Written: Volume II of the Previously Uncollected Writings of Gertrude Stein*, ed. Robert Bartlett Haas (Los Angeles: Black Sparrow Press, 1974), pp. 33–6.
——, *The Making of Americans: Being a History of a Family's Progress* [1925], foreword by William H. Gass, intro. Stephen Meyer (Normal, IL: Dalkey Archive Press, 1995).
——, *Narration: Four Lectures by Gertrude Stein*, intro. Thornton Wilder (Chicago: University of Chicago Press, 1935).
——, 'Subject-Cases: The Background of a Detective Story' [1923], *As Fine as Melanctha*, with a foreword by Natalie Clifford Barney (New Haven: Yale University Press, 1954), pp. 3–32.
——, *Three Lives* [1909], intro. Ann Charters (New York: Penguin, 1990).
——, 'A Water-fall and a Piano' [1937], in *How Writing is Written: Volume II of the Previously Uncollected Writings of Gertrude Stein*, ed. Robert Bartlett Haas (Los Angeles: Black Sparrow Press, 1974), pp. 31–2.
——, 'Why I Like Detective Stories' [1937], in *How Writing is Written: Volume II of the Previously Uncollected Writings of Gertrude Stein*, ed. Robert Bartlett Haas (Los Angeles: Black Sparrow Press, 1974), pp. 146–50.
Stephen, Leslie, 'Sir Walter Scott', in *Hours in a Library: Volume I* [1874] (London: Smith, Elder & Co., 1892), pp. 137–68.
Stephensen, P. R., illustrations by Hal Collins, *The Well of Sleevelessness: A Tale for the Least of These Little Ones* (London: Scholartis Press, 1929).
Strachey, Lytton, *Eminent Victorians* [1918] (Oxford: Oxford University Press, 2003).
Tey, Josephine, *Miss Pym Disposes* [1946], intro. Robert Barnard (New York: Simon & Schuster, 1998).
Toklas, Alice B., illustrations by Sir Francis Rose, *The Alice B. Toklas Cook Book* (London: Michael Joseph, 1954).
Van Dine, S. S., 'Twenty Rules for Writing Detective Stories' [1928], in *The Art of the Mystery Story: A Collection of Critical Essays*, ed. Howard Haycraft (New York: Grosset & Dunlap, 1946), pp. 189–93.
Vivien, Renée, *A Woman Appeared to Me* [1904], trans. Jeanette H. Foster, intro. Gayle Rubin ([n.p.]: Naiad Press, 1976).

West, Rebecca, 'Man and Religion', in *Man, Proud Man*, ed. Mabel Ulrich (London: Hamish Hamilton, 1932), pp. 249–85.
Woolf, Virginia, *A Change of Perspective: The Letters of Virginia Woolf Volume 3: 1923–1928*, ed. Nigel Nicholson and Joanna Trautmann (London: The Hogarth Press, 1977).
——, *Collected Essays Volume One* (London: The Hogarth Press, 1966).
——, *Collected Essays Volume Two* (London: The Hogarth Press, 1966).
——, *Collected Essays Volume Three* (London: The Hogarth Press, 1967).
——, *The Complete Shorter Fiction of Virginia Woolf*, ed. Susan Dick (San Diego: Harcourt, 1989).
——, *The Diary of Virginia Woolf: Volume 3: 1925–1930*, ed. Anne Olivier Bell assisted by Andrew McNeillie (London: The Hogarth Press, 1980).
——, *The Diary of Virginia Woolf: Volume 5, 1936–1941*, ed. Anne Oliver Bell assisted by Andrew McNeillie (London: The Hogarth Press, 1984).
——, *The Essays of Virginia Woolf: Volume I 1904–1912*, ed. Andrew McNeillie (London: The Hogarth Press, 1986).
——, *The Essays of Virginia Woolf: Volume II 1912–1918*, ed. Andrew McNeillie (London: The Hogarth Press, 1987).
——, *The Essays of Virginia Woolf: Volume III 1919–1924*, ed. Andrew McNeillie (London: The Hogarth Press, 1994).
——, *The Essays of Virginia Woolf: Volume IV 1925–1928*, ed. Andrew McNeillie (London: The Hogarth Press, 1988).
——, *Granite and Rainbow: Essays by Virginia Woolf* (London: The Hogarth Press, 1958).
——, 'The Journal of Mistress Joan Martyn', *The Complete Shorter Fiction of Virginia Woolf*, ed. Susan Dick (San Diego: Harcourt, 1989), pp. 33–62.
——, *Moments of Being: Autobiographical Writings* [1976], ed. Jeanne Schulkind (London: Pimlico, 2002).
——, *Orlando: A Biography* (London: The Hogarth Press, 1928).
——, 'A Professor of Life: The Letters of Walter Raleigh, A Brilliant Commentary on the Life and Work of a Great Professor of English Literature', *Vogue*, May 1926, 68–9.
——, *A Room of One's Own and Three Guineas* [1929; 1938] (London: Penguin, 1993).
——, *The Voyage Out* [1915] (London: Vintage, 2000).
Yourcenar, Marguerite, 'Reflections on the Composition of *Memoirs of Hadrian*', in *Memoirs of Hadrian* [1951], trans. Grace Frick (Harmondsworth: Penguin, 1983), pp. 255–77.

<small>Secondary Sources</small>

Abraham, Julie, *Are Girls Necessary? Lesbian Writing and Modern Histories* (New York: Routledge, 1996).

Adorno, Theodor W., and Max Horkheimer, 'The Culture Industry: Enlightenment as Mass Deception', in *Dialectic of Enlightenment* [1944], trans. John Cumming (London and New York: Verso, 1997), pp. 120–67.
Aird, Catherine, 'Josephine Tey, The Person', in *Josephine Tey: A Celebration. A Festscrift on the Life and Work of Josephine Tey*, ed. Geraldine Perriam and Catherine Aird (Glasgow: Black Rock Press, 2004), pp. 69–71.
Albinski, Nan Bowman, *Women's Utopias in British and American Fiction* (London: Routledge, 1988).
Attebery, Brian, *The Fantasy Tradition in American Literature From Irving to Le Guin* (Bloomington: Indiana University Press, 1980).
——, *Strategies of Fantasy* (Bloomington: Indiana University Press, 1992).
Bacon, Catherine, 'English Lesbians and Irish Devotion: The Manipulation of Sexual Discourse in Molly Keane's *The Rising Tide*', *Tulsa Studies in Women's Literature*, 28.1 (2009), 97–119.
Bartowski, Frances, *Feminist Utopias* (Lincoln: University of Nebraska Press, 1989).
Beauman, Nicola, *A Very Great Profession: The Woman's Novel 1914–1939* (London: Virago, 1983).
Bell, Kathleen, 'Cross-Dressing in Wartime: Georgette Heyer's *The Corinthian* in its 1940 Context', in *War Culture: Social Change and Changing Experience in World War Two Britain*, ed. Pat Kirkham and David Thoms (London: Lawrence and Wishart, 1995), pp. 151–9.
——, 'Writing a Man's World: an Exploration of Three Works by Rosemary Sutcliff, Mary Renault and Cecil Woodham Smith', in *Women's Writing 1945–60: After the Deluge*, ed. Jane Dowson (Basingstoke: Palgrave, 2003), pp. 148–61.
Benstock, Shari, 'Expatriate Modernism: Writing on the Cultural Rim', in *Women's Writing in Exile*, ed. Mary Lynn Broe and Angela Ingram (Chapel Hill: University of North Carolina Press, 1989), pp. 19–40.
——, *Women of the Left Bank: Paris, 1900–1940* (Austin: University of Texas, 1986).
Berman, Marshall, *All That is Solid Melts into Air: The Experience of Modernity* (New York: Penguin, 1988).
Bland, Lucy, and Laura Doan (eds), *Sexology Uncensored: The Documents of Sexual Science* (Cambridge: Polity, 1998).
Bloom, Clive, *Bestsellers: Popular Fiction Since 1900* (New York: Palgrave, 2002).
Bourdieu, Pierre, *Distinction: A Social Critique of the Judgement of Taste*, trans. Richard Nice (London: Routledge & Kegan Paul, 1984).
Bourdieu, Pierre, *The Field of Cultural Production: Essays on Art and Literature*, ed. Randal Johnson (Cambridge: Polity Press, 1993).

Bowlby, Rachel, *Feminist Destinations and Further Essays on Virginia Woolf* (Edinburgh: Edinburgh University Press, 1997).
Bravmann, Scott, *Queer Fictions of the Past: History, Culture, and Difference* (Cambridge: Cambridge University Press, 1997).
Bray, Alan, *Homosexuality in Renaissance England* (London: Gay Men's Press, 1982).
Brody, Miriam, 'The Haunting of *Gaudy Night*: Misreadings in a Work of Detective Fiction', *Style*, 19.1 (1985), 94–116.
Brookes, Barbara, 'A Corresponding Community: Dr Agnes Bennett and her Friends from the Edinburgh Medical College for Women of the 1890s', *Medical History: A European Journal for the History of Medicine and Health*, 52.2 (2008), 237–56.
Brown, Erica, and Mary Grover (eds), *Middlebrow Literary Cultures: The Battle of the Brows, 1920–1960* (New York: Palgrave Macmillan, 2012).
Buckley, Veronica, *Christina Queen of Sweden* (London: Harper Perennial, 2005).
Callow, John, 'Jacobite Rebellions', in *Celtic Culture: A Historical Encyclopedia Volume Three*, ed. John T. Koch (Santa Barbara: ABC-CLIO, 2006), pp. 1034–5.
Carey, John, *The Intellectuals and the Masses: Pride and Prejudice Among the Literary Intelligentsia, 1880–1939* (London: Faber & Faber, 1992).
Carlston, Erin G., *Thinking Fascism: Sapphic Modernism and Fascist Modernity* (Stanford: Stanford University Press, 1998).
Castle, Terry, *The Apparitional Lesbian: Female Homosexuality and Modern Culture* (New York: Columbia University Press, 1993).
——, *Noël Coward & Radclyffe Hall: Kindred Spirits* (New York: Columbia University Press, 1996).
——, 'Sylvia Townsend Warner and The Counterplot of Lesbian Fiction', *Textual Practice*, 4.2 (1990), 213–35.
Chessman, Harriet Scott, *The Public is Invited to Dance: Representation, the Body, and Dialogue in Gertrude Stein* (Stanford: Stanford University Press, 1989).
Cohler, Deborah, 'Sapphism and Sedition: Producing Female Homosexuality in Great War Britain', *Journal of the History of Sexuality*, 16.1 (2007), 68–94.
Cook, Blanche Wiesen, '"Women Alone Stir My Imagination": Lesbianism and the Cultural Tradition', *Signs: Journal of Women in Culture and Society*, 4.4 (1979), 718–39.
Coward, Rosalind, and Linda Semple, 'Tracking Down the Past: Women and Detective Fiction', in *From My Guy to Sci-Fi: Genre and Women's Writing in the Postmodern World*, ed. Helen Carr (London: Pandora Press, 1989), pp. 39–57.

Cranny-Francis, Anne, *Feminist Fiction: Feminist Uses of Generic Fiction* (London: Polity Press, 1990).

Croft, Andy, 'Worlds Without End Foisted Upon The Future – Some Antecedents of *Nineteen Eighty-Four*', in *Inside the Myth: Orwell: Views from the Left*, ed. Christopher Norris (London: Lawrence and Wishart, 1984), pp. 183–216.

DeJean, Joan, *Fictions of Sappho, 1546–1937* (Chicago: University of Chicago Press, 1989).

Dettmar, Kevin J. H., and Stephen Watt (eds), *Marketing Modernisms: Self-Promotion, Canonization, Rereading* (Ann Arbor: University of Michigan Press, 1996).

Doan, Laura, *Fashioning Sapphism: The Origins of a Modern English Lesbian Culture* (New York: Columbia University Press, 2001)

——,'Introduction', in *Old Maids to Radical Spinsters: Unmarried Women in the Twentieth-Century Novel*, ed. Laura L. Doan (Urbana and Chicago: University of Illinois Press, 1991), pp. 1–16.

——, '"The Outcast of One Age is the Hero of Another": Radclyffe Hall, Edward Carpenter and the Intermediate Sex', in *Palatable Poison: Critical Perspectives on The Well of Loneliness*, ed. Laura Doan and Jay Prosser (New York: Columbia University Press, 2001), pp. 162–78.

——, '"Woman's Place *Is* the Home": Conservative Sapphic Modernity', in *Sapphic Modernities: Sexuality, Women and National Culture*, ed. Laura Doan and Jane Garrity (New York: Palgrave, 2006), pp. 91–107.

Doan, Laura, and Jane Garrity, 'Introduction' to *Sapphic Modernities: Sexuality, Women and National Culture*, ed. Laura Doan and Jane Garrity (New York: Palgrave, 2006), pp. 1–13.

Doan, Laura, and Jay Prosser, 'Introduction: Critical Perspectives Past and Present', in *Palatable Poison: Critical Perspectives on The Well of Loneliness*, ed. Laura Doan and Jay Prosser (New York: Columbia University Press, 2001), pp. 1–31.

Doan, Laura and Sarah Waters, 'Making up Lost Time: Contemporary Lesbian Writing and the Invention of History', in *Territories of Desire in Queer Culture: Refiguring Contemporary Boundaries*, ed. David Alderson and Linda Anderson (Manchester: Manchester University Press, 2000), pp. 12–28.

Dollimore, Jonathan, *Sex, Literature and Censorship* (Cambridge: Polity Press, 2001).

Donoghue, Emma, *Inseparable: Desire Between Women in Literature* (New York: Knopf, 2010).

Dubino, Jeanne, 'Virginia Woolf: From Book Reviewer to Literary Critic, 1904–1918', in *Virginia Woolf and the Essay*, ed. Beth Carole Rosenberg and Jeanne Dubino (Basingstoke: Macmillan, 1997), pp. 25–40.

Duff, David, *Modern Genre Theory* (Harlow: Longman, 2000).
Duggan, Lisa, *Sapphic Slashers: Sex, Violence, and American Modernity* (Durham, NC: Duke University Press, 2000).
Dydo, Ulla E., with William Rice, *Gertrude Stein: The Language that Rises 1923–1934* (Evanston: North Western University Press, 2003).
Edson, Laura Gwyn, 'Kicking off her Knickers: Virginia Woolf's Rejection of Clothing as Realistic Detail', in *Virginia Woolf and the Arts: Selected Papers from the Sixth Annual Conference on Virginia Woolf*, ed. Diane F. Gillespie and Leslie K. Hankins (New York: Pace University Press, 1997), pp. 119–24.
Elliott, Bridget, and Jo-Ann Wallace, *Women Artists and Writers: Modernist (Im)positionings* (London: Routledge, 1994).
Engelking, Tama Lea, 'Translating the Lesbian Writer: Pierre Louÿs, Natalie Barney, and "Girls of the Future Society"', *South Central Review*, 22.3 (2005), 62–77.
Faderman, Lillian, *Odd Girls and Twilight Lovers: A History of Lesbian Life in Twentieth-Century America* (London: Penguin, 1991).
Finnan, Joseph P., *John Redmond and Irish Unity, 1912–1918* (Syracuse: Syracuse University Press, 2004).
Fitzgerald, Jennifer, '"Persephone Come Back From the Dead": Maude Violet Clarke (1892–1935)', in *Women Medievalists and the Academy*, ed. Jane Chance (Madison: University of Wisconsin Press, 2005), pp. 381–98.
Fleishman, Avrom, *The English Historical Novel: Walter Scott to Virginia Woolf* (Baltimore: Johns Hopkins Press, 1971).
Fletcher, Lisa, *Historical Romance Fiction: Heterosexuality and Performativity* (Aldershot: Ashgate, 2008).
Fowler, Alastair, *Kinds of Literature: An Introduction to the Theory of Genres and Modes* (Oxford: Oxford University Press, 1982).
Frye, Northrop, *Anatomy of Criticism: Four Essays* [1957] (Toronto: University of Toronto Press, 2006).
Fuller, Nicholas, 'Introduction' to *Sleuth's Alchemy: Cases of Mrs. Bradley and Others* (Norfolk, VA: Crippen & Landru, 2005), pp. 7–21.
Fuss, Diana, 'Inside/Out', in *Inside/Out: Lesbian Theories, Gay Theories*, ed. Diana Fuss (New York: Routledge, 1991), pp. 1–10.
Gallagher, Catherine, 'Undoing', in *Time and the Literary*, ed. Karen Newman, Jay Clayton, Marianne Hirsch (New York: Routledge, 2002), pp. 11–29.
Garber, Marjorie, *Vested Interests: Cross-dressing and Cultural Anxiety* (New York: Routledge, 1992).
Garrity, Jane, 'Encoding Bi-Location: Sylvia Townsend Warner and the Erotics of Dissimulation', in *Lesbian Erotics*, ed. Karla Jay (New York: New York University Press, 1995), pp. 241–68.

——, *Step-daughters of England: British Women Modernists and the National Imaginary* (Manchester: Manchester University Press, 2003).
Gilbert, Geoff, *Before Modernism Was: Modern History and the Constituency of Writing* (Basingstoke: Palgrave Macmillan, 2004).
Gilbert, Sandra M., 'Costumes of the Mind: Transvestism as Metaphor in Modern Literature', *Critical Inquiry*, 7.2 (1980), 391–417.
Gill, John Herbert, *Detecting Gertrude Stein and Other Suspects on the Shadow Side of Modernism* (New York: Democritus Books, 2003).
Gilmore, Leigh, 'Obscenity, Modernity, Identity: Legalizing *The Well of Loneliness* and *Nightwood*', *Journal of the History of Sexuality*, 4.4 (1994), 603–24.
Glendinning, Victoria, *Vita: The Life of V. Sackville-West* (London: Phoenix, 2005).
Goldman, Jonathan, *Modernism is the Literature of Celebrity* (Austin: University of Texas Press, 2011).
Greenberg, Clement, 'Avant-Garde and Kitsch' [1939], in *Clement Greenberg: The Collected Essays and Criticism Volume 1 Perceptions and Judgements 1939–1944*, ed. John O'Brian (Chicago and London: University of Chicago Press, 1988), pp. 5–22.
Griffin, Gabriele, 'Introduction', in *Outwrite: Lesbianism and Popular Culture*, ed. Gabriele Griffin (London: Pluto Press, 1992), pp. 1–8.
Gubar, Susan, 'Blessings in Disguise: Cross-dressing as Re-dressing for Female Modernists', *The Massachusetts Review*, 22.3 (1981), 477–508.
——, 'Sapphistries', *Signs: A Journal of Women in Culture and Society*, 10.1 (1984), 43–62.
Gygax, Franziska, *Gender and Genre in Gertrude Stein* (New York: Greenwood Press, 1998).
Hackett, Robin, *Sapphic Primitivism: Productions of Race, Class, and Sexuality in Key Works of Modern Fiction* (Piscataway, NJ: Rutgers University Press, 2004).
Hankins, Leslie Kathleen, '*Orlando*: "A Precipice Marked V" Between "A Miracle of Discretion" and "Lovemaking Unbelievable: Indiscretions Incredible"', in *Virginia Woolf: Lesbian Readings*, ed. Eileen Barrett and Patricia Cramer (New York: New York University Press, 1997), pp. 180–202.
Hart, Linda, *Fatal Women: Lesbian Sexuality and the Mark of Aggression* (Princeton: Princeton University Press, 1994).
Hartley, Jenny, 'Clothes and Uniform in the Theatre of Fascism: Clemence Dane and Virginia Woolf', in *Gender and Warfare in the Twentieth Century: Textual Representations*, ed. Angela K. Smith (Manchester: Manchester University Press, 2004), pp. 96–110.

Henderson, Linda Dalrymple, 'Einstein and 20th-Century Art: A Romance of Many Dimensions', in *Einstein for the 21st Century: His Legacy in Science, Art, and Modern Culture*, ed. Peter L. Galison, Gerald Holton, and Silvan S. Schweber (Princeton: Princeton University Press, 2008), pp. 101–29.

——, *The Fourth Dimension and Non-Euclidean Geometry in Modern Art* (Princeton: Princeton University Press, 1983).

——, 'The "Fourth Dimension" as Sign of Utopia in Early Modern Art and Culture', in *Utopianism and the Sciences, 1880–1930*, ed. Mary Kemperink and Leonieke Vermeer (Leuven: Peeters, 2010), pp. 1–15.

——, 'Modernism's Quest for Invisible Realities', in *Make It New: The Rise of Modernism*, ed. Kurt Heinzelman (Austin: University of Texas Press, 2003), pp. 135–9.

——, 'Vibratory Modernism: Boccioni, Kupka, and the Ether of Space', in *From Energy to Information: Representation in Science and Technology, Art, and Literature*, ed. Bruce Clarke and Linda Dalrymple Henderson (Stanford: Stanford University Press, 2002), pp. 126–49.

Hoberman, Ruth, *Gendering Classicism: The Ancient World in Twentieth-Century Women's Historical Fiction* (Albany: State University of New York Press, 1997).

Holmes, Rachael, 'Clothing and The Body: Motifs of Female Distress in Virginia Woolf and Katherine Mansfield', *Virginia Woolf Bulletin*, 3 (2000), 9–15.

Hoshi, Kumiko, 'Modernism's Fourth Dimension in *Aaron's Rod*: Einstein, Picasso, and Lawrence', in *Windows to the Sun: D. H. Lawrence's 'Thought-Adventures'*, ed. Earl Ingersoll and Virginia Hyde (Madison, NJ: Fairleigh Dickinson University Press, 2009), pp. 99–117.

Hughes, Helen, *The Historical Romance* (London: Routledge, 1993).

Humble, Nicola, *The Feminine Middlebrow Novel, 1920s to 1950s: Class, Domesticity, and Bohemianism* (Oxford: Oxford University Press, 2001).

Humm, Maggie, *Snapshots of Bloomsbury: The Private Lives of Virginia Woolf and Vanessa Bell* (New Brunswick, NJ: Rutgers University Press, 2006).

Huyssen, Andreas, *After the Great Divide: Modernism, Mass Culture, Postmodernism* (Bloomington: Indiana University Press, 1986).

——, 'High/Low in an Expanded Field', *Modernism/Modernity*, 9.3 (2002), 363–74.

Ingram, Angela, '"Unutterable Putrefaction" and "Foul Stuff": Two "Obscene" Novels of the 1920s', *Women's Studies International Forum*, 9.4 (1986), 341–54.

Jackson, Rosemary, *Fantasy: The Literature of Subversion* (London: Routledge, 1981).

Jameson, Fredric, 'Magical Narratives: Romance as Genre', *New Literary History*, 7.1 (1975), 135–63.

Jardine, Lisa, *Still Harping on Daughters: Women and Drama in the Age of Shakespeare* (Hemel Hempstead: Harvester Wheatsheaf, 1983).

Jay, Karla, *The Amazon and the Page: Natalie Clifford Barney and Renée Vivien* (Bloomington: Indiana University Press, 1988).

——, 'Lesbian Modernism: (Trans)Forming the (C)Anon', in *Professions of Desire: Lesbian and Gay Studies in Literature*, ed. George E. Haggerty and Bonnie Zimmerman (New York: The Modern Language Association of America, 1995), pp. 72–83.

Jay, Karla, and Joanne Glasgow (eds), *Lesbian Texts and Contexts: Radical Revisions*, ed. Karla Jay and Joanne Glasgow (London: Onlywomen Press, 1992), pp. 204–16.

Jeffreys, Sheila, *The Spinster and Her Enemies: Feminism and Sexuality 1880–1930* (London: Pandora Press, 1985).

Jones, Ann, *Women Who Kill* [1980] (London: Gollancz, 1991).

Jones, Danell, 'The Chase of the Wild Goose: The Ladies of Llangollen and *Orlando*', in *Virginia Woolf: Themes and Variations Selected Papers from the Second Annual Conference on Virginia Woolf*, ed. Vara Neverow-Turk and Mark Hussey (New York: Pace University Press, 1993), pp. 181–9.

Kaplan, Cora, 'An Unsuitable Genre for a Feminist?', *Women's Review*, 8 (1986), 18–19.

Katz, Jonathan Ned, *Gay American History: Lesbians and Gay Men in the U.S.A* (Harmondsworth: Meridian, 1992).

Kean, Danuta, 'Ian Rankin: The Singing Detective', *The Independent*, 22 October 2006, <www.independent.co.uk/news/people/ian-rankin-the-singing-detective-421060.html> [accessed 28 July 2010].

Kenney, Catherine, 'Detecting a Novel Use for Spinsters in Sayers's Fiction', in *Old Maids to Radical Spinsters: Unmarried Women in the Twentieth-Century Novel*, ed. Laura Doan (Urbana and Chicago: University of Illinois Press, 1991), pp. 123–38.

Knight, Stephen, *Form and Ideology in Crime Fiction* (Basingstoke: Macmillan, 1980).

——, 'The Golden Age', in *The Cambridge Companion to Crime Fiction*, ed. Martin Priestman (Cambridge: Cambridge University Press, 2003), pp. 77–94.

Koestenbaum, Wayne, *Double Talk: The Erotics of Male Literary Collaboration* (New York: Routledge, 1989).

Koppen, R. S., *Virginia Woolf, Fashion and Literary Modernity* (Edinburgh: Edinburgh University Press, 2009).

Kungl, Carla T., *Creating the Fictional Female Detective: The Sleuth Heroines of British Women Writers, 1890–1940* (Jefferson, NC: McFarland, 2006).

Laing, Kathryn S., 'Addressing Femininity in the Twenties: Virginia Woolf and Rebecca West on Money, Mirrors and Masquerade', in *Virginia Woolf and the Arts: Selected Papers from the Sixth Annual Conference on Virginia Woolf*, ed. Diane F. Gillespie and Leslie K. Hankins (New York: Pace University Press, 1997), pp. 66–75.

Lamos, Colleen, 'Queer Conjunctions in Modernism', in *Gender in Modernism: New Geographies, Complex Intersections*, ed. Bonnie Kime Scott (Urbana and Chicago: University of Illinois Press, 2007), pp. 336–43.

Landon, Brooks, '"Not Solve It But Be In It": Gertrude Stein's Detective Stories and the Mystery of Creativity', *American Literature*, 53.3 (1981), 487–98.

Latham, Sean, *'Am I a Snob?': Modernism and the Novel* (Ithaca: Cornell University Press, 2003).

Latimer, Tirza True, *Women Together/Women Apart: Portraits of Lesbian Paris* (New Brunswick, NJ: Rutgers University Press, 2005).

Lee, Hermione, *Edith Wharton* (London: Chatto & Windus, 2007).

——, *Virginia Woolf* (London: Vintage, 1997).

Leonardi, Susan J., 'Murders Academic: Women Professors and the Crimes of Gender', in *Feminism in Women's Detective Fiction*, ed. Glenwood Irons (Toronto: University of Toronto Press, 1995), pp. 112–26.

Levay, Matthew, 'Remaining a Mystery: Gertrude Stein, Crime Fiction and Popular Modernism', *Journal of Modern Literature*, 36.4 (2013), 1–22.

Lincoln, Victoria, *A Private Disgrace: Lizzie Borden by Daylight* (London: Gollancz, 1968).

London, Bette, 'Mediumship, Automatism, and Modernist Authorship', in *Gender in Modernism: New Geographies, Complex Intersections*, ed. Bonnie Kime Scott (Urbana: University of Illinois Press, 2007), pp. 623–32.

——, *Writing Double: Women's Literary Partnerships* (Ithaca, NY: Cornell University Press, 1999).

Lukács, Georg, *The Historical Novel* [1937], trans. Hannah and Stanley Mitchell (London: Merlin Press, 1962).

Maitzen, Rohan, '"This Feminine Preserve": Historical Biographies by Victorian Women', *Victorian Studies*, 38.3 (1995), 371–93.

Malcolm, Janet, *Two Lives: Gertrude and Alice* (New Haven: Yale University Press, 2007).

Marchino, Lois A, 'The Female Sleuth in Academe', *Journal of Popular Culture*, 23.3 (1989), 89–100.

Marcus, Jane, 'A Wilderness of One's Own: Feminist Fantasy Novels of the Twenties: Rebecca West and Sylvia Townsend Warner', in *Women Writers and the City: Essays in Feminist Literary Criticism*, ed. Susan Merrill Squier (Knoxville: University of Tennessee Press, 1984), pp. 134–60.

Marcus, Laura, 'Detection and Literary Fiction', in *The Cambridge Companion to Crime Fiction*, ed. Martin Priestman (Cambridge: Cambridge University Press, 2003), pp. 245–67.

——, 'Virginia Woolf and the Hogarth Press', in *Modernist Writers and the Marketplace*, ed. Ian Willison, Warwick Gould and Warren Chernaik (Basingstoke: Macmillan, 1996), pp. 124–50.

Marshik, Celia, *British Modernism and Censorship* (Cambridge: Cambridge University Press, 2006).

——, 'History's "Abrupt Revenges": Censoring War's Perversions in *The Well of Loneliness* and *Sleeveless Errand*', *Journal of Modern Literature*, 26.2 (2003), 145–59.

Maxwell, Richard, 'Historical Novel', *Encyclopedia of The Novel Volume 1*, ed. Paul Schellinger (Chicago: Fitzroy Dearborn, 1998), pp. 543–8.

McFadden, Marya, 'Queerness at Shrewsbury: Homoerotic Desire in *Gaudy Night*', *Modern Fiction Studies*, 46.2 (2000), 355–78.

Medd, Jodie, 'Séances and Slander: Radclyffe Hall in 1920', in *Sapphic Modernities: Sexuality, Women and National Culture*, ed. Laura Doan and Jane Garrity (New York: Palgrave, 2006), pp. 201–16.

Meese, Elizabeth, *(Sem)erotics: Theorizing Lesbian: Writing* (New York: New York University Press, 1992).

Miller, Arthur, *Einstein, Picasso: Space, Time, and the Beauty that Causes Havoc* (New York: Basic Books, 2001).

Miller, Meredith, *Historical Dictionary of Lesbian Literature* (Lanham, MD: Scarecrow Press, 2006).

Minow, Makiki, 'Versions of Female Modernism: Review-Article', *News From Nowhere*, 7 (1989), 64–9.

Mirkin, Ronnie, 'The Portrait of Elizabeth Cary in the Ashmolean Museum: "Cross-dressing" in the English Renaissance', in *The Renaissance Theatre: Texts, Performance, Design Volume 1*, ed. Christopher Cairns (Aldershot: Ashgate, 1999), pp. 77–106.

Morris, Virginia B., 'Arsenic and Blue Lace: Sayers' Criminal Women', *Modern Fiction Studies*, 29.3 (1983), 485–95.

Moylan, Tom, *Demand the Impossible: Science Fiction and the Utopian Imagination* (New York: Methuen, 1986).

Mullin, Katherine, 'Poison More Deadly than Prussic Acid: Defining Obscenity after the 1857 Obscene Publications Act (1850–1885)', in *Prudes on the*

Prowl: Fiction and Obscenity in England, 1850 to the Present Day, ed. David Bradshaw and Rachel Potter (Oxford: Oxford University Press, 2013), pp. 11–29.

Munt, Sally R., *Murder by the Book? Feminism and the Crime Novel* (London: Routledge, 1994).

Nair, Sashi, *Secrecy and Sapphic Modernism: Reading 'Romans À Clef' Between the Wars* (Basingstoke: Palgrave Macmillan, 2012).

Neroni, Hilary, *The Violent Woman: Femininity, Narrative, and Violence in Contemporary American Cinema* (New York: State University of New York Press, 2005).

Newton, Esther, 'The Mythic Mannish Lesbian: Radclyffe Hall and the New Woman', in *Hidden From History: Reclaiming the Gay and Lesbian Past* [1989], ed. Martin Bauml Duberman, Martha Vicinus and George Chauncey Jr (Harmondsworth: Penguin, 1991), pp. 281–93.

Oram, Alison, '"Embittered, Sexless or Homosexual": Attacks on Spinster Teachers 1918–1939', in *Not a Passing Phase: Reclaiming Lesbians in History 1840–1985*, ed. Lesbian History Group (London: Women's Press, 1989), pp. 99–118.

——, *Her Husband Was a Woman!: Women's Gender-Crossing in Modern British Popular Culture* (Abindgon: Routledge, 2007).

——, 'Telling Stories About the Ladies of Llangollen: The Construction of Lesbian and Feminist Histories', in *Re-presenting the Past: Women and History*, ed. Ann-Marie Gallagher, Cathy Lubelska, and Louise Ryan (Harlow: Pearson, 2001), pp. 44–72.

Oram, Alison, and Annmarie Turnbull (comp.), *The Lesbian History Sourcebook: Love and Sex Between Women in Britain from 1780–1970* (London: Routledge, 2001).

Orel, Harold, *Popular Fiction in England 1914–1918* (Hemel Hempstead: Harvester Wheatsheaf, 1992).

Pacteau, Francette, 'The Impossible Referent: Representations of the Androgyne', in *Formations of Fantasy*, ed. Victor Burgin, James Donald and Cora Kaplan (London: Methuen, 1986), pp. 62–84.

Palmer, Paulina, 'The Lesbian Feminist Thriller and Detective Novel', in *What Lesbians Do In Books*, ed. Elaine Hobby and Chris White (London: Women's Press, 1991), pp. 9–27.

——, *Lesbian Gothic: Transgressive Fictions* (London: Cassell, 1999).

Parkes, Adam, *Modernism and the Theater of Censorship* (New York: Oxford University Press, 1996).

Patai, Daphne, 'Imagining Reality: The Utopian Fiction of Katharine Burdekin', in *Rediscovering Forgotten Radicals: British Women Writers 1889–1939*, ed. Angela Ingram and Daphne Patai (Chapel Hill: University of North Carolina Press, 1993) pp. 226–43.

Payne, Kenneth, 'Grania, "a mad woman ... Doomed to attempt the impossible": Imagining Utopia in Katherine [sic] Burdekin's *The End of This Day's Business*', *Lamar Journal of the Humanities*, 30.2 (2005), 33–42.

Pearson, Neil, *Obelisk: A History of Jack Kahane and the Obelisk Press* (Liverpool: Liverpool University Press, 2007).

Plain, Gill, *Twentieth-Century Crime Fiction: Gender, Sexuality and the Body* (Edinburgh: Edinburgh University Press, 2001).

Potter, Rachel, *Obscene Modernism: Literary Censorship and Experiment, 1900–1940* (Oxford: Oxford University Press, 2013).

Prosser, Jay, '"Some Primitive Thing Conceived in a Turbulent Age of Transition": The Transsexual Emerging from *The Well*', in *Palatable Poison: Critical Perspectives on The Well of Loneliness*, ed. Laura Doan and Jay Prosser (New York: Columbia University Press, 2001), pp. 129–44.

Radford, Jean, 'Introduction', in *The Progress of Romance: The Politics of Popular Fiction*, ed. Jean Radford (London: Routledge & Kegan Paul, 1986), pp. 1–20.

Rado, Lisa, 'Would the Real Virginia Woolf Please Stand Up? Feminist Criticism, the Androgyny Debates, and *Orlando*', *Women's Studies*, 26.2 (1997), 147–69.

Raitt, Suzanne, 'Sex, Love and the Homosexual Body in Early Sexology', in *Sexology in Culture: Labelling Bodies and Desires*, ed. Lucy Bland and Laura Doan (Cambridge: Polity Press, 1998), pp. 150–64.

——, *Virginia and Vita: The Work and Friendship of V. Sackville-West and Virginia Woolf* (Oxford: Oxford University Press, 1993).

Rauve, Rebecca, 'An Intersection of Interests: Gurdjieff's Rope Group as a Site of Literary Production', *Twentieth-Century Literature*, 49.1 (2003), 46–81.

Ray, Chelsea, 'Decadent Heroines or Modernist Lovers: Natalie Clifford Barney's Unpublished *Feminine Lovers or the Third Woman*', *South Central Review*, 22.3 (2005), 32–61.

Reddy, Maureen T., 'Women Detectives', in *The Cambridge Companion to Crime Fiction*, ed. Martin Priestman (Cambridge: Cambridge University Press, 2003), pp. 191–207.

Rives, Darcie D., 'Fantastic Writing, Real Lives: Gender, Race, and Sexuality in Early Twentieth-Century American Women's Speculative fiction' (unpublished doctoral dissertation, University of Nebraska, 2006). <http://digitalcommons.unl.edu/dissertations/AAI3216433> [accessed 15 January 2010].

Robbin, Tony, *Shadows of Reality: The Fourth Dimension in Relativity, Cubism, and Modern Thought* (New Haven: Yale University Press, 2006).

Rohr, Susanne, '"Everybody sees, and everybody says they do": Another Guess at Gertrude Stein's *Blood on the Dining-Room Floor*', *Amerikastudien/ American Studies*, 41.4 (1996), 592–602.

Rose, Jonathan, *The Intellectual Life of the British Working Classes* [2001], 2nd edn (New Haven: Yale University Press, 2010).

Rzepka, Charles J., *Detective Fiction* (Cambridge: Polity Press, 2005)

Samuels, Charles, and Louise Samuels, *The Girl in the House of Hate* (New York: Fawcett, 1953).

Sargent, Lyman Tower, 'Themes in Utopian Fiction in English Before Wells', *Science Fiction Studies*, 3.3 (1976), 275–82.

Schleiner, Winfried, 'Male Cross-Dressing and Transvestism in Renaissance Romances', *The Sixteenth Century Journal*, 19.4 (1988), 605–19.

Scholes, Robert, *Parodoxy of Modernism* (New Haven: Yale University Press, 2006).

Sedgwick, Eve Kosofsky, *Epistemology of the Closet* [1990], 2nd edn (Berkeley and Los Angeles: University of California Press, 2008).

Seed, David, '"Psychical" Cases: Transformations of the Supernatural in Virginia Woolf and May Sinclair', in *Gothic Modernisms*, ed. Andrew Smith and Jeff Wallace (Basingstoke: Palgrave, 2001), pp. 44–61.

Slide, Anthony, *Gay and Lesbian Characters and Themes in Mystery Novels: A Critical Guide to Over 500 Works in English* (Jefferson, NC: McFarland, 1993).

Smith, Patricia Juliana, *Lesbian Panic: Homoeroticism in Modern British Women's Fiction* (New York: Columbia University Press, 1997).

Smith-Rosenberg, Carroll, 'Discourses of Sexuality and Subjectivity: The New Woman, 1870–1936', in *Hidden from History: Reclaiming the Gay and Lesbian Past* [1989], ed. Martin Bauml Duberman, Martha Vicinus and George Chauncey Jr (Harmondsworth: Penguin, 1991), pp. 264–80.

Souhami, Diana, *Gertrude and Alice* [1991] (London: Weidenfeld & Nicolson, 1999).

——, *The Trials of Radclyffe Hall* [1998] (London: Virago Press, 1999).

——, *Wild Girls: Paris, Sappho and Art: The Lives and Loves of Natalie Barney and Romaine Brooks* (London: Weidenfeld & Nicolson, 2004).

Stec, Loretta, 'Dystopian Modernism vs. Utopian Feminism: Burdekin, Woolf, and West Respond to the Rise of Fascism', in *Virginia Woolf and Fascism: Resisting the Dictators' Seduction*, ed. Merry M. Pawlowski (Basingstoke: Palgrave, 2001), pp. 178–93.

Straub, Kristina, 'The Guilty Pleasures of Female Theatrical Cross-Dressing and the Autobiography of Charlotte Charke', in *Body Guards: The Cultural Politics of Gender Ambiguity*, ed. Julia Epstein and Kristina Straub (New York: Routledge, 1991), pp. 142–66.

Strychacz, Thomas, *Modernism, Mass Culture, and Professionalism* (Cambridge: Cambridge University Press, 1993).
Suvin, Darko, *Defined by a Hollow: Essays on Utopia, Science Fiction and Political Epistemology* (London: Peter Lang, 2010).
Sword, Helen, *Ghostwriting Modernism* (Ithaca, NY: Cornell University Press, 2002).
Symons, Julian, *Bloody Murder From the Detective Story to the Crime Novel: A History* (Harmondsworth: Viking, 1985).
Tamagne, Florence, *A History of Homosexuality in Europe: Berlin, London, Paris 1919–1939 Volume II* (New York: Algora, 2004).
Taylor, Clare L., *Women, Writing, and Fetishism 1890–1950: Female Cross-Gendering* (Oxford: Oxford University Press, 2003).
Taylor, Melanie A., '"The Masculine Soul Heaving in the Female Bosom": Theories of Inversion and *The Well of Loneliness*', *Journal of Gender Studies*, 7.3 (1998), 287–96
Thurschwell, Pamela, *Literature, Technology and Magical Thinking, 1880–1920* (Cambridge: Cambridge University Press, 2001).
Todorov, Tzvetan, *The Fantastic: A Structural Approach to a Literary Genre* (Ithaca, NY: Cornell University Press, 1980).
——, 'The Typology of Detective Fiction' [1966], in *The Poetics of Prose*, trans. Richard Howard (Oxford: Basil Blackwell, 1977), pp. 42–52.
Turner, Catherine, *Marketing Modernism Between the Two World Wars* (Amherst: University of Massachusetts Press, 2003).
Vanderham, Paul, *James Joyce and Censorship: The Trials of Ulysses* (Basingstoke: Macmillan, 1998).
Vicinus, Martha, 'Distance and Desire: English Boarding-School Friendships', *Signs: Journal of Women in Culture and Society*, 9.4 (1984), 600–22.
——, '"A Legion of Ghosts": Vernon Lee (1856–1935) and the Art of Nostalgia', *GLQ: A Journal of Lesbian and Gay Studies*, 10.4 (2004), 599–616.
Villarejo, Amy, *Lesbian Rule: Cultural Criticism and the Value of Desire* (Durham, NC: Duke University Press, 2003).
Wachman, Gay, *Lesbian Empire: Radical Crosswriting in the Twenties* (New Brunswick, NJ: Rutgers University Press, 2001).
Wallace, Diana, *The Woman's Historical Novel: British Women Writers, 1900–2000* (Basingstoke: Palgrave, 2005).
Wallace, Jo-Ann, 'Edith Ellis, Sapphic Idealism, and *The Lover's Calendar* (1912)', in *Sapphic Modernities: Sexuality, Women and National Culture*, ed. Laura Doan and Jane Garrity (New York: Palgrave, 2006), pp. 183–99.
Warthling Roberts, Joan, 'Amelia Butterworth: The Spinster Detective', in *Feminism in Women's Detective Fiction*, ed. Glenwood Irons (Toronto: University of Toronto Press, 1995), pp. 3–11.

Waters, Sarah, '"A Girton Girl on a Throne": Queen Christina and Versions of Lesbianism, 1906–1933', *Feminist Review*, 46 (1994), 41–60.

——, 'Wolfskins and Togas: Maude Meagher's *The Green Scamander* and the Lesbian Historical Novel', *Women: A Cultural Review*, 7.2 (1996), 176–88.

White, Patricia, 'Female Spectator, Lesbian Specter: *The Haunting*', in *Inside/Out: Lesbian Theories, Gay Theories*, ed. Diana Fuss (New York: Routledge, 1991), pp. 142–72.

Wilson, Leigh, *Modernism and Magic: Experiments with Spiritualism, Theosophy and the Occult* (Edinburgh: Edinburgh University Press, 2013).

Wilt, Judith, 'Steamboat Surfacing: Scott and the English Novelists', *Nineteenth Century Fiction*, 35.4 (1981), 459–86.

Winning, Joanne, *The Pilgrimage of Dorothy Richardson* (Madison: University of Wisconsin Press, 2000).

——, 'Wilde Identifications: Queering the Sexual and the National in the Work of Eve Langley', *Australian Literary Studies*, 20.4 (2002), 301–15.

——, 'Writing by the Light of *The Well*: Radclyffe Hall and the Lesbian Modernists', in *Palatable Poison: Critical Perspectives on The Well of Loneliness*, ed. Laura Doan and Jay Prosser (New York: Columbia University Press, 2001), pp. 372–93.

'Woman's Hour', BBC Radio 4, 23 November 2006, <www.bbc.co.uk/radio4/woman'shour/02/2006_47_thu.shtml> [accessed 28 July 2010].

INDEX

androgyny, 41–4, 52, 67, 71, 72, 75, 76, 122–3, 124–5, 126, 129
avant-garde, the, 13, 109

Barney, Natalie Clifford, 59–78, 65–6, 79n, 79–80n, 87, 192
  relationship with Renée Vivien, 76–7
  spiritual love and, 65–78
  WORKS
  Feminine Lovers or the Third Woman, 73
  In Memory of Dorothy Ierne Wilde, 66–7, 68
  The One Who is Legion, 29–30, 61, 66, 67–78, 190
Biron, Sir Chartres (Chief Magistrate), 7, 9
Bloch, Iwan, 168n
Bodkin, Sir Archibald (Director of Public Prosecutions), 6, 7–8
Borden, Lizzie, 142, 173–7, 186, 187n
Bourdieu, Pierre, 16, 109
Bowen, Marjorie, 116
Brand, Christianna, 156

Brooks, Romaine, 70–1, 79n
Bryher, 34, 35, 132n
Burdekin, Katharine, 17, 23n, 29–30, 31–55, 55n, 189–90, 191, 192
  censorship and, 39–40, 54, 56–7n, 189–90
  Edward Carpenter and, 47–9, 50, 54
  collaboration with Margaret Goldsmith, 93, 94, 106n
  focus on the invert as revolutionary, 46–9, 54–5
  interest in Radclyffe Hall's *The Well of Loneliness*, 38–41, 49, 54, 56n
  problematic treatment of desire, 49–54
  pseudonym, Murray Constantine, 33, 34, 35, 38, 93
  relationship with Havelock Ellis, 35, 38, 50, 54, 56n
  relationship with H.D., 33, 34–5, 38, 54, 55n, 56n, 58n
  spirituality, spiritual love and, 40–1, 49–50, 52–4

Burdekin, Katharine (*cont.*)
  treatment of male homosexuality as dystopian, 43, 51
  treatment of reincarnation, 52–3
  treatment of transgenderism, 50–1, 52
  unpublished narratives about sexual inversion, 38–41, 49, 50, 52, 53–4
  utopian project for sexuality, 49–55
  writing in *Life and Letters To-Day*, 34
  WORKS
  'Dolly', 53
  Proud Man, 35, 38, 41–4, 46, 47 49, 51, 52, 54, 189–90
  'Snakes and Ladders', 38, 56n
  Swastika Night, 33, 44, 51
  The End of this Day's Business, 44–6, 48, 49, 50, 52, 54, 58n, 189–90
  The Rebel Passion, 48–50, 51, 52, 54, 57n, 189–90
  'The Stars Shine in Daylight', 38–41, 52, 57n
  'Two in a Sack', 38–41, 56n, 56–7n
  Venus in Scorpio, 93, 94
  'Walking to Mark', 52–3

Carpenter, Edward, 47–9, 50, 54, 57n, 58n, 95
censorship
  as commercially profitable, 11–12, 22n
  First World War and, 2, 3–4, 5, 19n
  Fortune Press/Sequana book shop raid and, 11, 20n
  gender and, 3–7
  government censorship, 1–12, 20n, 21n, 22n
  James Joyce and, 2
  D. H. Lawrence and, 2, 6, 7, 21n
  lesbian literature and, 9–10, 11–12

London Public Morality Council and, 9, 11, 21n
  Naomi Mitchison and, 1–2, 16, 20n, 41, 189
  modernism as a response to, 8–9, 14, 15, 21n
  nationalism and, 5–6, 7
  Obscene Books Bill (1936) and, 11
  Obscene Books Commission and, 11
  Publishers' Association and, 11
  Time and Tide and, 10, 21n
  see also Hall, Radclyffe; James, Norah; Mackenzie, Compton; Woolf, Virginia
Chesterton, G. K., 137, 138, 166
class, 16, 108–10, 162, 165–6
clothes and costume, 114–30, 131n, 132n, 133n
Constable (publisher), 1
cross-dressing and disguise, 88, 94, 97, 99, 115–30, 132n, 150–1, 153

Daily Mail, 11–12
Dane, Clemence, 148
Defence of the Realm Act (DORA, 1918), 5–6, 19n, 20n
Detection Club, The, 138
detective fiction, 137–42, 142n, 144–66, 167n, 169–86, 190
  education in, 155–66
  Golden Age, 137–9, 141, 142n, 142–3n, 170, 180
  lesbian crime fiction, 139, 142–3n
  modernism and, 169–70, 173
Donisthorpe, G. Sheila, 11, 12
Douglas, James, 3, 6, 7
Dunn, J. W., 64–5

Einstein, Albert, 63, 64, 70
Ellis, Edith, 50, 53, 62
Ellis, Havelock
  on criminality, violence and inversion, 140–1, 152, 160
  on education and inversion, 157
  Edith Ellis and, 62

Radclyffe Hall and, 2–3
Studies in the Psychology of Sex: Sexual Inversion, 20n, 36, 50, 56n, 58n, 157
see also Burdekin, Katharine
erotics of literary collaboration, 103, 106n, 106–7n

fantasy fiction, 27–30, 30n, 31–55, 59–78
Ferenczi, Sándor, 69
First World War, 2, 3, 5, 19n, 32, 37, 59, 86
Freud, Sigmund, 27–8, 62, 68–9, 96, 162, 165, 181–2

genre fiction
as a creative strategy, 1–2, 8, 15–17, 18–19, 189–93
cultural value and, 12–16, 22n, 108–10, 193
escapism and, 12–13
the lesbian writer/reader and, 18–19
the middlebrow and, 110
Goldsmith, Margaret, 17, 87–8, 92–4, 105–6n, 189, 190, 191, 192
collaboration with Katharine Burdekin, 93, 94, 106n
relationship with Vita Sackville-West, 93, 105–6n
treatment of psychoanalysis, 94–9, 98
treatment of sexology, 94–9, 106n
WORKS
Christina of Sweden, 93–9, 104–5
Frederick the Great, 106n
Sappho: A Psychological Reconstruction of Her Life, 93, 94, 104
Venus in Scorpio, 93, 94
Gordon, Mary, 17, 87–8, 92–4, 106n, 189, 190, 192
Chase of the Wild Goose, 99–105, 106n
connection to *Orlando* and Woolf, 107n

Greenberg, Clement, 13
Gurdjieff, George Ivanovitch, 78

Hall, Radclyffe
interest in the occult, 59–60, 61, 62, 79n
'Miss Ogilvy Finds Herself', 12, 22n, 59–60
The Well of Loneliness, 21n, 37, 57–8n, 59–60, 61, 71, 86, 95, 104: attempt to republish, 11, 22n; censorship of, 2–12, 15, 57n, 189; Havelock Ellis, sexology and, 2–3, 37–8; legal judgement on, 7, 9; parody of, 5; reception of, 3; struggle to publish, 3; transgenderism and, 50–1, 52; treatment compared to Mackenzie's *Extraordinary Women*, 5–8, 20–1n, 21n
see also Burdekin, Katharine
Hammett, Dashiell, 170, 187n
H.D. see Burdekin, Katharine
heterosexual crime, 169–86
Heyer, Georgette, 85
The Masqueraders, 117–18, 127
These Old Shades, 118
Hicklin test case, 2
historical biography, 87–8, 90–105, 105n, 190
historical fiction, 83–8, 88n, 89n, 90–105, 105n, 108–30
historical romance, 108–30, 132n, 193n
history (as discourse), 83–4, 86–7, 90–1, 104–5, 190
homoerotic nostalgia, 77
homosexuality (male), as dystopian, 43, 51
Hutton, Dr Laura, 9–10, 11

James, Norah
on censorship, 8
Sleeveless Errand, 3–4, 5, 6, 20n, 22n

217

Jameson, Storm, 31–2, 33
John Lane (publisher), 1
Jonathan Cape (publisher), 1, 3, 20n, 20–1n
Joynson-Hicks, Sir William (Home Secretary), 21n
Jung, Carl, 106n

Kahane, Jack, 4, 22n
Keane, Molly, 153
Knox, Ronald, 142n, 169–70, 186
Krafft-Ebing, Richard von, 36, 37

Ladies of Llangollen, 87–8, 92, 93, 99–105
Larsen, Nella, 153
Lawrence, Hilda, 139, 156
lesbian criminal, 138–42, 144–66, 173–7, 182–6, 191
lesbian detective, 144–66, 191
lesbian modernism
  definition of, 13–18, 22n, 191–2
  queer modernism and, 17–18
  sapphic modernism and, 17
lesbian occult, 29–30, 59–78, 78n, 99–105, 190; *see also* the occult; spiritualism
lesbian panic, 153–4
lesbian sexuality and identity
  attempt to criminalise (1921), 57n
  education and, 37, 97–8, 155–66, 167n
  feminism and, 5, 37, 43–4, 97, 100–1, 103, 168n, 191, 192
  First World War and, 3–4, 5, 59
  historical narrative and, 86–7, 89n, 128
  nationalism and, 5–6
  as political, 31–55
  professional work and, 37, 98, 146–66
  spinster and, 145–50, 152, 154, 156–7, 159, 167n

spirituality and, 44–55, 59–78, 99–104
as utopian, 31–55, 190
violence and, 139–41, 143n, 144–66, 174–7, 185–6
Life and Letters To-Day, 34
Loddon, D. L., 11, 12
Lukács, Georg, 84–5, 86

Mackenzie, Compton
  Extraordinary Women, 5, 6, 7, 8, 20–1n, 116
  Sinister Street, 116
  The Early Life and Adventures of Sylvia Scarlett, 116
McDermid, Val, 143n
Man, Proud Man (collection of essays), 31–2
Middlebrow, 108–10, 111, 112, 128, 130n
Mirrlees, Hope, 87, 113
Mitchell, Alice, 140–1
Mitchell, Gladys, 17, 141–2, 145, 156, 166, 190–1, 192
  Speedy Death, 138–9, 144–5, 150–5, 162, 163, 166–7n, 174
Mitchison, Naomi, 1, 2, 3, 16, 19n, 20n, 189
Mitre Press, 11–12
Moberly, Anne and Eleanor Jourdain, 64–5
modernism
  definition of, 13–14, 16–18, 21n, 23n, 192, 193n
  the 'great divide' and, 13

Obscene Publications Act (1857), 2
Obscenity (definition of), 2, 21n
occult, the
  the fourth dimension and, 63–5, 69–70, 72, 78
  psychoanalysis and, 62, 65, 68–9
  science and, 63–5, 68, 70
  see also lesbian occult; spiritualism
Olivier, Edith, 64–5

psychoanalysis, 94–9, 98, 104, 120, 139, 151, 152, 192
  the androgyne and, 124
  fantasy and, 27–8
  homosexuality and, 68–9
  mourning and, 181–2
  see also the occult

Queen Christina of Sweden, 88, 92, 93–9, 104, 105
queer
  texts and characters as, 35, 78, 153, 154, 160
  use of the term, 52, 144, 152, 154, 166–7n, 167n

Rankin, Ian, 143n
Renault, Mary
  on historical fiction, 85–6
  the western and, 18–19, 23n
Riding, Laura, 38, 56n
Riviere, Joan, 120
romantic friendships, 101–2, 149, 150, 158, 163
Ross, Martin (Edith Somerville and Violet Martin), 62

Sackville-West, Vita, 63–4, 91, 93, 105–6n, 111, 130n, 133n
sapphic idealism, 50
Sappho, 66, 87, 92–3, 94, 104
Sayers, Dorothy L., 17, 141–2, 145, 158, 165, 166, 190–1, 192
  on detective fiction, 12–13, 22n
  Gaudy Night, 158–62, 163, 165–6
  Strong Poison, 158, 160
  Unnatural Death, 139, 145–50, 160, 161, 162, 167n, 174
Scott, Sir Walter, 84, 113–14, 116–17, 131n
sexology and sexual inversion, 2–3, 5, 6, 7, 8, 29, 31–55, 56n, 57n, 58n, 59, 71, 72, 94, 95, 101, 102, 104, 106n, 140–1, 152, 157, 168n, 189, 190, 192

Shakespeare, William, *The Tempest*, 123
Sitwell, Edith, 176
Spain, Nancy, 139, 156
speculative fiction, 31–55, 190
  sex-role reversal in, 31–2, 44–6
  utopian fiction, 32–3, 55n
spinster *see* Lesbian sexuality and identity
spiritualism, 54, 61–2, 68, 75
Stein, Gertrude, 142, 169–86, 190, 191, 192
  Lizzie Borden and, 173–6, 187n
  interest in detective fiction and crime, 170–2, 187n
  mourning in the work of, 181–2, 186
  WORKS
  'A Water-fall and a Piano', 170, 171, 184, 185
  'American Crimes and How They Matter', 171, 175–6, 180
  Blood on the Dining-Room Floor, 170, 171–4, 176–86, 187n
  Everybody's Autobiography, 172, 173, 177, 178–9, 181, 183, 184–5
  'How Writing is Written', 179
  'Is Dead', 170
  Narration: Four Lectures by Gertrude Stein, 171
  'Subject-Cases: The Background of a Detective Story', 170
  The Autobiography of Alice B. Toklas, 172
  The Making of Americans, 181
  Three Lives, 180
  'Why I Like Detective Stories', 170, 171, 180, 187n
Stephen, Leslie, 113–15, 131n
Stephenson, Sir George (Deputy to the Director of Public Prosecutions), 6
Strachey, Lytton, 105
supernatural fiction, 59–78, 190
Sylvia Scarlett (dir. George Cukor), 116

Tey, Josephine (Elizabeth Mackintosh), 17, 141–2, 145, 190–1, 192
  Miss Pym Disposes, 139, 162–6
time travel, 63–5
Toklas, Alice B., 173, 184, 187n
Troubridge, Una, 11, 22n, 61–2

Ulrichs, Karl Heinrich, 36
Uranism, 36

Van Dine, S.S., 142, 167n, 170
Victor Gollancz (publisher), 1
Vivien, Renée, 66, 76–7, 87

Wallace, Edgar, 170
Weininger, Otto, 36
West, Rebecca, 31–2, 33
Wharton, Edith, 187n
wild goose as symbol, 107n
Wilde, Dorothy, 66–7, 74, 76, 77, 79–80n
Woolf, Virginia, 130n, 192
  as book reviewer, 112–13, 116, 131n
  on censorship, 10, 21n
  on clothes and fashion, 115, 128–9, 131n, 133n
  dreadnought hoax and, 115, 131–2n
  historical fiction and, 112–15, 116–17, 131n
  on history as a discourse, 83–4, 114–15
  on Sir Walter Scott, 113, 116–17
  WORKS
  A Room of One's Own, 83, 90, 112, 126, 192
  'A Society', 115
  'Middlebrow' and the marketplace, 108–10, 111, 112, 115, 128, 131n, 192
  'Modern Fiction', 128–9
  Orlando: A Biography, 12, 71, 87, 88, 110–12, 114–15, 118–30, 133n, 190: connection to *The Chase of the Wild Goose*, 107n; escape from censorship, 9, 16; sales of, 110–12, 130n; Woolf on, 12, 120
  'The Journal of Mistress Joan Martyn', 84
  'The "Movie" Novel', 116
  The Voyage Out, 118

Yourcenar, Marguerite, on historical fiction, 85–6

EU representative:
Easy Access System Europe
Mustamäe tee 50, 10621 Tallinn, Estonia
Gpsr.requests@easproject.com

www.ingramcontent.com/pod-product-compliance
Lightning Source LLC
Chambersburg PA
CBHW062220300426
44115CB00012BA/2148